Samuel Beckett's Signature in Years 1929-1938

TRANSATLANTIC STUDIES IN BRITISH AND NORTH AMERICAN CULTURE

Edited by Marek Wilczyński

VOLUME 37

Rafał Borkowski

Samuel Beckett's Signature in Years 1929–1938
Reflecting on the Thought Process: Language, the Neutrum and Memory

Bibliographic Information published by the Deutsche Nationalbibliothek
The Deutsche Nationalbibliothek lists this publication in the Deutsche Nationalbibliografie; detailed bibliographic data is available online at http://dnb.d-nb.de.

Library of Congress Cataloging-in-Publication Data
A CIP catalog record for this book has been applied for at the Library of Congress.

Cover illustration: Courtesy of Benjamin Ben Chaim.

This work has been reviewed by: David Malcolm (SWPS University) and Grzegorz Maziarczyk (John Paul II Catholic University of Lublin).

ISSN 2364-2882
ISBN 978-3-631-88484-3 (Print)
E-ISBN 978-3-631-88486-7 (E-Book)
E-ISBN 978-3-631-88690-8 (EPUB)
DOI 10.3726/b20059

© Peter Lang GmbH
Internationaler Verlag der Wissenschaften
Berlin 2022
All rights reserved.

Peter Lang – Berlin · Bern · Bruxelles · New York ·
Oxford · Warszawa · Wien

All parts of this publication are protected by copyright. Any utilisation outside the strict limits of the copyright law, without the permission of the publisher, is forbidden and liable to prosecution. This applies in particular to reproductions, translations, microfilming, and storage and processing in electronic retrieval systems.

This publication has been peer reviewed.

www.peterlang.com

For Marcel and Magdalena

Table of Contents

Introduction 9

Part One 15

Chapter 1: The Concept of the Signature 17

Chapter 2: The Signature of Samuel Beckett 31

Chapter 3: The Language 45

Chapter 4: The Neutrum 59

Chapter 5: Memory and time 89

Part Two 103

Chapter 1: Early criticism in *Dante... Bruno. Vico.. Joyce.*
(1929) and *Proust* (1931) 105

Chapter 2: *More Pricks Than Kicks* (1934) 127

Chapter 3: *Murphy* (1938) 145

Chapter 4: 'Echo's Bones:' A short story (wr. 1933 – publ.
2014) 165

Conclusions 183

Bibliography 187

Index of Names 199

Introduction

The aim of this dissertation is to trace the origins of the artistic signature in the earliest works of Samuel Beckett (1906–1989). The time frame discussed in the thesis includes the years 1929–1938, the former date refers to Beckett's double debut in a literary magazine *transition*, where he published his short story 'Assumption' and a critical text *Dante ... Bruno. Vico.. Joyce*, whereas the latter date indicates the year of publishing the novel *Murphy*. The research material is limited to six texts including two early works of criticism *Dante ... Bruno. Vico.. Joyce* (published 1929) and *Proust* (published 1931), one collection of short stories *More Pricks Than Kicks* (published 1934) from which were selected two short stories, the opening 'Dante and the Lobster' and the third in the collection 'Ding-Dong;' one novel *Murphy* (published 1938), and one short story entitled 'Echo's Bones' that was rejected to be published in 1933 and was published posthumously in 2014. In my work, it was decided to scrutinise neither early Beckett's poems nor his other rejected novel *Dream of Fair to Middling Women* (written 1932, published 1992). Such a choice was a result of a vast interpretational material that the selected six texts offer. Nevertheless, the fragments of some poems such as 'Echo's Bones' (which should be distinguished from the same-titled short story) and fragments of *Dream* will also appear in this thesis.

In the early years of his artistic carrier Samuel Beckett struggled with publishing his texts. For this reason, there can be observed an artistic process of incorporating already written texts into others works. For example, fragments of *Dream* can be found in a short story 'What a Misfortune.' One can also observe that the discussed texts appear in the chronological order, including 'Echo's Bones' that functions as a coda to the whole pre-war *oeuvre* of Samuel Beckett. The reasons for including this story in my dissertation are as follows: firstly, the text allows us to examine the writer's artistic process from the perspective of the twenty-first century Beckett researcher to be more precise. Secondly, the motifs and themes that appear in this story, such as the search of the unnamable, the body—mind relation and the endless work of the subject to constitute itself through the language can be used for further research both in the context of Beckett's pre- and post-war works.

The second aspect that needs further explanation is the notion of the 'signature' that is used in the title of this thesis. The starting point for my research is a physical quality of signature, i.e., the graphical sign that allows the receiver to recognise one's work. The examples of signatures that appear in William

Shakespeare, Heinrich Isaac and Michelangelo's hand-writing function as a pretext to illustrate the switch from the signature's physical to abstract features. It is also taken into consideration that a certain degree of physicality that is epitomised in the natural language is indispensable.

The abstract qualities of my definition of the signature will be predominantly based on notions introduced by Yuri Lotman. My main interests will pivot around the concept of the 'semiosphere,' the uniformed semiotic space that generates meanings on the semiotic signs and that uses the 'boundary' to filter the signs from the outer, the non-textual world. That juxtaposition between the external—internal and the text—non-text is also visible in other Lotman's notions, i.e., 'I' and 'other.' All these terms suggest that the act of signature is happening in-between these two spheres, where the 'I' of the artist needs to intermingle with the 'other,' understood as the receiver of the text. Owing to that the artist's signature requires a certain degree of recognition in the collective consciousness of the 'others,' such a consciousness allows the receiver to decode the artist's signature without a need of its physical representation, such as a painting or a sculpture.

The third aspect of the signature is the role that the natural language plays in it. The language should be recognised as a transmitter that not only conveys meanings between these two spaces but also play a role of a generator of new meanings. The motifs, notions and ideas that a language has cumulated in itself will allow the artist, in our case Beckett, to artistically modulate and create new meanings. In that case, the significance of Lotmanian 'I' needs to be discussed once again. On the one hand, the 'I' conveys in itself the artist's individuality and uniqueness, on the other the 'I' intermingles with the 'other,' where that sense of uniqueness is multiplied and infiltrated by the 'Is' of the 'others.' That feature of the signature finds its reflection in Derek Attridge's term of 'singularity,' the singular experience that is happening within the artist's work and that allows the receiver to reveal his or her signature. Thus, the sense of uniqueness (singularity) is recognised as an intellectual act where the artist's well-known signature is revealed to the receiver as a singular experience every time the receiver encounters the work of art.

Having defined my understanding of the signature, I would like to discuss the reasons that stand behind choosing that particular period of time in Beckett's writing carrier. First and foremost, the pre-war period of Beckett's literary activity is still not fully explored. Nowadays, we can observe that the increasing number of researchers concentrate on the writer's early works. For example, Mark Nixon has published *Samuel Beckett's German Diaries 1936–1937* (2011), *Samuel Beckett's Library* (together with Dirk van Hulle, 2013) and edited Beckett's short story *Echo's Bones* (2014). The other book collection that has allowed to reveal new aspects of Beckett's early years are the four volumes of *The Letters of Samuel Beckett* (edited by Martha Dow Fehsenfeld, Lois More Overbeck, 2009–2016). Volume I covering the years 1929–1940 is particularly vital for my study as the author's letters to his friends and editors allow us to trace the artistic process that stands behind Beckett's early writings.

I also found useful Brigitte Le Juez's *Beckett before Beckett: Samuel Beckett's Lectures on French Literature* (2008) that analyses the memories on Beckett as a literary scholar at Trinity College Dublin in 1930–1931, John Pilling's *Beckett before Godot* (2004) that concentrates on the write's formative years as well as Ruby Cohn's *A Beckett Canon* (2005) which attempts to describe all Beckett's works, including less-known pre-war texts. In the recent years the critical versions of the early writings are becoming more and more popular. In addition to the already mentioned scrupulously edited 'Echo's Bones,' we should mention Christopher Ackerley's *Demented Particulars: The Annotated Murphy* (2010) that scrutinise Beckett's first published novel. Samuel Beckett's texts that I work on are, in general, versions published in *The Selected Works of Samuel Beckett Volumes I-IV* (2010). The only exceptions are *Dream of Fair to Middling Women* (2012) and *Echo's Bones* (2014) since they were published separately.

As the above examples well illustrate, one can notice that the intensified research in the area of the pre-war texts covers the last 20 years, which means that this period of Beckett's *oeuvre* has not been fully revealed and elaborated yet. The main reason of researching the pre-war texts of Beckett is the publication of 'Echo's Bones' in 2014. The short story that was originally to be a part of the *More Pricks Than Kicks* yet was dismissed by the publisher, when read from the diachronic perspective through the prism of the whole *oeuvre* reveals that the motifs that eventually become significant in his late works, can be traced in its embryonical form in 'Echo's Bones.' These motifs include: the importance of the voice, the search of the neutral language and the reduction of the meanings to its pure forms. Thus, the research on that particular period of Beckett's artistic activity allows us to indicate that his works, even though written almost one hundred years ago, are still a vital, evolving element of the contemporary culture. The ideas developed in this doctoral thesis were preceded by my two papers, namely 'Beckett przed Beckettem? Poszukiwania początków sygnatury Beckettowskiej na przykładzie opowiadania 'Echo's Bones' ['Beckett before Beckett? In Search of the Origin of Beckett's Signature based on 'Echo's Bones']. In: Wiśniewski, Tomasz (ed). *Beckett w XXI. Wieku. Rozpoznanie*. Gdańsk University Press, 2017 and 'Bergson—Beckett—Lotman: A Semiotic Analysis of Samuel Beckett's "A Wet Night" from *More Pricks Than Kicks*.' In: *Beyond Philology*, Gdańsk

University Press, 14.2/2017. My research covered in these papers concentrated on recognising what Samuel Beckett's signature is as well as how Lotman's notion of semiosphere can be juxtaposed with Beckett's texts in general.

My decision to write the thesis in English has been motivated not only by my background of an English philologist but also by the lack of translations of the discussed works in Polish. Among the works that were translated into Polish and are discussed or appear in this thesis there is *Dream of Fair to Middling Women* (*Sen o Kobietach Pięknych i Takich Sobie*, translation Barbara Kopeć-Umiastowska, Sławomir Magala, 2003). The translations of *Dante... Bruno. Vico.. Joyce* and *Proust* appear in Antoni Libera's anthology *Samuel Beckett. Utwory wybrane* (2017), whereas 'Dante and the Lobster' was translated by Marek Kędzierski, Antoni Libera and Ewa Jankowska in *Twórczość* (4/1981). Thus, the choice of writing in English is both practical, as instead of working on non-ideal philological translation of my own, I can concentrate on the analysis of the works discussed in the thesis and personal as it is grounded in my educational background. Moreover, that particular period of Beckett's writing is still not fully discovered by the Polish academia;[1] thus, raising that subject can be a good starting point to the discussion on Beckett's early texts.[2]

---

1 Polish reception of Samuel Beckett was summarised, for example, in Marek Kędzierski's article 'Samuel Beckett i Polska (w latach 1981–2008),' (*Tekstualia*, 4/2018: 63–78), however, the article presents only Beckett's post-war texts. The more systematic reception of the writer in Poland can be found in Brzeska, Ewa. *Recepcja twórczości Samuela Becketta w Polsce*. Wydawnictwo Naukowe Uniwersytetu Mikołaja Kopernika, Toruń 2020.
2 The author of this thesis is aware of an undoubtful significance that Antoni Libera has played in popularising Beckett's *oeuvre* in Poland and in Polish language. Among his translation one can evoke such collections as *no właśnie co. Dramaty i Proza* (PIW, Warszawa 2010) and a two volume of essays, fiction and poems *Samuel Beckett. Utwory wybrane*, (PIW, Warszawa 2017). Libera's academic research in the field of Beckett studies can be found in his articles written in *Kwartalnik Artystyczny* (e.g., 'Dante, Vico a Towarzystwo Becketta,' Bydgoszcz 4/1996: 134–140), *Tekstualia* (e.g., 'Beckettowska negacja niczego nie przesądza,' Warszawa 3/2009) or *Topos* (translation of Beckett's text, e.g., 'Z Tekstów na nic,' Sopot 5/2010). Among his books of criticism written in Polish one can mention *Błogosławieństwo Becketta i inne wyznania literackie*, SIC!, Warszawa 2004, *Godot i jego cień*, Znak, Kraków 2013 and, written with Janusz Pyda, *Jesteście na Ziemi, na to rady nie ma! Dialogi o teatrze Samuela Becketta*. PIW, Warszawa 2018. However, due to the construction of the present thesis, i.e., written in English and focused on the works that, in majority, are not translated into Polish, Libera's viewpoint on Beckett's works is not dominant in the dissertation.

The thesis is divided into two parts, Part One consists of five chapters while Part Two of four chapters. Whereas Part One is of a theoretical character and attempts to define the notion of the signature in general, not only in Beckett's context, Part Two concentrates on interpretation of Beckett's texts in a chronological order through his signature. Chapter 1 of Part One concentrates on distinguishing the qualities of the signature – in particular, on its relation with physical qualities (1.1). It is also presented why I have decided on the term 'signature; instead of 'manner,' 'style' or 'poetics' (1.2). Section 1.3. examines the features of the signature as an act and event, following Derrida and Attridge.

Chapter 2 of Part One focuses on the definition of signature in general terms as well as on defining the artistic signature of Samuel Beckett. It needs to be mentioned that Sections 2.1 to 2.3 cover more general views on the definition of signature and do not focus on Samuel Beckett's signature as the latter will be examined from Section 2.4. Section 2.1 concentrates on the role of the receiver in the signature seen in light of Eco's principles. Section 2.2. presents differences between the terms 'signature' and 'poetics,' whereas section 2.3 attempts to define the term 'signature.' Section 2.4 concludes the principles of Beckett's artistic signature by evidencing three leading themes that appear to be the core for the author's interests, namely language, neutrum and memory. The search of 'pure' language, i.e., the language that, without conveying any meaning, can only exist in a neutral space and is aimed at a maximal reduction, to a single sign, as understood by Blanchot, appear to be the second theme of Beckett's interests. Even though Beckett became familiar with Blanchot's text as late as after the Second World War, he presents similar observations in his early works. The next three chapters attempt to characterise core elements of Beckett's signature defined in this book. Chapter 3 presents the origins of the writer's interests in the language itself, including information on Beckett's early language education. Chapter 4 attempts to define the neutrum, by referring to different philosophers and notions such as Blanchot's 'neutrum,' Hill's 'aporia,' and Husserl's 'epochē.' It is worth mentioning that information about Beckett's reading covered in *Samuel Beckett' Library* are a vital element of tracing what books or ideas could have influenced Beckett's intellectual development, thus a vast number of names used in the whole thesis can find its reflection in Nixon and van Hulle's book.

Chapter 5 describes the mind-body relations, especially in Bergsonian terms. All three elements of Beckett's artistic signature – language, the neutrum, memory – are discussed in section 5.3, where I argue that Beckett finds natural languages as a non-sufficient tool that he uses to arrive at the neutrum in order to identify the end of language. The never-ending struggle is epitomised in reducing notions to single signs that Beckett uses in his art, the signs that will be examined in detail in chapters 1 to 4 of Part Two. The third element of the triad, memory, is used by Beckett, to 'arrest the flow of durée with concepts or symbols' (Gontarski 2011: 65); Beckett's reduced symbols are equivalents to the 'image memory' that is used for grasping a metaphysical representation of meanings, or in another words, the neutrum.

Chapter 1 of Part Two concentrates on two works of criticism: *Dante... Bruno. Vico.. Joyce.* and *Proust*. In both examples one can indicate how Beckett's work on signs, for example, the sequence church—marriage—burial presented in *Dante* that evokes the reduction of one's life span to a maximum, is anchored in the thought of philosophers who are discussed in the essays. The concepts used in *Dante*, for example Vico's philosophy of eternal returns or Bruno's maximal-minimal, depict the writer's interests in the circular sequence of events as well as the reduction of notions to a single sign. Similarly, Beckett uses the concept of involuntary memory in *Proust* that Beckett uses as a drill to reach the neutrum.

Chapter 2 concentrates on two short stories selected from *More Pricks Than Kicks*, 'Dante and the Lobster' and 'Ding-Dong.' In the case of these two stories, the author takes symbols from Dante's *The Divine Comedy* and Shakespeare's *The Tempest* to reinvent them for the purposes of his own language. Whereas the symbol of the 'lobster' allows to indicate a movement from motionlessness to dynamism, the travel through Dublin in 'Ding-Dong' is concentrated on the spherical movement of the protagonist. Such a work on symbols allows Beckett to explore the notions of neutrum and memory through artistically recycled signs. Similarly, in Chapter 3, Beckett explores the possibilities of signs in the world of *Murphy*. However, what is the most visible is the attempt of defying the system of the neutral space that is not interfered by the external world, the world of signs.

Finally, Chapter 4 concentrates on 'Echo's Bones' but also serves as pretext to summarise Beckett's artistic signature through the text. The story uses a vast number of symbols as references to other early works such as 'Lord Gall,' 'the Alba,' 'Belacqua.' These symbols allow us to indicate that their role is not only to communicate with the external texts but also with other texts of Beckett. Owing to that, through these symbols the author is able to build the world of the story based on the motifs that will eventually become the core of his signature.

Part One

Chapter 1: The Concept of the Signature

1.1. Physicality of the signature

The Oxford English Dictionary offers the following definition of the term *signature*: 'A person's name written in a distinctive way as a form of identification in authorizing a cheque or document or concluding a letter.' The importance of the physical activity of signing covered in the dictionary definition correlates with the term's origin; from Latin *signare* ('to mark with a stamp, to sign') through French and Scottish *signature* (the sixteenth century legal term meaning 'one's own name written in one's own hand') until the modern meaning of the word. Intriguingly, the very act of writing a signature in one's hand, even if it is only written as a symbol X, causes that the signature gains its formality and authenticity as 'by signing a document one authenticates it: the signatory gives it the same legal power in his absence as if he were physically present to swear its truth' (MacNeil 2000: 4–17). The notion of the simultaneous absence and non-absence of the signer within the signature has concerned many literary scholars, such as Jacques Derrida's *Signature, Event, Context* (1988) and Derek Attridge's *The Singularity of Literature* (2004). Their observations will be further discussed and applied in this thesis, and at this point I would like to focus on the basic feature of the signature, namely its physicality.

The aforementioned basic definition of the signature covers in itself two main features: the physical aspect, namely being written by one's own hand and a lack of formal requirements that need to be fulfilled to treat the signature as a valid one (a symbol X). The following three examples of artists representing music, literature and sculpture seem to confirm MacNeil's proposal. Firstly, as Rob C. Wegman writes in his *Isaac's Signature*:

> one of the curious things about signatures is that it does not actually matter whether they look formal or not, or whether they spell out the person's proper name or simply form a graphic symbol like the letter X. The point about signatures is that they have to be written *in one's own hand*. (2011: 13).

Such an approach to the definition of signature corresponds to the one presented by MacNeil. The protagonist of Wegman's article, Heinrich Isaac (1450–1517), a Dutch Renaissance composer, promotes the idea that the signature represents the output of labour, or in modern marketing categories, a product produced by a professional composer. He signed his works as *Isaac de manu sua*. 'this piece is by Isaac in his own hand,' as if the composer wanted to assure his receiver about the authenticity of his work.[1] Secondly, the concept of a written-in-one's-own-hand signature can be also visible in the case of William Shakespeare (1564–1616) who was hardly concerned with the spelling of his surname using such forms as Willm Shaks, William Shaksper, Wm Shakspe or Willm Shakspere (Dawson 1992: 76), the multiplicity of forms used by Shakespeare only proves Wegman's assumption concerning the lack of formality of the author's signature.

Another intriguing example of the written signature used by an artist, is the one by Michelangelo (1475–1564). In his example the most crucial is the fact that he wrote his signature only once, on the famous Pietà (1497–99). Michelangelo wrote his name diagonally across the Virgin's chest in the following manner: MICHAEL·AGELVS·BONAROTVS· FLORENT·FACIEBA. According to Giorgio Vasari's biography of Michelangelo (1550), the artist only added his signature to the Pietà because the audience started thinking that the sculpture had been made by Cristoforo Solari da Angerra, not by Michelangelo (Wang 2004: 450). The artist's behaviour, even though considered as the output of Vasari's imagination, correlates with the legal function of the signature applied in the case of Heinrich Isaac. Besides, the authentication of the author, Michelangelo's signature covers one vital aspect that corresponds to Jacques Derrida's view on the signer that 'marks, and retains his having been present in a past now or present which will remain a future now or present' (1982: 20), namely the usage of the word 'facieba[t]', an imperfect form of a much popular in Michelangelo's time 'faciebat', meaning 'done'.[2] The sculptor's innovation in the usage of the progressive tense in the signature, contrary to other significant artists of that time as, for example, Albrecht Dürer, Giovanni Bellini or Andrea Sansovino, who used only perfect tenses in their signatures, suggests that for Michelangelo the artistic creation is a never-ending process that cannot be completed, or, in Derrida's categories, implicating 'the actual or empirical nonpresence of the signer' (1982: 20).[3]

---

1 Worth mentioning is the fact how forgers were perceived in the Renaissance society. Suitable traces can be found in Dante's *Divine Comedy* where falsifiers such as impersonators, liars, forgers and alchemists were located near bottom of Dante's hell, in the 9th circle, 10th chasm, and only traitors were considered more evil (Inferno, Cantos XXIX-XXX).
2 Lisa Pon recognises Michelangelo's choice of the verb's imperfect form as an ongoing process that the artist is 'continuing into the future' (1996: 19).
3 Michelangelo's measure of using an imperfect form 'facieba' instead of finished 'faciebat' correlates with Pliny the Elder's viewpoint on importance of the artist's modesty as well as the assumption that the art is always an unfinished process, while the art of these

Michelangelo's 'facieba' brings the reader up before the most vital, and definitely most problematic question concerning the signature, namely its never-ending possibility, or in George Steiner's nomenclature its 'inexhaustibility'. The ephemeral duality of signature, its simultaneous being and non-being on several, structurally contradictory layers, or as Derrida points out in his *Signéponge/Signsponge*, its feature of 'remain[ing] in order to disappear, or disappear in order to remain' (1984: 56) leads to such significant questions as the origin of the signature, where it starts, ends, and which factors distinguish the signature of one artist, in the case of this dissertation of Samuel Beckett, from another.

Having described the physical features of signature, at this point one important voice in the discussion upon its tangibility must be evoked, namely George Steiner's notion of 'the character'. In *Real Presences* he suggests that 'the word "character" does mean the actual marker on the page' (2013: 149), moreover he suggests that the role of the signature does not end on the physical mark on the paper, but starts existing beyond the actual idiom:

> And there is undoubtedly a sense in which an Odysseus, a Falstaff, an Anna Karenina are 'characters,' which is to say no more and no less than assemblages of lexical grammatical signs on a page. But it is, very exactly, the quantum leap between the character as letter and the character as presence, and as a presence often far richer, more exigent of exploring assent, far more lasting than our own, which makes the point. (2013: 149).

---

artists who confidently use the finished form 'faciebat' in their signature, tends to be 'very unpopular:'
'I should like to be accepted on the lines of those founders of painting and sculpture who, as you will find in these volumes, used to inscribe their finished works, even the masterpieces which we can never tire of admiring, with a provisional title such as *Apelles faciebat* or *Polyclitus* [faciebat], as though art was always a thing in process and not completed, so that when faced by the vagaries of criticism the artist might have left him a line of retreat to indulgence, by implying that he intended, if not interrupted, to correct any defect noted. Hence it is exceedingly modest of them to have inscribed all their works in a manner suggesting that they were their latest, and as though they had been snatched away from each of them by fate. Not more than three, I fancy, are recorded as having an inscription denoting completion-*Ille fecit* [he made this] (these I will bring in at their proper places); this made the artist appear to have assumed a supreme confidence in his art, and consequently all these works were very unpopular.' (Pliny the Elder, *Natural History*. Harvard University Press, Cambridge 1979, pp. 16–19)

The transformation of an idiom, in this case of literary characters like Odysseus or Falstaff, from a physical mark on the paper into a construct that begins to function in a different, cultural dimension, reveals a kind of collision, the collision that occurs within the signature causing the birth of a 'character' that functions both inside and outside of the signature, or, as this term would be used synonymously in this thesis, the semiosphere of the author's work.[4] I adapt the term 'character' from Steiner as it encapsulates two instances within which the signature functions, i.e. the physical one, where a character is represented by a particular letter, number or symbol, and the non-physical, where the character stops functioning only within its physical representation, for instance a novel, painting or a piece of music,[5] and begins to function outside the actual signature

---

4   The concept of semiosphere is understood as it is defined and presented by Yuri Lotman in such works as *On the semiosphere*. Signs System Studies 17, Tartu 1984 and *The Universe of the Mind*. I.B. Tauris & CO. LTD, London 1990. The term *Semiosphere* has been coined as the mutual word for the term *biosphere*. According to Vladimir Vernadsky, biosphere is '[a] cosmic mechanism, which occupies a specific structural place in planetary unity. Situated on the surface of our planet and including within itself the totality of living things, the biosphere transforms the radiated energy of the sun into the chemical and physical [objects] and is concerned with the transformation of the inert inanimate materials' (Lotman 1984: 207). In the definition there can be found a variety of analogies with the semiosphere recognised as the totality of individual texts and isolated languages which relate to each other. Lotman recognises semiosphere as a unified semiotic space which resembles a mechanism or even an organism. He points out that semiosis cannot exist without semiosphere. The separate semiotic units cannot create a semiotic universe, as the bricks recognised separately cannot create a house, however the existence of a superior universe, in this case semiosphere, transmits meanings upon the semiotic signs.
Moreover, Lotman points out that semiosphere cannot exist without the notion of the *boundary*. In this case the boundary is recognised as a filter which separates the semiotics and non-semiotic texts. The non-semiotic texts may be incorporated to semiosphere on condition of being adapted. It causes that strange, outer non-texts become the familiar ones. In contrast to the semiosphere, which is structured and unified on many different strata, the structure of border is patchy and disordered. However, the disorder introduced by the non-texts to semiosphere is a significant element of its development. Additionally, the existence of a boundary allows to differentiate the semiospheric and non-semiospheric universe and, paradoxically, to confirm the existence of semiosphere.
5   Jacques Derrida notices that the musician is the only creator who is not able to inscribe his nominal signature in the work due to the lack of the langue space for it. Derrida proposes a remedy for the musician who should overcode 'his work on the basis of

as an idiom within a particular cultural context, e.g. Shakespeare's *Hamlet*, Leonardo's *Mona Lisa* or Beethoven's *The Symphony No. 9*. The latter function of the character, or the signature, is especially haunting due to its functioning not only in the non-text contexts understood in Yuri Lotman's categories,[6] but also leads to an important notion of the proper name of the signature.

1.2. The proper names, manner and style

In *Culture and Explosion* Lotman defines 'proper names' as a distinctive human quality (i.e. not available to animals) that allows humans to distinguish the notions of 'I' and 'other'. The sense of individuality and uniqueness, 'I,' correlated with the awareness of the 'other,' is a foundation on which a network of proper names is built, bearing in mind the paradox that one cannot exist without the other. He argues that human beings, belonging to both spheres, i.e. the sphere of an individual and the sphere in which the individual functions, for instance, in a society, contradict each other. For Lotman it is crucial to observe the dichotomy of naming oneself and simultaneously being named by others (2009: 31).[7]

Lotman's notion of proper names corresponds to the theory of the signature recognised as a character that functions both in a signed work of art and in an external world, for instance, the culture in which the signer functions. Such a

---

another semiotic system, one of musical notation, for example' (*Signéponge/Signsponge* 1984: 54).

6   The concept of the systematic and extra-systematics features of the artistic text are explained in detail in chapter 4, 'Text and System,' of *The Structure of the Artistic Text*, University of Michigan, 1977.

7   The signature and the roles it performs in the society can be portrayed on the example of coins as the word *signere* in Latin also means 'to coin.' As Giorgio Agamben in his *The Signature of All Things. On Method*. Zone Books, New York 2009 suggests:
'Now consider the example of a signature stamped on a coin which determines its value. In this case, too, the signature has no substantial relation with the small circular metal object that we hold in our hands. It adds no real properties to it at all. Yet once again, the signature decisively changes our relation to the object as well as its function in society. Just as the signature, without altering in any way the materiality of Titan's painting inscribes it in the complex network of relations of 'authority,' here it transforms a piece of metal into coin, producing it as money' (40).
The word 'coin' in the above quotation functions as a proper name, however without an external world, a society, it cannot be fully defined existing only as a piece of metal. Started functioning not only within its semiosphere as a 'coin' but also in the external sphere as 'money,' its proper name functions in Lotmanian categories.

definition of signature emphasises two elementary aspects of the author's signature; the recognition both by the author himself, and, even more importantly, by an external world in which the signature functions. At that point, there may arise the question if the term signature should not be replaced with more popular terms such as 'manner' or 'style'. Nonetheless, in my dissertation I insist on employing the term 'signature' for the following reasons.

The term 'manner' etymologically originates from Latin *mano*, meaning the 'hand' and referring to the artist's working method that gives 'the visible results of that method' (Atkins 2012: 148). The importance of a physical output of the manner is concurrent with the definition of signature as a physical object; however, similarities end here. Paradoxically, the importance of the visible output of the manner is its major limitation, as such a definition suggests that not being able to actually see the artist's working method, eliminates the receiver from fully perceiving it.[8] In practice, if one wants to understand Leonardo's 'manner' ('signature') of *Mona Lisa*, he or she should visit the Louvre to witness the paining on his own; thus, the term 'manner', albeit functioning synonymously to the term 'signature', is not sufficient in our research as the notion focuses predominantly on the method – on how the piece of art is created, the factor that cannot be captured by the receiver, for example in a written text.[9]

As far as the definition of 'style' is concerned, Meyer Schapiro defines the term as 'a system of forms with a quality and meaningful expression through which the personality of the artist and the broad outlook of a group are visible' (1953: 287). In his definition, which predominantly concentrates on style in art, Schapiro proves that the notion of style is inextricably connected with the time

---

8   If one is interested in observing the actual Beckett's writing process, 'The Beckett Manuscript Project' edited by Mark Nixon and Dirk Van Hulle offers the complete textual history of the writer's works. Since 2011 the project is aimed both at publishing the critical editions of all Beckett's works, including the writers' marginalia (so far ten volumes have been published including such works as *Molloy, Krapp's Last Tape or Waiting for Godot*) and at developing a website (https://www.beckettarchive.org) where Beckett's manuscripts are digitally archived.

9   The similar recognition of the term 'manner' meaning method can be found, for example, in Karel van Mander's *The Lives of the Illustrious Netherlandish and German Painters*, Vol. 2 where he defines the term as follows:
    '*Maniere*' was until recently understood as a deliberately aimed-at style. I have felt that this view needs some modification: maniere means nothing more than method or manner of working, and the outwardly-visible results of this, which together make up the style, are only one component of this.'(251)

and space during which it occurs, additionally pointing out its dependency on the particular historical events within which the style is anchored. Additionally, he speaks about the 'inner form' of the style that reflects the 'collective thinking and feeling' (1953: 287) of the particular culture, functioning in a defined time and space. At that point, Schapiro's definition is concurrent with Lotman's 'proper names,' where the 'I' is named by 'others,' or where 'the style' exists in a collective mind of a given culture; however, Schapiro depicts an additional point where he sets the role of the shared qualities of the style that developed during a distinct time above the importance of an individual art. That statement, on the one hand contradicts the Lotmanian idea of 'I' in proper names, and on the other does not fulfil the need for a profound definition of the signature. Furthermore, Schapiro suggests that 'every style is peculiar to a period of a culture and that, in a given culture or epoch of culture, there is only one style or a limited range of styles' (1953: 288) that only limits the term's usefulness in the context of the definition of the signature.

However, Derrida points out that the term 'style' can be identified with the notions of 'the proper name' and eventually, with the signature. He recognises 'the style' as 'the inimitable idiom of a writer, sculptor, painter, or orator' (1984: 54). That idiom allows the receiver, whether it is a spectator or a reader, to immediately recognise that a given piece of art was created by a particular artist. Even more absorbing is the fact that the idiom left by the creator does not have to be necessarily left on purpose. Suffice it to say that we do not need to find the creator's signature, whether in a form of a full name or merely an X sign, in the work. Moreover, no correspondence between the piece of art and the artist's proper name is necessary. Even under these circumstances we are still able to recognise the creator's idiom.[10] In fact, the view on 'the style' proposed and used interchangeably with the signature and proper names by Derrida inscribes in the definitions of 'the signature' that have been proposed so far. However, using the word 'inimitable' in the definition contradicts with other viewpoints upon what the signature is and how it is understood by the author of this thesis.

Derek Attridge introduces the notion of *singularity* that he defines as 'the singularity of a cultural object [that] consists in its difference from all other such objects, not simply as a particular manifestation of general rules but as a peculiar nexus within the culture that is perceived as resisting or exceeding all

---

10 Derrida concludes that 'we will say that the work is signed Ponge or X without having to read the proper name' (1984: 54).

pre-existing general determinations' (2004: 63).[11] Such a definition is explicably in favour of defining the idiom we are deliberating on as the signature, not a style. Attridge's viewpoint opens new possibilities for understanding the signature. He characterises the singularity as 'a peculiar nexus within the culture,' and suggests that the creator does not live in a cultural vacuum, and his or her artistic output must be a variation upon the pre-existing forms of art. Thus, at that point Attridge's viewpoint strongly contradicts Derrida's; what is more, Attridge adds that '[s]ingularity is not *pure*; it is constitutively impure, always open to contamination, grafting, accidents, reinterpretation, and recontextualisation. Nor is it inimitable (highlighted by R.B.): on the contrary, it is eminently imitable, and may rise to a host of imitations' (2004: 63).

The abovementioned quotations add two vital points to the definition of the signature: firstly, that the signature, though a unique output of one's invention,[12] does not exist in void, but needs to cohabitate within the particular cultural network (similarly to the mentioned Lotman's semiosphere). And secondly, that the signature can be, and very often is, taken from the original creator and can be artistically re-contextualised – Lotman's idea of 'I' and 'other' can be applied in the latter example. The features of singularity – such as: 1) carrying a meaning, focusing on situatedness and datedness rather than on particular place and time; 2) being recognisable by the reader, for example by an act of memory; 3) the recognition of the importance of the form as a 'performed mobility' rather than an 'empirical structure' (Attridge 2004: 111),[13] and 4) implication that the act of repetition is different every time – define the meaning of the term 'signature' as it

---

11 He also indicates that 'singularity functions like a signature.' (2004: 64).
12 Attridge understands invention as 'a new device, program, or technology, but the act (which is also, as we have seen, an event) of invention is a mental feat, a step into the unknown, which makes possible both the manufacture of the new entity and, even more importantly, new instances of inventiveness in the culture at large.' (2004: 42).
13 In this distinction, Attridge recognises 'the form' as a performance, 'a performance of reading answering to a performance of writing' (2004: 111). He suggests that a literary work encrypted in a written form implies in itself an 'act-event' image, an image that can be re-enacted through reading. Thus, for Attridge the singularity is understood more as a 'performed mobility' as the singularity's performative factor is, to some extent, decoded in a written form and subsequently encoded in reading. That mobility, which the author of this thesis finds as a vital one in the process of coining the definition of signature as well as the performative particle allow to get rid of the physical aspect of the signature that the original definition conveys.

1.3. The Signature as an act and event

The recognition of the signature, as the inimitable, or imitable as we have already presented, idiom of a creator that a culturally literate receiver is able to recognise without looking for a proper name, provokes further questions, namely of our ability to recognise the artist's signature, and of when it happens that a receiver knows that a particular idiom belongs to a particular creator. Finally, it is vital to discuss how it is possible that even when one makes an attempt to imitate someone else's signature, we are still able to recognise the *mano* of the original creator.

Derrida's definition of the signature evokes one more modality, namely its state of happening or being an act of creation that occurs while the receiver communes with the text. He points out that:

> …we may designate as general signature, or signature of the signature, the fold of the placement in abyss where, after the manner of the signature in the current sense, the work of writing designates, describes, and inscribes itself as act (action and archive), signs itself before the end by affording us the opportunity to read; I refer to myself, this is writing, I am a writing, this is writing – which excludes *nothing* since, when the placement is abyss succeeds, and is thereby decomposed and produces an event, it is the other, the thing as other, that signs (1984: 54).

The suggestion that the signature functions as an act that occurs between the work of art and the receiver correlates not only with Derrida's but also Attridge's point of view. While Attridge notices that the signature is not only pure but can also undergo further processing, whether it is re-contextualisation or re-interpretation, Derrida in 'Signature, Event, Context' writes about 'the impossibility of their [signatures' – R.B.] rigorous purity' (1982: 20) without which the signature is unable to function properly. In addition, Derrida presents a certain paradox when saying that the true reproducibility of a pure event can only be achieved by the act of replication and repetition (1982: 20). Attridge writes in a similar manner, suggesting that 'singularity can inhere as much in a photograph reproduced a million times as in the coloured plaster of Leonardo's 'Last Supper' in the refectory of the monastery of Santa Maria delle Grazie' (2004: 64).

The next point in our discussion should concentrate on the explanation of how the term *event* is understood for the purpose of this thesis. Thus, we do not concentrate on understanding the event in either historic[14] or literary[15] categories, but see it as a uniqueness that is produced – as an emergence of an extraordinary quality. As Attridge notices:

> Singularity ... is not a property but an event, the event of singularizing which takes place in reception: it does not occur outside the responses of those who encounter and thereby constitute it. It is produced, not given in advance; and its emergence is also the beginning of its erosion, as it brings about the cultural changes necessary to accommodate it (2004: 64).

Attridge's understanding of singularity (signature) in the context of an event, i.e. an action that must take place in order to prompt the beginning of a new idiom that creates value, opens a new perspective upon the understanding what the signature is, and what is more significant for our understanding, where it begins. So far, the signature has been presented either as a physical object anchored in language, more precisely in writing, or as a certain notion, an idiom equivalent to the style or manner that allows the receiver to identify the particular signature, and prospectively, to detect whether the signature had not been borrowed from somebody else. However, the role of the receiver in this process was only passive, reducing his or her role to a mere observer of the signature. By claiming that singularity is produced, Attridge suggests that the process demands three subjects in order to take place: the author, the signature included in a piece of art and the receiver.[16]

In this model the author and his or her signature stays in the state of suspension, it means that the signature is merely a proper name if the receiver of the piece of art does not have an idiosyncratic knowledge that allows him or her to recognise the author's signature. Such a state does not allow to constitute in advance, as Attridge notices, any kind of activity reducing it to a mere possibility, or as Umberto Eco defines it in *Lector in fabula*, to the state of the *unspeakable* (1994a: 73). In fact, there can be noticed an analogy between the role of the receiver presented by Eco, for instance in *The Limits of Interpretation*, to the receiver of the singularity in Attridge's *The Singularity of Literature*.

---

14 See Paul Ricoeur, *Time and Narrative I*, The University of Chicago Press, Chicago 1984.
15 See Maurice Blanchot, *The Space of Literature*. University of Nebraska Press, Lincoln, London 1989.
16 For a better understanding these roles, the author is to be recognised as a creator of the piece of art, the signature as a carrier of a meaning that covers in itself the author's 'I' and the receiver that can be juxtaposed with the role of a reader, but following Attridge's thought, that role can be extended to a performer or a director as well.

Eco's understanding of a model reader can be reduced to two main points: 1) the reader plays a vital role in the process of creating the meaning of the literary text, 2) the receiver's power upon the text is limited and can occur under certain conditions.[17] Eco's theory, even though it concentrates on the literary text, can be useful in our understanding what role the receiver needs to play in the process of the event that, as it has been already pointed out, is indispensable in decoding and understanding the signature.

We will return to the second modality of Eco's model upon the importance of some restriction imposed on the receiver; however, at this point we should concentrate upon the features of an event. Derrida in 'A Certain Impossible Possibility of Saying the Event' (2007) enumerates several points to characterise the features of the event:[18]

a) The event should occur as a surprise which means that it should not incorporate any features of anticipation. Derrida writes that 'it has to come as a surprise, from the other or to the other; it has to extend beyond the confines of the economic circle of exchange (448) – indicating that the singularity of the event evinces in its uniqueness.

b) Furthermore, he points out that the event cannot be expected as if we expect that the event occurs, it loses its quality of being an event: '[h]orizontally, I see it [the event – R.B.] coming, I fore-see it, I fore-say it, and the event is that which can be said [*dit*] but never predicted [*prédit*]. A predicted event is not an event. The event falls on me because I do not see it coming.' (451).

c) In addition, the language of the event should consist in exceeding 'all pre-established and pre-dictable notions (Rowner 2015: 99). The language should leave us 'disarmed' causing the continuous sense of unpredictability: '[we] should remain disarmed, utterly disarmed by this very impossibility, baffled in face of the always unique, exceptional, and unpredictable arrival of the other, of the other, and that I must remain absolutely disarmed' (452) – the notion of the event as the other is intriguing in this context as it suggests that

---

17 Umberto Eco's viewpoint upon the role of the reader in the literary act can be found in such books, as e.g. *The Limits of Interpretation*, Indiana University Press, 1994 or *Lector in fabula*, PIW, 1994 (English version was published in: *The Role of the Reader. Explorations in the Semiotics of Texts*, Indiana University Press, 1984.).

18 Derrida's features of the event correspond with the definitions proposed in classical narratology, for example Wolf Schmid in *Narratology: An Introduction* recognises the event as the 'unprecedented incident' (2010: 8). See also Gérard Genette, *Narrative Discourse: an Essay in Method*. Cornell University Press, New York 1972.

the receiver should stay uninformed in order to allow the act of event to take place. The juxtaposition between the other that unexpectedly pours into the sphere of the receiver connotes Lotman's idea of the semiosphere, especially the notions of the non-text, text and explosion.

d) Despite the fact that the above insights upon the nature of the event may suggest a certain sense of impossibility, the author *Of Grammatology* adds one more interesting feature of the event, namely the importance of the repetition. It has already been suggested that the importance of repetition in the event is both significant to Attridge and Derrida. The latter suggests that 'the event cannot appear to be an event, when it appears, unless it is already repeatable in its very uniqueness' (452). The paradox of the event in this assumption is the following: the full apprehension of the event can only occur through the process of replication. On the one hand, the event cannot take place if it appears on the horizon of our expectations, on the other without a certain amount of presupposition the act of the event cannot fully materialise.[19] In order to better understand this paradox Derrida refers to Emmanuel Lévinas' concept of *substitution*[20] claiming that '[s]ubstitution is not simply the replacement of a replaceable uniqueness: substitution replaces the irreplaceable' (452). Taking from Lévinas the concept of the event's return to the uniqueness, despite fulfilling in a replication, Derrida calls it a *revenant*, noticing that '[t]he coming is absolutely new. But the novelty of this coming implicates in and itself the coming back' (453).

Derrida's argument on the paradox of the event corresponds with the above-mentioned Attridge's view on the importance of the receiver's idiosyncratic knowledge, the knowledge without which the signature cannot take place. Based on these two notions, one can suggest that author's signature cannot be recognised without a receiver's pre-supposed recognition of the signature's distinguished features that a given author represents. In the case of Beckett's signature the topics that are the core of his writing such as memory, the sound-silence

---

19 So as to illustrate that concept Derrida proposes the situation when we receive an unexpected visit of a guest, which contains in itself both the sense of uniqueness and novelty and a certain amount of presupposed codes how to react in such a situation (2007: 453).
20 Lévinas in *Otherwise than Being or Beyond Essence* (1991) presents the idea of substitution predominantly in reference to the multi-dimensionality of an inner life, especially in the context of psychology, however Derrida applied the notion of the substitution in a more philosophical context.

relation and the search of the unnamable that in this thesis is juxtaposed with the term neutrum, are universal topics used by any other authors. The originality that makes Beckett's signature unique is his work in language and expression of the above topics through the language. Beckett's phrase appears to be reserved and precise, by that statement I understand singular words or phrases such as 'womb-tomb' the encapsulate in themselves the vital notions for Christo-Judean culture. On the other hand, the motifs and notions that appear in Beckett's writings are often abstract and absurd (the lobster in 'Dante and the Lobster', the chat between characters at the party from 'A Wet Night' or the circumstances of the afterlife in which Belacqua finds himself in Echo's Bones).[21]

---

21 I am aware of the connotations that the term 'absurd' conveys, especially in Martin Esslin's definition of the 'Theatre of the Absurd' where, on the basis of on the post-war works of such authors as Ionesco, Pinter or Beckett, the researcher used Ionesco's definition of this term: 'Absurd is that which is devoid of purpose. [...] Cut off from his religious, metaphysical, and transcendental roots, man is lost; all his actions becomes senseless, absurd, useless.' (1961: xix). Nevertheless, such a usage of the term 'absurd' in the context of the whole Beckett's oeuvre seems not sufficient for the contemporary researcher of the Irishman's writing. Bearing in mind Beckett's viewpoint on the complexity of literature, searching for its essence as well as contemplating the world's complexity through the literature (Bennet 2011: 3).
Owing to that I opt for Bennet's definition of the absurd that is '[n]ot about absurdity, but about making life meaningful given our absurd situation (2011: 4). However, the term absurd usually refers to Beckett's post-war plays, I find Bennet's definition applicable for the writer's pre-war texts. For example Celia's observations of flying a kite from Murphy inscribes in Bennet's definition of absurd actions through which the deeper meaning on the human's condition is depicted.

Chapter 2: The Signature of Samuel Beckett

To illustrate how Derrida and Attridge's respective views on the event work in practice, an example taken from Samuel Beckett's poetry will be used, namely the poem entitled 'Echo's Bones' written in 1933. Even though Beckett's pre-war poetry is not discussed in detail in this dissertation, the poem 'Echo's Bones' has been selected to indicate how certain motifs function within Beckett's signature. The poem holds the same title as the short story that is discussed in detail in Chapter 4 of Part Two, and is the output of the author's disappointment when he found out that the short story 'Echo's Bones' had been rejected by a publisher (*Letters I*, 2009: 171). Both the short story and the poem share similar themes, such as the sound-silence relation (however, while in the case of the short story such motifs are reduced to singular idioms, in the case of the poem they are even further reduced to single words):

> Echo's Bones
> asylum under my tread all this day
> their muffled revels as the flesh falls
> the gantelope of sense and nonsense run
> taken by the maggots for what they are[1]

The core of the poem are the letters, the twenty-six letters of the English alphabet to be precise, the letters that are the graphic representation of the English phonemes. Thus, we can treat letters as the means of representing the language in the written form. This assumption inscribes in Derrida's notion of a certain dose of presupposition without which the event cannot take place. Subsequently, the thirty-one words used in the poem, and built of twenty-six letters, are arranged in a way that creates its uniqueness, or in Derrida's categories, a surprise. Such a combination of words creates in the receiver not only the sense of novelty but also unpredictability; the receiver while joining the creator's game, i.e. his or her signature inscribed in a piece of art, could not expect that the arrangement of words in such a particular way.

Moreover, the poem can be used as an example employed to display the notion of invention, especially in its structural form (five unrhymed lines that can be read as a rough pentameter, Cohn 2005: 60) and the restrained usage

---

1 *The Selected Works of Samuel Beckett*. Volume IV. Grove Press, New York, 2010, p. 32.

of vocabulary that cumulates in itself a multitude of meanings connected with the theme of confinement and death ('asylum,' 'muffled' 'gantelope'). Attridge's notion of invention would be particularly useful in this matter. As it has been mentioned, the terms 'invention' and 'act' are strongly related; thus, we may treat them as indispensable ingredients of the event. Without the creator's invention, an act of singularity cannot take place. In the case of 'Echo's Bones' Beckett's act of invention is displayed through the motifs that appear in the poem and that can be further recognised by the receiver as characteristic features of the writer's signature, such as an ambiguous persona that only appears in the first line ('asylum under my tread'),[2] similar to a voice from *Company*, the condensation and reduction of certain motifs, in this case the motif of live and death to single expressions ('muffled revels') combined with a state of in-betweenness (living beings whose 'flesh falls').

However, the act is singular, unique, and can still emerge in repetitions. Attridge notices that the piece of art can be manifested in a variety of forms: 'whether it be printed, written, spoken, sung, illuminated, or recorded, and in whatever font, style of handwriting, delivery, musical setting, mode of decoration, or type of transcription …; all the different manifestations, that is, are types of a single token' (2004: 66). And even though the transmitter can be different, the replication of the signature incorporated in the poem allows the act of the event to take place.

Grounded predominantly on Derrida and Attridge's assumptions, the definition of signature that I am trying to forge, will be complemented by Lotman's view on the event. In *The Structure of the Artistic Text*, Lotman defines an event as 'the smallest indivisible unit of plot construction' (1977: 232). It is visible in this way that Lotman concentrates mainly on the relation of the plot to the artistic text, whether there can exist a plot-less text and how the event, as 'the indivisible unit' builds both the boundary and the secondary modelling system (ibid.). However, from our perspective of understanding the event through Derrida and Attridge's notions, the importance of the plot may play a secondary role.[3] Besides being a basic unit in the plot construction, the event, according to Lotman, conveys one additional modality, namely the 'probability.' He writes

---

2 The persona's walk on an asylum-grave while being passed by other live beings indicates the persona's sense of suspension between the worlds of dead and alive corresponds with May's back and forth walk from *Footfalls*.

3 Moreover, Lotman recognises that both the hierarchy and the sequence of events results in the plot (1977: 233–234).

that 'an event is that which did occur, though it could also not have occurred. The less probability that a given event will take place …, the higher the rank of that event on the plot scale' (236). Lotman uses the notion of the probability predominantly for determining whether texts are plot-based or plot-less, but what is more useful for our understanding of the role that the probability plays in the event is, the probability suggests that a certain event takes place within the text, but simultaneously it 'need not have taken place' (1977: 236). Thus, one can juxtapose the notion of the 'probability' with the 'possibility', the concept that plays a crucial role in defining what the 'signature' is. The above-mentioned definition of Derrida's 'impossibility' with reference to the event suggests that the state of the 'impossibility' is the condition of the possible (Rowner 2015: 97). Similarly, Lotman's probability conveys a suggestion that may or may not happen within the event. Such a possibility allows the receiver who attempts to experience or decipher the author's signature through the event.

That event can be also recognised as the act of Attridge's singularity, the singular experience with the author's work of art that may allow the receiver to reveal the artist's well-known signature through the singular experience of an event. 'Echo's Bones' serves here as an example of such a singular experience, where the primary motif of the poem, i.e., the suspension between the live and death, the in-betweenness, is continually explored through expressions used in the poem. The reduction of these motifs to single words and expressions, on the one hand illustrates the author's work in the matter of the language to distillate the precise meaning, on the other hand allows the receiver to recognise Beckett's signature through the act of singularity, i.e., the singular act where the receiver with a background knowledge about the author's signature is able to recognise elements of such a signature while reading the poem.

2.1. The role of the receiver in the signature

The next point in the discussion should lead to the role of the receiver in the concept of signature as without the role of the receiver the act of signature cannot fully take place. For the purpose of this thesis, I would like to concentrate on the concept of model reader proposed by Umberto Eco as his ideas correspond with those proposed by Attridge and Lotman. Eco's concept suggests that one should investigate the receiver's limitations, and scrutinise how they function in the case of the signature. In *The Limits of Interpretation*, Eco presents two contradictory ways of interpretation: a finite one,[4] i.e. that which is intended by the creator, and an infinite one, i.e. that which allows to an unrestricted interpretation.[5] The second way, which Eco calls 'Hermetic semiosis' or 'Hermetic drift' is simultaneously an example of how Eco understands the notion of the signature:

> I shall call Hermetic drift the interpretive habit which dominated Renaissance Hermetism and which is based on the principles of universal analogy and sympathy, according to which every item of the furniture of the world is linked to every other element (or to many) of this sublunar world and to every element (or to many) of the superior world by means of similitudes or resemblances. It is through similitudes that the otherwise occult parenthood between things is manifested and every sublunar body bears the traces of that parenthood impressed on it as a *signature*. (1994b: 24)

From the above quotation one can formulate a hypothesis that besides the infinity of the receiver's interpretation, he or she is still able to trace the roots of the creator's signature. That viewpoint is surprising as the infinity of possibility should, at least theoretically, be an impediment in the process of deciphering the signature. Eco's understanding of signature and the role of the receiver in its interpretive process may derive from his attempt to redefine the notion of meaning in the interpretative process. He says that '[t]he problem is not to challenge the old idea that the world is a text which can be interpreted, but rather to decide whether it has a fixed meaning, many possible meanings, or none at all' (1994b: 23). On the one hand the signature requires its uniqueness and singularity but on the other allows to be replicated and interpreted by the receiver in infinite ways, then there should be raised the question about the border that separates the signature from the receiver, namely where the signature representing the creator ends and where the limitless interpretation of the receiver starts.

---

4 Eco recognises the finite interpretation as the *metaphysical realism* (1994b: 24).
5 Eco claims that the both ways of interpretation are strongly anchored in the historical periods, referring both to the Medieval duality and univocality and equivalence, through the Renaissance refusal of dualism until the modern polysemy of interpretation:
'Medieval interpreters were wrong in taking the world as a univocal text; modern interpreters are wrong in taking every text as an unshaped world. Texts are the human way to reduce the world to a manageable format, open to an intersubjective interpretive discourse. Which means that, when symbols are inserted into a text, there is, perhaps, no way to decide which interpretation is the 'good' one, but it is still possible to decide, on the basis of the context, which one is due, not to an effort of understanding 'that' text, but rather to a hallucinatory response on the part of the addressee.' (1994b: 21).

The notion of the border separating a non-text from a text has been already discussed as prominent in Lotman's model of the semiosphere. However, its role and usefulness in answering the above question should be developed. Lotman notices that the processes that happen within the border can be treated as filters that translate the non-texts from texts and *vice versa*. He points out that 'the border represents a multiplicity of points, belonging simultaneously to both the internal and external space' (2005: 208). So far the definition of the border corresponds with Eco's hermetic semiosis, dealing with the infinity of interpretations, and eventually, the signature's ability of replication. Thus, we can postulate to read the creator's signature through the model of the semiosphere defined by Lotman. The model in which the receiver of the text is located in the space of non-texts, i.e., the texts that are beyond the semiosphere. Subsequently, the receiver is only capable of deciphering the creator's signature (semiosphere) through the border's infiltration (translation) that allows the received to get into the text of the semiosphere. That is why one can postulate that the function of the border as a transmitter appears to be indispensable.[6]

In Attridge's quotation concerning the definition of the event, there appears one more interesting expression that merges both Attridge and Lotman's theories. Attridge writes about 'the beginning of its erosion, as it brings about the cultural changes necessary to accommodate it [the event – R.B]' (2004: 64). The term 'erosion' plays a primary role in the understanding of this concept. When something is erosive, it does not necessarily destroy the object but it modifies it in an unexpected way. The process of the erosion in natural environment may have a destructive effect on the structure of the rock but also soil or sand. By infiltrating into the dissolved material, the erosion can destroy the rock, but what is more important for our discussion, can also transport the dissolved material into a different location. Owing to that the erosion can contribute to the changes in the landscape, which result in creating a new, unexpected space.

Lotmanian notion of the 'explosion' works in a similar manner. Explosions are the processes that happen within the semiosphere, eventually shaping the semiosphere's internal structure; by that explosions appear to be indispensable in the process of creating the semiosphere. The concept of the 'explosion' was adopted by Lotman from the research on the phenomena of bifurcation and fluctuation.[7]

---

6 'Thus only with the help of the boundary is the semiosphere able to establish contact with non-semiotic and extra-semiotic spaces.' (2005: 210).

7 Lotman refers predominantly to Vladimir Vernadsky's biosphere: '[a] cosmic mechanism, which occupies a specific structural place in planetary unity. Situated on the surface of our planet and including within itself the totality of living things, the biosphere

These terms refer to the processes observed in natural sciences, and may be defined as the dynamic processes whose results cannot be predictable. Lotman suggests that such a phenomenon may be observed in the sphere of culture as well. When two, or more, ideas collide with each other, there exists a possibility that something new and unpredictable emerges. According to Lotman, the collision between ideas derives predominantly from language; he claims that 'each generation has a language for describing yesterday and principally lacks a language for tomorrow' (1992: 4, as cited in *Culture and Explosion*, 2004: xxvi). That statement not only illustrates that the collision of different ideas may bring an effect but also allows to understand that the semiosphere consists predominantly of three ingredients: the natural language, time and space. In addition, both time and space should be understood in the non-linear categories.

The second fundamental feature of the explosive act is its dynamism, without which the collision cannot be fulfilled.[8] The movement of ideas within the semiosphere can be both non-lineal and diachronic. Thus, the collision of certain ideas is usually unpredictable, being simultaneously pre-assumed. The discovery of America by Columbus in 1492 can serve as an example that helps to illustrate how the explosion works in practice. As is generally known, before Columbus the Vikings arrived to the cost of Newfoundland in the eleventh century but they abandoned the idea of further exploration.[9] After four centuries Columbus arrived at the cost of the Caribbean, which developed into a turning point, or an explosion, in the process of the colonisation of America as this event had a profound impact the culture, history and politics.

The analogies as well as differences of the Lotmanian concept of explosion and that of Attridge's erosion can be adjusted to the role of the receiver in the process of deciphering the signature. The receiver, weather he or she is absorbing the piece of art through a written text, painting, dance, or music, is involuntarily

---

transforms the radiated energy of the sun into the chemical and physical [objects] and is concerned with the transformation of the inert inanimate materials.' (Lotman 1984: 5–23).

8 'All explosive dynamic processes occur via a dynamically complex dialogue with stabilising mechanisms. We must not be deceived by the fact that in historical reality they appear to be enemies striving for the full destruction of the other pole. Any such destruction would be fatal to culture but, luckily, it is not feasible. Even when people are strongly convinced that they are putting into practice some kind of ideal theory the practical sphere also includes within itself opposing tendencies: they may adopt abnormal forms but they cannot be destroyed' (2005: 7).

9 See Parker, Philip. *The Northmen's Fury: A History of the Viking World*. Vintage, 2014.

responding to it. The meeting between the receiver and a piece of art is, in fact a collision of different, or similar, experiences that start to push against each other. Such a collision leads to creating a nucleus that eventually leads to the production of a cultural event. As Lotman notices, the collision of different ideas should be dynamic and its output, unpredictable. It is noteworthy that the process is bidirectional; both the creator and the receiver undergo the process of accommodation, similar collisions are taking place in Lotman's semiosphere where non-semiotic spaces infiltrate, through the boundary, the extra-semiotic, simultaneously changing the structure of the semiosphere (2005: 210).

2.2. Signature and poetics

Having presented the modalities upon which we understand and define the term 'signature,' one may ask a justified question: why should we not use a term that accompanies the literary tradition much longer and speak of a 'poetics' rather than 'signature.' I would like to point out why this term is not fully suitable and should not be used in the present study.

The attempts of defining the term 'poetics' can usually be divided into two categories: historical and theoretical. The historical sources of poetics can be found in the Ancient Greece, especially in the works of Pindar, Plato, and Aristotle. Aristotle was the first philosopher who attempted to create a taxonomy for a coherent and systematic study of literature. In *Poetics*, he defines the notion as 'the poetic art itself and the forms of it, what a specific capacity each has and how one ought to put together stories' (2006: 19). Aristotle is more concerned with the skill of making poetry rather than the nature and origin of it. After Aristotle, numerous authors attempted to characterise the nature of poetics; one might wish to mention such works as Nicolas Boileau's *Art of Poetry* (1674), William Wordsworth's preface to *Lyrical Ballads* (1802) and Samuel Taylor Coleridge's *Biographia Literaria* (1817). However, this historical development will not be our concern here.[10]

While Aristotle concentrates mainly on the art of poetry rather than on attempts to theoretically define it, Percy Bysshe Shelley presents a slightly different viewpoint. In *A Defence of Poetry* (1840) he proposes that '[p]oetry in

---

10 A historical overview of the notion of poetics and its development can be found in the monumental *The New Princeton Encyclopedia of Poetry and Poetics*. Preminger, A., Brogan, T.V.F. (ed.). Princeton University Press, Princeton 1993, especially pages 934–938.

general sense, may be defined to be 'the expression of the imagination:' and poetry is connate with the origin of man' (2002: 635). While the first part of Shelley's definition of poetics may be correlated with the importance of invention in the process of singularity presented by Attridge, the second part reveals a religious aspect of poetics. In fact, further in *A Defence of Poetry* Shelley imputes artists, whose domain is the work of imagination, to reveal the foundations of the civil society, namely the art.[11] Both Aristotle and Shelley's viewpoints on poetics, i.e. as the art of poetry and as a basis of a religious system, do not inscribe into our understanding of what the signature is. However, they share one common feature with our understanding what the signature is, namely all of the conceptions are recognised as a system: Aristotle sees poetics as a system of craftsmanship whereas Shelley as a metaphysical one. Moreover, the signature holds one unique feature that differs from the presented viewpoint on the poetics, namely besides being a system, the signature is also a dynamic process.

The second type of definitions concentrates on a theoretical aspect of poetics. *The New Princeton Encyclopedia of Poetry and Poetics* points out that the term 'poetics; can refer to the 'implicit principles' of the author, or more narrowly, it depicts 'the theory of literature' (2002: 929–930). The authors of the *Encyclopedia* go even further arguing that '[poetics] has been applied to almost every human activity, so that often it seems to mean little more than 'theory' … such usage is the most general and least useful' (929). A similar amount of generality can be observed in, for instance, Marjorie Perloff's definition of poetics, who in *Differentials. Poetry, Poetics, Pedagogy* (2004) observes:

> As someone trained in the discipline of English and Comparative Literature, I want to take a look at what traditionally has been one of the central branches of the humanities: the study of literature or, as I prefer to call it, *poetics*. 'Literature' is an imprecise designator that came into use only in the eighteenth century, whereas discussions of the poetic have a much more ancient and cross-cultural lineage. (5–6)

Perloff's viewpoint inscribes the term poetics into a much broader context characterising it as the name for the whole branch of the humanities. Nevertheless, such a definition is also too vague to be used in our definition of signature.

---

11 'But poets, or those who imagine and express this indestructible order, are not only the authors of language and of music, of the dance, and architecture, and statuary, and painting: they are the institutors of laws, and the founders of civil society, and the inventors of the arts of life, and the teachers, who draw into a certain propinquity with the beautiful and the true that partial apprehension of the agencies of the invisible world which is called religion.' (2002: 637).

Despite Perloff's viewpoint on the poetics, in *Differentials. Poetry, Poetics, Pedagogy* one can find at least four definitions what the poetics is and how it has been treated through centuries namely:

a) poetics as a branch of rhetoric, i.e. the art of 'finding the available means of persuasion' (2002: 6) that one can find in the works of Aristotle, Cicero and Quintilian;
b) poetics as a branch of philosophy, especially concentrated on 'a potential expression of truth and knowledge'[12] (2002: 7);
c) poetics as one of the arts next to music, dance, architecture or visual arts arguing that Plato in Ion describes the act of poetry as techné kai episteme, where the Greek techné means 'skill,' 'craft' or 'art' (2002: 8);
d) finally, she notices that poetics can be viewed as 'a historical or cultural formation' (2002: 9).

The aforementioned definitions have been referred to by numerous authors and scholars; however, neither of them corresponds to the definition of the signature presented in this thesis. Whereas Perloff characterises poetics as a branch of rhetoric, philosophy, craftsmanship, and even sociology, the signature should be perceived more as an intellectual act that can pivot around the abovementioned topics, yet should not be recognised *as* a branch of the above. We may notice that the notion of poetics very often indicates the state of 'in-betweenness' attempting to simultaneously belong to manifold categories. Tzvetan Todorov in *Introduction to Poetics* defines the notion as follows:

> Poetics breaks down the symmetry thus established between interpretation and science in the field of literary studies. In contradistinction to the interpretation of particular works, it does not seek to name meaning, but aims at a knowledge of the general laws that preside over the birth of each work. (1981: 6).

Todorov focuses on finding the general laws of poetics trying to indicate that they are independent from the creator and suggesting that a piece of art is the outcome of these laws. The role of the creator in this process is minimalised to that of a transmitter between the general laws of poetics and a work of art: such an approach diminishes the role of invention in the process. The problem of conceptualizing poetics as something between literary theory and philosophy

---

12 Perloff argues that the authors can be divided into two groups: those who use the theory of poetry-as-rhetoric including in this group, e.g. James Joyce and Ezra Pound, and those who represent the theory of poetry-as-philosophy like Paul Celan and Samuel Beckett (2002: 7).

has been, and still is, the core of the discussion upon this notion. Lyn Hejinian in *The Language of Inquiry* notices that '*[p]oetics* ... seems as much a philosophical realm as a literary one' (2000: 2), whereas Linda Hutcheon in *A Poetics of Postmodernism. History, Theory, Fiction* suggests that 'poetics would not seek to place itself in a position *between* theory and practice ..., but rather would seek a position *within* both' (2004: 17).[13]

Hutcheon's idea of anchoring poetics in practice, to some extent, overlaps with the definition of signature; however, that anchoring, in my opinion, does not connect these two definitions strongly enough for us to start using these names interchangeably. In fact, it is possible to find some traces of the signature structure in the definitions proposed by Todorov and Hejinian, yet these authors introduce them under completely different terms. Todorov, for instance, notices that '[w]hereby this science [poetics] is no longer concerned with actual literature, but with a possible literature in other words, with the abstract property that constitutes the singularity of the literary phenomenon: *literariness*' (1981: 7). Such a definition of literariness has more in common with the signature, just to point out the importance of possibility that is a significant factor in the act of establishing the singularity. On the other hand, Hejinian introduces the term *acknowledging* indicating that it 'is a process not a definitive act; it is an inquiry, a thinking on. And it is a process in and of language' (2000: 2). Hejinian's view concentrates on the process immersed in the language, the language that functions as a transmitter for both the creator and the receiver. However, the literariness and acknowledging inscribe in our understanding of what the signature to some extent, mainly due to recognising these two terms as processes, nevertheless their usefulness in our research seems limited, predominantly because they function as separate terms that function within the notion of poetics, but they are not defined *as* poetics.

2.3. The definition of the signature

So as to sum up the way in which the definition of signature will be understood in the context of characterising the artistic signature of Samuel Beckett, a

---

13 Hutcheon notices as well that the creation of a fixed definition of poetics is difficult to achieve due to its 'ever-changing theoretical structure' (2004: 14). Thus, she proposes to concentrate more upon the mix of cultural practice and theory than solely on studying a literary discourse (ibid.).

summary of what has already been presented is needed. The main features of the definition are as follows:

a) The term 'signature' corresponds with Steiner's 'character,' Attridge's 'singularity,' Lotman's 'proper name,' and Derrida's 'event' as all these notions cover one common ingredient, namely the act of production. Because of that, the terms 'style' (existence in a collective mind of a given culture), 'manner' (visible physical output) and 'poetics' (understood as a theory of literature or humanities in general, or a philosophic system) are not applicable in the context analysed here.

b) The functioning of the signature is limited by the boundaries of what Lotman called the 'semiosphere.' It means that all the notions, themes and subjects that exist within the semiosphere of the signature are beforehand infiltrated and accumulated in the notion of 'I.' Nevertheless, there can exist a relation between 'I' and the 'other,' or between semiotic and extra-semiotic spheres that, due to the process of collision, may result in explosions or erosions, and eventually, in the origin of new notions.

c) The signature encapsulates a never-ending possibility of generating new meanings. That possibility contributes to two apparently contradictory notions, of surprise and pre-assumption, without which the event of singularity cannot take place.

d) Among pre-assumed factors, one can distinguish the importance of the natural language that constitutes the basic element of the signature, simultaneously referring to the physicality of the signature. Moreover, the natural language is used to create other languages (Lotman's secondary modelling systems) that allow the creator to leave the receiver 'disarmed,' i.e. surprised. The disarmament results in a certain amount of unpredictability, namely words that are known for the receiver used by the author in a new context allow to generate new meanings.

e) One of the most important constituents in the process of the signature is the receiver (spectator, listener or reader) without whom, following Eco's assumptions, the signature cannot be constituted and remains in the realm of possibility. In addition, the receiver's influence on the act of constituting the signature is limited and can only happen under certain conditions (vide the structure of Lotman's semiosphere).

f) Finally, the signature cannot function in itself without the act of the repetition, creating the paradox of repetitive uniqueness. Namely, every act of encountering the artist's work by the receiver is unique, i.e., singular, however the work of art requires to encapsulate in itself certain pre-suppositions that the receiver is able to recognise in order to decipher the signature.

The above qualities of what the signature is will eventually lead us to a definition of notion as an intellectual act where, applying Lotman's notions of 'I,' 'other,' 'proper names,' and 'semiosphere,' the artist is using the natural language and all the motifs, notions and ideas that the natural language conveys in itself as a material to produce new meanings. Moreover, one may add that the indispensable feature of signature is a certain degree of the artist's recognition. The interwoven relation between the artist's 'I' and 'the other' creates a space for the artist's recognition. The internal text epitomised in the 'I' understood as the artist's unique phrase should be traced in the realm of 'common' names, the collective collection of signs that function in 'the other' (the external text). Only that condition allows the receiver to decode the characteristic features of a given artist, to recognise him or her. Owing to the recognition, the receiver is able to initiate the process that constitutes the signature and that does not require the artist's physical sign as it happens in a painting or a sculpture.

The forthcoming chapters of this thesis will concentrate on presenting Samuel Beckett's artistic signature as it appears in on his early works. The three main elements that I recognise in these works are the notions of the natural language, the neutrum and the memory; the elements that are the core of the pre-war texts and the motifs that appear to accompany Beckett's writing until his late works.

2.4. The artistic signature of Samuel Beckett

Having defined the concept of signature as used in this dissertation, I shall now proceed to examine how the afore-mentioned assumptions can be applied in the case of the artistic signature of Samuel Beckett. Chapter 2 will concentrate mainly on three aspects of my understanding of the concept of Beckett's signature, i.e.; the language, the neutrum and the memory. These three pillars will be discussed in this sub-chapter in a theoretical way. The practical aspects of the discussed theory will be further examined in Chapters 1–4 of Part Two where I focus solely on the writer's pre-war criticism, short stories and novels.

To begin characterising the main points of the artistic signature of Samuel Beckett, one should take into consideration the artist's own viewpoint on that matter. It seems remarkable that Beckett attempts to define his artistic manifesto, albeit does not do it directly. In *Beckett before Beckett*, a study that gathers the notes of Rachel Burrows, Beckett's student when the writer worked as a 1930–31 academic lecturer of French literature at Trinity College Dublin, one can find the writer's critique on Honoré de Balzac's writing. Although his criticism refers directly to Balzac's novels, one can notice that Beckett's thoughts encapsulate the concepts that he eventually applies to his own writing. Burrows observes: 'He hated Balzac, of course. He hated what he called the snowball act, which means that you do something that has causes, causes, causes, causes so that it's perfectly consistent' (2009: 28).

That inconsistency, or the opposition of 'the snowball act,' which is also defined by Beckett as a 'fatal mechanical chain of circumstances' ('enchaînement mécanique, fatal, de circonstances') (2009: 28), appears to be an essential point in characterising the writer's artistic signature. Manifold examples of Beckett's early writings only justify that thesis, repeatedly being the source of the author's failures, especially during his attempts to have his works published. His idea of inconsistency met with the reluctance of publishers who repeatedly dismissed his early works,[14] which, eventually led to a sense of disheartening in the young artist.[15] Despite the early failures, Beckett seemed to follow the path of inconsistency in his artistic expressions in such works as *More Pricks Than Kicks* or *Dream of Fair to Middling Women*. He himself defines that state of inconsistency as the state of flux. Rachel Burrows in her interview on her student years at Trinity College expands that idea as follows:

> The artist himself was changing all the time and his material was constantly in a state of flux, hence you had to do something to organize this mess, but not to make puppets and set them in motion, and not to fantasize in the way the Romantics did. He's

---

14 Edward Garnett from London publishing house Jonathan Cape expressed his opinion on *Dream of Fair to Middling Women* as 'I wouldn't touch this with a barge pole. Beckett probably is a clever fellow, but here he has elaborated a slavish, & rather incoherent imitation of Joyce, most eccentric in language & full of disgustingly affected passages – also *indecent;* this school is damned – & you wouldn't sell the book even on its title. Chatto was right to turn it down' (*Letters, Vol. I*, 120). Then, Charles Prentice from Chatto and Windus dismissed in 1933 the short story *Echo's Bones* arguing, in a sincere letter, why the story is not suitable for publishing:
'It is a nightmare. Just too terribly persuasive. It gives me the jim-jams. Th same horrible and immediate switches of the focus, and the same wild unfathomable energy of the population. There are chunks I don't connect with. I am so sorry to feel like this. Perhaps it is only over the details, and I may have a correct inclining of the main impression. I am sorry, for I hate to be dense, but I hope I am not altogether insensitive. 'Echo's Bones' certainly did land on me with a wallop.' (Beckett 2014: xii)
15 In a letter to Thomas McGreevy from 6 December 1933, Beckett says that the dismissal of 'Echo's Bones' 'discouraged me [him] profoundly.' (*Letters*, vol I., 171).

[Beckett – R.B.] concerned with digging into the real as he sees it at that moment, and even that was relative, because the artist is changing, the material is changing, and the moment is changing. (2009: 28)

The above fragment encapsulates the main fields of interests that are manifested in Beckett's works from the earliest 'Assumption' (1929) until the last 'what is word' (1990), for example his profound interests in literature, languages, philosophy, art, psychology, and in general, the human condition. Nevertheless, it is evident that the element that joins all these fields together, is the idea of flux, the artistic recycling, reorganisation, and eventually, the infinite process of creating new meanings.

Chapter 3: The Language

3.1. The concept of language in Beckett's early writings

In order to search for Beckett's deep interest in languages, one needs to move back to the author's school days. As far as French is concerned, it seems to have been the first language that was learnt by him. In *Damned to Fame*, James Knowlson notices that Beckett's first teacher of French was Ida Elsner, a German-born who ran a small kindergarten on the Leopardstown Road, near Foxrock with her sister, Pauline (1996: 42–43). Beckett attended Misses Elsners' Academy between he was five and nine, which only depicts how early his education in the field of foreign languages started. His education in French continued at Earlsfort House, a school located in Dublin that Beckett attended between 1915 and 1919, owing to the school's headmaster, Alfred E. Le Peton, who helped Beckett with French.[1] In the spring of 1920, Beckett started Portora Royal School, a prominent boarding school located in Enniskillen, famous for its over-three-hundred-year-long tradition and located in a picturesque area of the Irish lake district. During that time, the author's interest in arts flourished, unlike that in chemistry, physics or mathematics. At that time, despite being taught by a talented French teacher, Evelyn Tennant, his interests in that language declined significantly and were replaced by his enthusiasm to Latin taught by A.T.M. Murfet. As it turned out later, this allowed Beckett to deal with complex Latin texts of classical authors (1996: 57).[2] There is no trace that at Portora he learnt either German or Greek.

In October 1923, Beckett started, as an undergraduate, to study for an arts degree, at Trinity College in Dublin. There he met his Romance languages professor, Thomas Brown Rudmose-Brown, who had an enormous impact on Beckett's

---

1 It seems that at that period Beckett started learning Latin that was being taught by the Earlsfort House's coprincipal, William Ernest Exshaw (1996: 49).
2 Deirdre Bair in *Samuel Beckett: A Biography* notices that the writer's interest both in French and Latin, eventually decreased:
'In his third year at Portora, Beckett's grades were average or above in four of his ten subjects: Latin, arithmetic, algebra and trigonometry. His French was decidedly mediocre – two hundred out of a possible four hundred – and his English, history, geometry, physics, and chemistry were slightly worse. His grades declined in his last year at Portora, with only three of his subjects – arithmetic, geometry and English – normal or above. His Latin had dropped to 184, which was far below normal, and his French remained at the midpoint of two hundred.' (1990: 30).

interest in the matter of French language and French literature. Rudmose-Brown not only awoke Beckett's interests in the nineteenth century French poets such as Paul Valerie and Henri de Regnier but also presented and actually taught the young student about modern French authors such as Proust, Gide and Valery Larbaud. Rudmose-Brown's evident reluctance towards the canon, for instance towards Corneille, influenced young Beckett as well, as it has been already illustrated on the author's attitude towards Balzac.[3]

Besides French, Italian was another compulsory honour subject for Beckett. The Italian literature, just to include such authors as Petrarch, Machiavelli, Ariosto and above all Dante, was taught both by Rudmose-Brown and Walter Starkie. However, it was a private tutor, Bianca Esposito, who had tremendous influence on Beckett's love of *The Divine Comedy* (1996: 67).[4] Esposito was portrayed in 'Dante and the Lobster,' the first story in *More Pricks Than Kicks* collection, as Signorina Adriana Ottolenghi:

> Signorina Adriana Ottolenghi was waiting in the little front room off the hall, which Belacqua was naturally inclined to think of rather as the vestibule. That was her room, the Italian room. On the same side, but at the back, was the French room. God knows where the German room was. Who cared about the German room anyway? (2010: 84–85)

The description not only correlates with Beckett's experience with Bianca Esposito's private lessons[5] but also shows the writer's attitude towards the German language, the one that was not at that time in his area of interests.

---

3 The amicable relationship between Beckett and Rudmose-Brown left a vivid mark on Beckett's attitude both towards literature and towards life. For instance, the professor was famous for organising parties for his favourite students that impressed young Beckett who called them to be 'very sexy affairs' (1996: 65). In addition, Beckett commemorated Ruddy as he was called colloquially in *Dream of Fair to Middling Women* and *More Pricks Than Kicks,* where the professor is presented in a mocking way as a figure of the Polar Bear, a tight-fisted person who makes advances to young women.

4 In *Samuel Beckett. The Last Modernist* Anthony Cronin suggests that Beckett discovered Dante with the help of Esposito. This was '[a] discovery which came with the force of a revelation' (1999: 64).

5 Beckett attended to private classes in Italian to a school of languages and music located at 21 Ely Place in Dublin. Worth noting is the fact that Bianca Esposito's father, Michele, was a well-known pianist teacher and a musician of Italian origin. In addition, the Espositio and Beckett families were acquainted with each other through generations (see: Bowyer Bell, John. 'Waiting for Mario: The Espositos, Joyce, and Beckett.' In: *Éire-Ireland*, 30.2/1995: 7–26). Contrary to the relation presented in 'Dante and the Lobster,' where a certain amount of sexual tension between Belacqua and Ottolenghi is presented (Pilling 1997: 99), Samuel Beckett did not display such entanglement with

As far as German is concerned, it seems that the initial reason for learning this language can be rooted a romantic affair Beckett had with his cousin Ruth Margaret 'Peggy' Sinclair whom he met for the first time in Dublin in 1928. Beckett and 'Peggy' enchanted each other to such an extent that when she returned to her home in Kassel, Germany, Beckett '[b]egan to apply himself assiduously to learning German' (Knowlson 1996: 91). However, it is highly probable that he must have taken some lessons of German while visiting Kassel between 1928 and 1932, as in the letter to his cousin Morris Sinclair dated 27th January 1934, Beckett claims that '[i]n no way troubled the very imperfect understanding that I have of the German language' (*Letters I*, 2009: 180). Finally, his trip to Germany between 1936 and 1937[6] contributed to improving his language skills. His commitment to improving German can be illustrated by the fact of buying, for instance, Emil Otto's *German Conversation-Grammar; Methode Gaspey-Otto-Sauer*, the book that was found many years later in his private library (Van Hulle-Nixon 2013: 82).

One of the most fundamental characteristics of Beckett's writing is his life-long struggle with the matter of language. He deliberately chose the path of a bi-lingual writer and playwright, writing both in English and French, to expose himself to the 'resistance' of language. Daniel Katz assumes that the Beckettian resistance towards language materialises both in meaning and reference, simultaneously pointing out that '[t]his resistance itself can be transferred from one particular language to another, that any statement about language as a whole must be made from within a particular language and that this positioning has its own retinue of effects and implications' (2013: 361). Katz's viewpoint on the resistance recognised not as a universal phenomenon for every language, but the one that is becoming independent and is provisioned by the features of a particular language, corresponds with a theory of language proposed by Fritz Mauthner (1849–1923) in his *Beiträge zu einer Kritik der Sprache* (*Contributions to a Critique of Language*), a theory that had a decisive impact on Beckett's own understanding of what language is and how it can be treated not only in solely linguistic but also philosophic categories. The influence of Mauthner's thought on Beckett's writing will be discussed in this section; however, at this point one

---

Bianca, especially due to a serious gap between their age. However, Beckett was seriously bewildered with Esposito's wit and intelligence (Knowlson 1996: 68).

6 See Nixon, Mark. *Samuel Beckett's German Diaries 1936–1937*. Continuum, New York-London 2011, especially chapter 1.

should discuss the traces that indicate the beginning of Beckett's struggle with language.

As it has been already mentioned, Beckett's exposure to foreign languages started in his early childhood. Later, by mastering French, Latin, Italian, German, and later Spanish[7] he had to unconsciously develop interest in the language and, more precisely, in the word and its meaning(s). Beckett's private library proves this assumption: among many books dealing with the topic of language, one can find many dictionaries.[8] The most haunting seems to be the discovery of several etymological dictionaries in English, French and German, for instance Ernest Weekley's *A Concise Etymological Dictionary of Modern English* (1924), Albert Dauzat's *Dictionnaire étymologique* (1938) and Friedrich Kluge's *Etymologisches Wörterbuch der Deutschen Sprache* (1960) (Van Hulle-Nixon 2013: 195). The concise study in the etymology of words, eventually developed in Beckett the skill of playing with words as well as using them in new contexts and creating extraordinary meanings. These exercises in language fundamentally influenced the idiosyncrasy of Beckettian idiom that had been developed through his whole artistic carrier. Nonetheless, it cannot be forgotten that a certain amount of resistance towards language is visible in his early attempts at writing in different languages than English.

As far as French is concerned, Beckett started to write in this language, especially to his friends and acquaintances for whom English was not a native language or who had problems with it. An increase of letters written in French can be observed in 1937 when the young writer settled down in France. However, before that period, it was common for him to interweave French words and

---

7   In this thesis, I do not focus on the importance of Spanish in Beckett's education, as the writer explored on this language predominantly after World War II. However, it is worth noting that he started learning Spanish on his own in 1933, revealing it in a letter to Thomas MacGreevy from 22 June 1933 ('I started to work hard at Spanish, and though the occasion to use it has receded I suppose I may as well keep it on,' Van Hulle-Nixon 2013: 197), it seems that he abandoned that project shortly. Beckett's renaissance in the acquisition of Spanish started in the 1950s, when he translated *Anthology of Mexican Poetry* (1958). The process of translating this anthology is described at length in Carrera, María José. 'Handicapped by my Ignorance of Spanish:' Samuel Beckett's Translations of Mexican Poetry.' In: Wiśniewski, Tomasz (ed.). *Back to the Beckett Text*. Wydawnictwo Uniwersytetu Gdańskiego. Gdańsk-Sopot 2012: 93–105.
8   For example, Samuel Johnson's *Dictionary of English Language* (1799), *Oxford English Dictionary*, Melzi's *Italian-English/English-Italian Dictionary*, or *Der Sprach-Brockhaus* (Van Hulle—Nixon 2013: 193–196).

expressions to his English letters.[9] Despite his proficiency in colloquial French that he could use in non-formal conversations, he encountered some difficulties with more formal and legal French. In a letter dated 2 March 1936 to Sergei Eisenstein, which served as the writer's CV, one can notice a mixture of colloquial and formal French with a number of spelling errors (*Letters I*, xxxiii-xxxiv). Moreover, in the texts written in French, it was still palpable that French is not a native language for the author.

A similar situation can be applied to texts written in German. Beckett did not feel as comfortable in German as he did in French: the resistance of the former language was more evident. His writing in German had neither practical nor professional purpose. As it was more writing for writing's sake, focused on practising that language. His earliest German letter was written in 1934 to his cousin Morris Sinclair (*Letters I*, xliii, 200–203) and is full of grammatical and syntactical mistakes. The writer's afore-mentioned trip to Germany between 1936 and 1937 vividly influenced his writing skill as well. The letter to Axel Kaul, written in July 1937 proves that Beckett had not only broadened his knowledge of German, but also developed his erudition in that area.[10]

The struggle with language is noticed in the playwright's artistic texts as well. His fascination with etymology can be illustrated with the following fragment of *Murphy* (1938):

> He lit the tall thick candle from the radiator and went down to the w.c. to shut off the flow. What was the etymology of gas? On his way back he examined the foot of the ladder. It was only lightly screwed down, Ticklepenny could rectify it. He undressed to the regulation shirt, stuck the candle by its own tallow to the floor at the head of the bed, got in and tried to come out in his mind. But his body was still too busy with its fatigue. And the etymology of gas? Could it be the same word as chaos? Hardly. Chaos was yawn. But then cretin was Christian. Chaos would do, it might not be right but it was pleasant, for him henceforward gas would be chaos, and chaos gas. It could make you yawn, warm, laugh, cry, cease to suffer, live a little longer, die a little sooner. (2010a: 106)

The above fragment involves the points that have been discussed so far in the case of Beckettian understanding of language. First and foremost, the etymology

---

9   For instance, the letter dated 17 July 1930 to Thomas MacGreevy ends with a surprising mixture of French and English: 'Gaudin is collé, poor creature, & he wanted to get married. Réclame pour moi!' (*Letters I*, 27), whereas the letter to Philippe Soupault dated 5 August 1930 is entirely in French (*Letters I*, 38).

10 See Cohn, Ruby (ed.). *Disjecta. Miscellaneous Writings and a Dramatic Fragment*. Grove Press, New York 1984, especially chapter 4 of Part I entitled 'German Letter of 1937.'

serves here as a pretext to a deepen meditation upon the nature of language, raising such fundamental questions as the language origin and its limitations. The juxtaposition of the word 'gas'[11] with the word 'chaos,' where the latter alludes to the Greek creation myth ('first there were Chaos and Earth.,' Pinsent 1969: 16), subconsciously steers the reader's attention to the topic of the word's origin. Intriguingly, in the very next sentence the narrator shifts the perspective by evoking the Christian founding myth known from the Gospel of St. John ('In the beginning was the Word, and the Word was with God, and the Word was God.,' 1: 1). The artistic measure applied in the discussed example would turn out to be characteristic for Beckett's entire *oeuvre*; the maximum reduction of a particular notion to a single word that, by being located in an apparently noncongruent context, allows the author of *Murphy* to create his own language of signs.

Secondly, the process of wringing the essence of words is not an easy task for the author but, it evinces as the source of endless struggle with the matter of language. The author examines the persistence of language, for instance, by the process of changing the meanings ('for him henceforward gas would be chaos, and chaos gas'). Behind this artistic move stands the idea of resistance that can only happen within a particular language that is occurring within a specific cultural context.[12] Moreover, the notion of language inextricably interlinks with the problem of language failure, a never-ending process of getting to the essence of matter, in Beckett's case, to the essence of language. That issue, related to the notion of 'neutrum,' would be further discussed in Chapter 4 of Part One. However, at this point it needs to be mentioned that the idea of 'neutral language' constitutes as one of the fundamental aspects of Beckettian signature that start to crystallise in his early writings.[13]

---

11 Worth noting is the fact that the elusive nature of 'gas' corresponds with Beckett's predilection for another biblical sentiment, namely 'for dust thou art, and unto dust shalt thou return' (Genesys 3: 19). For further see: Auckley, Chris. 'The Bible.' In: Uhlman, Anthony (ed.). *Beckett in Context*. Cambridge University Press, Cambridge 2013: 324–335.
12 Katz notices: 'Beckett never let us forget that any speculation about language happens not in 'language' but in a specific language, at a specific time' (2013: 361).
13 The traces of Beckett's profound interests in the notion of neutrum can be found in his very first published short story 'Assumption' (1929), where he *de facto* juxtaposes neutrum with the act of reduction: '[t]o avoid the expansion of the commonplace is not enough; the highest art reduces significance in order to obtain that inexplicable bombshell perfection.' (2010b: 58).

The next characteristic feature of Beckettian idiosyncrasy is the perception of language as a process of the multiplication and reversal of meanings. In the above example taken from *Murphy*, the narrator lists a number of activities that usually collocate with the word gas ('It could make you yawn, warm, laugh, cry, cease to suffer, live a little longer, die a little sooner.'). However, in the previous sentence the author purposely reversed the word 'gas' with 'chaos' and *vice versa*. In such a context, the word 'chaos,' already reduced to a sign of Western philosophy, by the references to the Greek mythology, and the Bible, reveals the new meanings, or, the new possibilities.[14]

In the case of the above example, it is worth delimiting another characteristic feature of Beckett's play with language, namely the juxtaposition of low- and high-brow topics,[15] very often in the same sentence. Next to a laughing gas, he sets a gas that can cause suffering. Such an artistic strategy is intentional and occurs in many Beckettian works corresponding with his bitter-sweet sense of humour and irony.[16]

The above-mentioned qualities of Beckett's language, namely its limitation, reduction, resistance, word-play, functioning in the specific language, at a specific time, and finally, perusing to reach the state of neutrum started to clarify in Beckett's early writing in the 1930s. His reluctance towards Balzac, who represented the stream of predictable, cause-effect literature, only indicates that from

---

14 The multiplication of synonyms used for a similar artistic purpose can be noticed, for example, in the post-war novels, just to evoke *The Unnamable* (1953), where in one fragment the narrator plays with the expressions connected with locomotion:
'the ball would start a-rolling, the disturbance would spread to every part, locomotion itself would soon appear, trips properly so called, business trips, pleasure trips, research expeditions, sabbatical leaves, jaunts and rambles, honeymoons at home and abroad and long sad solitary tramps in the rain, I indicate the main trends, athletics, tossing in bed, physical jerks, locomotor ataxy, death throes, rigor and rigor mortis, emergal of the bony structure, that should suffice.' (2010b: 101).
15 See the opening part of a short story from *More Pricks Than Kicks* (1934) called 'A Wet Night,' where an elevated atmosphere of Christmas is juxtaposed with a supposedly urinating Hyam: 'Hark, it is the season of festivity and goodwill. Shopping is in full swing, the streets are thronged with revellers, the Corporation has offered a prize for the best-dressed window, Hyam's trousers are down again.' (2010c: 108)
16 The laughter, next to silence, functions in Beckett's writing as the final answer to the limitations of language. That notion has been presented in manifold studies such as Sailsbury, Laura. *Samuel Beckett: Laughing Matters, Comic Timing*. Edinburgh University Press, Edinburgh 2012 or Rabaté, Jean-Michel. *Think, Pig! Beckett at the limits of the Human*. Fordham University Press, New York 2016.

his earliest artistic activities Beckett opted for the insufficiency of language and dismissed traditional literary forms.[17] In *Dream of Fair to Middling Women* we can find a fragment where Belacqua expresses his expectations toward the book he would like to write. The following fragment, read from the diachronic point of view, can serve as a kind of artistic manifesto:

> I shall write a book, he mused, tired of the harlots of earth and air—I am hemmed in, he submused, on all sides by putes, in thought or in deed, hemmed in and about; a great big man must be hired to lift the hem—a book where the phrase is self-consciously smart and slick, but of a smartness and slickness other than that of its neighbours on the page. The blown roses of a phrase shall catapult the reader into the tulips of the phrase that follows. The experience of my reader shall be between the phrases, in the silence, communicated by the intervals, not the terms, of the statement, between the flowers that cannot coexist, the antithetical (nothing so simple as antithetical) seasons of words, his experience shall be the menace, the miracle, the memory, of an unspeakable trajectory. (2012: 138)

The above fragment reveals the foundations of literature that would be later recognised by the writer himself as the literature of the 'non-word.' The narrator not only wants to reduce the words to minimum but also to completely get rid of the language to reach to its essence.[18] It can be proven that Beckett's transformation in the perception of what the language is, should be correlated with his profound studies on Fritz Mauthner's *Beiträge zu einer Kritik der Sprache* (*Contributions to a Critique of Language*).

Beckett started his research on Mauthner's theory of language in 1932,[19] while studying at Trinity College in Dublin (Ben-Zvi 1980: 185). Undoubtedly,

---

17 In *Dream of Fair to middling Women* (1932/92), Belacqua openly expresses his resistance towards the traditional literature, personified by Balzac:
'To read Balzac is to receive the impression of a chloroformed world. He is absolute master of his material, he can do what he likes with it, he can foresee and calculate its least vicissitude, he can write the end of his book before he has finished the first paragraph, because he has turned all his creatures into clockwork cabbages and can rely on their staying put wherever needed or staying going at whatever speed in whatever direction he chooses. The whole thing, from beginning to end, takes place in a spellbound backwash.' (2012: 119–120).
18 'It is indeed getting more and more difficult, even pointless, for me to write in formal English. And more and more my language appears to me like a veil which one has to tear apart in order to get to those things (or the nothingness) lying behind it.' (*Letters I, 518*).
19 In his copy of Mauthner's *Beiträge*, Beckett marked over seven hundred pages (Van Hulle-Nixon 2013: 158–163). Moreover, he added a vast number of comments based on Mauthner's work in his 'Whoroscope' Notebook (ibid. 155–156). The detailed research

the work of the Austro-Bohemian philosopher had impact on the artistic development of the Irishman, as Mauthner's *Critique* accompanied Beckett through all his life.[20] Mauthner's thoughts on the nature of language can be described as nominalist and represent the philosophical current that was especially close to Beckett due to his earlier studies on other nominalists such as Vico, Kant or Schopenhauer.[21]

The core of Mauthner's philosophy is based on the assumption that there exists nothing but language. The language that is perceived not only in categories of a tool or a transmitter of thoughts but as an independent, '[c]entral concern in its own right' (Ben-Zvi 1980: 188). The opening section of *Beiträge* reflects the Christian idea of perceiving words as the founding element, upon which the world was created, however further similarities between the Christian theology and Mauthner's viewpoint differ radically:[22]

> In the Beginning was the Word. With the word, men stand at the beginning of their insight into the world, and if they stay with the world they'll stop there. He who wishes to move on, even if it be only a tiny step that may serve to advance the though efforts of an entire lifetime, *he must try to redeem the world from the tyranny of language*. (1921: 1)[23]

The philosopher claims that the beginning as well as ending of every man is constituted in language, without which man cannot be constituted. Moreover,

---

on the Beckett's introduction to Mauthner's writing was presented in Pilling, John. 'Beckett and Mauthner Revisited.' In: Gontarski, S.E., Uhlmann, Anthony (ed.), *Beckett after Beckett*. University Press of Florida, 2006: 158–166.

20 Pilling notices that the three-volume edition of *Critique* was found after the writer's death in his private library (2006: 164).

21 Their viewpoints on the nominalist nature of language can be found in such works as *Dante...Bruno. Vico.. Joyce* or *Dream of Fair to Middling Women*.

22 Mauthner recognises the concept of God only as a useful phantasm that allows us to name the unknowable or unnamable. For more see: Jakuszko, Honorata. 'Fritz Mauthner's Critique of Locke's Idea of God.' In: *Studies in Logic, Grammar and Rhetoric*, Uniwersytet w Białymstoku, 20/2010: 65–78.

23 ['Im Anfang war das Wort.' Mit dem Worte stehen die Menschen am Anfang der Welterkenntnis und sie bleiben stehen, wenn sie beim Worte bleiben. Wer weiter schreiten will, auch nur um den kleinwinzigen Schritt, um welchen die Denkarbeit eines ganzen Lebens wieter bringen kann, der muß sich vom Worte befreien und vom Wortaberglauben, der muß seine Welt von der Tyrannei der Sprache zu erlösen versuchen.']. Mauthner, Fritz. *Beiträge zu einer Kritik der Sprache*. J.G. Cotta'sche Buchhandlung Nachfolger, Berlin – Stuttgart, 1921. All translations based on Ben-Zvi, Linda. 'Samuel Beckett, Fritz Mauthner, and the Limits of Language.' In: PMLA, 95.2/1980: 183–200.

the source of all knowledge and thought is constituted solely in language, i.e. knowledge cannot exist without it. For Beckett, a viewpoint of subordinating the constitution of a subject solely to words seems to be especially attractive, as the attempts of implementing Mauthner's philosophy can be traced in the Irishman's early works. A suitable example is a meta-linguistic meditation on Belacqua's purpose in *Dream of Fair to Middling Women*. In the chapter *Und*, the narrator does not mask that Belacqua functions as a linguistic experiment that, unfortunately, did not fulfil his purpose. The narrator claims that '[w]e picked Belacqua for the job, and now we find that he is not able for it.' (2012: 126). The language plays a paradoxical role in the constituency of thought; it is something without which the thought cannot be established, yet the bonds of language do not allow to perceive the external, the unknowable that is located beyond the language.

The bonds of language are, according to Mauthner, the source of the everlasting confinement of the subject, the bonds from which every thinking man should try to get liberated:

> He who sets out to write a book with a hunger for words, with a love of words, and with the vanity of words, in the language of yesterday or of today or of tomorrow, in the congealed language of a certain and firm step, he cannot undertake the task of liberation from language. I must destroy language within me, in front of me, and behind me step for step if I want to ascend in the critique of language, which is the most pressing task for thinking man; I must shatter each rung of the ladder by stepping upon it. He who wishes to follow me must reconstitute the rungs in order to shatter them once again. (1921: 1–2)[24]

The never-ending process of liberation from language, the one that eventually ends with failure, presented in the above fragment, was to become the core of Beckett's thematic preoccupations that was scrutinised even in his very last work 'what is the word' (1990).[25] Both Mauthner and Beckett are aware of the confines that originate from language, and both are aware that the liberation from

---

24 ['Der kann das Werk der Befreiung von der Sprache nicht vollbringen, der mit Worthunger, mit Wortliebe und mit Worteitelkeit ein Buch zu schreiben ausgeht in der Sprache von gestern oder von heute oder von morgen, in der erstarrten Sprache einer bestimmten festen Stufe. Will ich emporklimmen in der Sprachkritik, die das wichtigste Geschäft der denkenden Menschheit ist, so muß ich die Sprache hinter mir und vor mir und in mir vernichten von Schritt zu Schritt, so muß ich jede Sprosse der Leiter zertrümmern, indem ich, sie betrete. Wer folgen will, der zimmere die Sprossen wider, um sie abermals zu zertrümmern.'].
25 A concise study on this work can be found in Salisbury, Laura. 'what is the word:' Beckett's Aphasic Modernism.' In: Journal of Beckett Studies, 17.1–2/2008: 78–126.

language is intrinsically connected with the state of failure. Nevertheless, both thinkers interpose the problem of failure in the central point of their work. The most appealing is the fact that, besides its inevitability, Beckett and Mauthner are completely aware of the failure and the consequences that the limitations of language carry with it.

In the case of Beckett's *Dream*, the narrator is aware that 'Belacqua was not free and therefore could not at will go back into his heart, could not will and gain his enlargement from the gin-palace of willing' (2012: 122–123), whereas Mauthner speaks about self-delusion in this way: '[t]he renunciation of self-delusion is contained in the insight: *I am writing a book against language in a rigid language*' (1921: 2).[26] Moreover, the narrator in *Dream* is aware of the limitations of the language as a structure, simultaneously pointing out, after Mauthner, that the logic that stands behind the language is not universal, and should be always adjusted to the structure of a particular language:

> It would scarcely be an exaggeration to maintain that the four-and-twenty letters make no more variety of words in diverse languages than the days and nights of this hopeless man produce variety. Yet, various though he was, he epitomised nothing. (2012: 126)

The process of methodical reaching of the 'unreachable' – the thought not infected by language – functions in Beckett's works as an artistic method, as an exercise within the artistic process.[27] That everlasting failure to reach the unreachable state of suspension between the thought infected by language and the *pure* thought can be also found in Beckett's viewpoint on the philosophy of Giambattista Vico (1668–1744). For Vico, the process of making was based on 'a subjectively unconditioned, concrete, linguistic fabrication of true things' (Rudnick Luft 2003: 25). Vico, similarly to Mauthner and Beckett's viewpoints, opts for the dualistic perception of the world, i.e. 1) the internal that happens within the language *vide* in the human's thought, and 2) the external that is philosophically abstract and cannot be penetrated by language. However, it is worth pointing out that Vico is not in favour of any options as they would cause '[t]he danger in neatness of identification' (2010c: 495). Beckett expresses his viewpoint on the philosophy of Vico in the opening of his essay *Dante... Bruno. Vico.. Joyce* (1929):

---

26 ['In diser Einsicht liegt der Verzicht auf die Selbsttäuschung, ein Buch zu schreiben gegen die Sprache in einer starren Sprache.'].
27 In the 1937 letter to Axel Kaun, Beckett writes: 'To drill one hole after another into it until that which lurks behind, be it something or nothing, start seeping through – I cannot imagine a higher goal for today's writer' (*Letters I*,518).

Giambattista Vico himself could not resist the attractiveness of such coincidence of gesture. He insisted on complete identification between the philosophical abstraction and the empirical illustration, thereby annulling the absolutism of each conception – hoisting the real unjustifiably clear of its dimensional limits, temporalizing that which is extratemporal. (2010c: 495).

Beckett's view on the tie between time and language proposed by Vico, connects with Mauthner's afore-mentioned idea on the same matter; thus, it can be assumed that the immersion in a particular language, functioning within particular structures and at a particular time period is one of the foundations of the artistic signature, particularly visible in case of Beckett's multilingualism, where his gradual switch from writing in English to French has influenced how his signature is constructed.[28]

Having presented the relations between Mauthner and Beckett's philosophy so far, one should not forget about one indispensable aspect of Beckett's signature: the importance of the act of speaking. As Mauthner notices in *Critique*:

> What stands most clearly in the path of knowing truth is that men all believe they themselves think, when actually they only speak, and also that scholars and students of the mind all speak of thinking for which speaking should be at most the instrument or the clothing. But this is not true; there is no thinking without speaking, i.e., without words. There is no thinking, there is only speaking. (1921: 176)[29]

The reduction of knowledge to the act of speaking allows Mauthner to claim that all we know is only what we say ('there is no thinking outside speaking,' 1921: 507),[30] it means that what we say reflects who we are and nothing more. For Beckett, the ideas covered in *Critique* answer his questions covered in the letter to Axel Kaun, about the 'non-word' literature. Namely, the reduction of knowledge

---

28 Brian Fitch notices a significant aspect of Beckett's bilingualism that corresponds with the definition of signature, namely with its surprise and pre-supposition aspects: '[i]n whichever of the two languages Beckett happens to be writing at a given moment, there is always the presence of the other language with its wholly different expressive potential hovering at his shoulder, always at arm's reach and within earshot' (1988: 156).

29 ['Dies steht der Erkenntnis der Wahrheit am starrsten im Wege, daß die Menschen alle glauben zu denken, während sie doch nur sprechen, daß aber auch di Denkgelehrten und Seelenforscher allesamt von einem Denken reden, für welches das Sprechen höchstens das Werkzeug sein soll. Oder das Gewand. Das ist aber nicht wahr, es gibt kein Denken ohne Sprechen, das heißt ohne Worte. Oder richtiger: Es gibt gar kein Denken, es gibt nur Sprechen. Das Denken ist das Sprechen auf seinen Ladenwert hin beurteilt.'].

30 ['daß es kein Denken gebe außer dem Sprechen'].

to the act of speaking allows Beckett to reduce words of his characters to signs of 'the failure of knowledge' (Ben-Zvi 1980: 188). Owing to that, words symbolise the failure of going beyond language, the leitmotif of Beckett's post-war works such as *Three Dialogues* (1949), *Malone Dies* (1951), and *The Unnamable* (1953). However, the traces of this artistic measure are visible in the pre-war period, such as a poem 'Cascando' (1936). In the poem, the subject struggles with the act of communication, simultaneously trying in vain to escape from the limitations of language or form, '[t]he churn of stale words' (2010c: 34). A similar measure can be noticed in, for instance, 'A Wet Night' from *More Pricks Than Kicks* where the Polar Bear encourages Belacqua to 'say[ing] his lines' (2010c: 135) or the opening chapter of *Dream*, where the act of failed communication is symbolised by young Belacqua's furious pedalling after 'Findlater's van' (2012: 1)

Chapter 4: The Neutrum

In *Murphy* (1938), one can find a peculiar description of Mr. Endon's wish concerning his preferable way of dying, namely the act of apnoea:

'Mr. Endon was on parchment and Murphy had his tab: 'Mr. Endon. Apnoea, or any other available means.'
Suicide by apnoea has often been tried, notably by the condemned to death. In vain. It is a physiological impossibility. But the Marcyseat was not disposed to take unnecessary chances. Mr. Endon has insisted that if he did it at all, it would be by apnoea, and not otherwise. He said his voice would not hear of any other method. ... It was not like a real voice, one minute it said one thing and the next minute something quite different.' (2010a: 111)

The apnoea, known also as asphyxia or breathlessness, is the cessation of both breathing and of the movement of the lungs. The state can be achieved, for instance, by closing the vocal cords or by blocking the nasal vestibule. The state of apnoea connotes the state of 'in-betweenness,' a kind of suspension between existence (the patient is still aware of his or her corporeality) and non-exitance (the prolonged cut-off from fresh air eventually leads to death). Thus, it is not surprising that such a metaphor is especially attractive for Beckett and re-appears in his later works.[1] As Alain Badiou notices, 'Beckett's method is ... a question of subtracting or suspending the subject so as to see what then happens to being' (2003: 108). Such an approach constitutes the core of Beckett's signature, namely a never-ending attempt to reach the state of neutrality or the state of *neutrum*, also understood as neutral language. Reaching that state should allow the writer to create not only a non-word literature but also the literature where the words are not seen and disappear, such a motif appears to be a core of the writer's complete *oeuvre* that is only further developed in his late works.[2] In the following section I would like to discuss in detail terms such as: 'neutrum,' 'aporia,' 'reduction,'

---

1   See: 'In Short. The Right Aggregate, the Grand Apnoea, and the Accusative of Inexistance' in: Blau, Herbert. *Sails of the Herring Fleet. Essays on Beckett.* The University of Michigan Press 2004, 180–195, where the author points out the references to apnoea, for example, in *Endgame* and *Texts for Nothing*.
2   The example of the word disappearance is epitomised in the phrase 'ooze' from *Worstward Ho*, where this phrase functions as an abstract hypothesis that serves to alarm the reader both the disappearance of words and '[t]he real end of the imperative of saying' (Badiou 2003: 108).

'le Dehors' and the 'Epochē'. In spite of certain amount of similarity between these terms, their precise meanings are subtly different. Such a broad perspective on the notion of the neutrum and how it is understood by different researchers and philosophers should eventually lead us to crystallising the definition of the neutrum that is applicable to Beckett's *oeuvre*.

4.1. The neutral language

Maurice Blanchot (1907–2003) indicates the main feature that can characterise the neutrum as follows: '[t]o think or to speak in the neuter, the neutral, is to think or to speak apart from every visible and every invisible' (1993: 301). Blanchot encapsulates in this sentence the main idea that stands behind attempts of defying the neutrum, namely to express the original ideas that are unspeakable and unthoughtful through the device of the language. Such a viewpoint on what the neutrum is in the context of Beckett's works will be a leading one in this thesis. I use Blanchot's ideas as a starting point for my discussion on the notion of neutrum even though I am aware of the achronological impact that Blanchot's thought had on Beckett's *oeuvre*.[3] In *The Space of Literature* (*L'Espace littéraire*, 1989), Blanchot, taking the example of Stéphane Mallarmé, introduces the category of the 'crude language,' the language understood as a pure silence, where there exists nothing, including words.[4] The most vital, in Blanchot's theory of the crude language, seems to be the notion of 'presence' understood not as the state of substantial presence or non-presence, but more as an enigmatic concept that functions beyond the natural language and is described by the author of *Thomas the Obscure* as the 'pure word' or the 'pure thought'.[5] The grasp of the pure word,

---

3   Derval Tubridy notices that Beckett received an article by Blanchot from Georges Duthuit in 1948, while working on *Three Dialogues* (2018: 2).
4   'Silent, therefore, because meaningless, crude language is an absence of words, a pure exchange where nothing is exchanged, where there is nothing real except the movement of exchange, which is nothing. But it turns out the same for the word confided to the questing poet – that language whose whole force lies in its not being, whose very glory is to evoke, in its own absence, the absence of everything. This language of the unreal, this fictive language which delivers us to fiction, comes from silence and returns to silence.' (39).
5   Leslie Hill in *Blanchot. Extreme Contemporary* attempts to explain the concept of Blanchotian presence in the following manner:
    'For "presence," in Blanchot's texts, evidently does not quite mean the same as "presence," but nor is it the same as "non-presence." It is, one might say, both presence itself, and something other (or less) than presence; it is presence mentioned rather than

i.e. the word that is not infected by the natural language but exists as the essential word in the realm of presence, seems to be impossible to fulfil. Blanchot describes the qualities of such a pure word in the following manner:

> But nothing is more foreign to the tree than the word *tree*, as it is used nonetheless by everyday language. A word which does not name anything, which does not represent anything, which does not outlast itself in any way, a word which is not even a word, and which disappears marvellously altogether and at once in its usage: what could be more worthy of the essential and closer to silence?' (1989: 39–40).

The qualities of the neutral language presented in the above fragment seem to be contradictory to any qualities that a natural language, i.e., the language whose primary aim is communication, should possess. Firstly, Blanchot claims that words used in any natural language like the 'tree', 'dog' or 'rain' function only as a mere reflection of the realm of 'presence', the realm that exists beyond the 'presence' of words and languages used in the acts of writing and speaking. Such an approach, to some extent, allows us to draw a conclusion that the world of pure words or the neutral language covers in itself a metaphysical aspect of the mystery, namely, suggests the existence of a realm of pure, original words, a realm that, in Lotmanian categories, is located beyond the borderline, and the access to this world is almost impossible due to the immediate contamination of the pure word-thought by the natural language.[6]

---

used, but thereby used rather than mentioned; as such, it is perhaps readable only as an enigmatic erasure of presence, as presence, so to speak, in its fragility as erasure, presence always already effaced and just about to be effaced, presence deferred and dispersed, transformed into a possibility of otherness, into a spectral "presence" or "non-presence."' (2001: 133).

6 The metaphysical aspect of the 'presence' in Blanchot's works corresponds with George Steiner's term 'real presence'. For Steiner, the 'real presence' is equivalent with the presence of God. In *Real Presences*, the act of the aesthetic experience, such as the literature or art are inextricable with a metaphysical presence of the absolute:
'It proposes that any coherent understanding of what language is and how language performs, that any coherent account of the capacity of human speech to communicate meaning and feeling is, in the final analysis, underwritten by the assumption of God's presence. I will put forward the argument that the experience of aesthetic meaning in particular, that of literature, of the arts, of musical form, infers the necessary possibility of this 'real presence.' (1989: 1)
Blanchot notices a similar dependency in poetry. Based on Mallarmé's poems, the 'Nothingness,' or the realm of neutrum is equivalent to the gods' absence. The act of 'digging into the verse' causes that the reader '[e]scapes from being as certitude, meets with the absence of the gods, lives in the intimacy of this absence, becomes responsible

The second distinguishing feature of Blanchot's pure word theory refers to its elusive nature. Here, Blanchot suggests that neutrum, or pure word, does not fulfil the basic role we should expect from it, namely that it conveys no meaning, that it 'does not represent anything.' Such an approach may be confusing as it deconstructs our perception of what the word is and which role it should play. To paraphrase Beckett, one may ask the question: what is the (pure) word? If the neutrum does not convey any semantic features, how should we classify it? Leslie Hill argues that '[t]he neutre, however is not just a name; it is a response to that which always exceeds the name' (2001: 134). Such a definition situates the neutrum, not necessarily at the top of the word hierarchy, but rather beyond it, simultaneously suggesting that the neutre is the source of all meaning, owing to which words can mean at all.[7] Even though the neutrum is the source of all meaning, it cannot be the source of meaning for itself, thus it stays 'beyond meaning' (2001: 134). Owing to that, the term neutrum should not be perceived in substantial categories but rather as a 'name for namelessness.'[8]

The next vital feature of the neutrum suggested by Blanchot is its ephemeral nature ('[it] disappears marvellously altogether and at once in its usage'). That ephemerality is inextricably connected with a vital question concerning the origin of the neutrum, or rather the place where the neutrum occurs. Because the verb 'occur' connotes a certain degree of physicality in its meaning, i.e. it suggests that the process of the neutrum creation is substantial, I would like to borrow, from Leslie Hill, the term 'manifestation:'

> So, if the neutre in Blanchot functions on one level as manifestation and erasure, it also exceeds those concepts, which it suspends and defers. Manifesting itself as erasure, the

---

for it, assumes its risk, and endures its favour.'(1982: 38). The metaphysical aspect of the neutrum will not be further developed in this thesis, however the author wants to indicate that the term 'God's absence' functions as the synonym of neutrum and as such can be applied to Beckett's concept of the absolute presented in his post-war novels and plays such as *Waiting for Godot*, *Endgame* or *The Unnamable*. The traces of the Western metaphysics in Beckett's narratives are described in detail, for instance, in Amiral, Eyal. *Wandering and Home: Beckett's Metaphysical Narrative*. Pennsylvania State University Press, 1993.

7 'If the neutre is what makes words mean other than what they mean, it is arguably also what allows them to mean at all.' (Hill 2001: 134).
8 'Despite the name, the neutre is not an entity, nor is it, properly speaking, a concept. It is rather a name for the namelessness of the name, a concept whose purpose is to conceptualise that which precedes all concepts.' (Hill 2001: 132).

neutre discreetly erases that manifestation; erasing itself as manifestation, it manifests itself as an absent erasure that has always already disappeared. (2001: 134)

The neutrum as a manifestation of the erasure displays the second, besides revealing the pure word, feature, namely its intransigent pursuit to achieve the state of suspension, a suspension that should allow us to observe the neutrum in its pure form. Ideally, the state of suspension should allow us to reduce the language, following the term coined by Roland Barthes, to 'the degree zero' ('le degré zéro'),[9] i.e. to the state of full neutrality, nevertheless such an attempt is doomed. The everlasting disappearance of the neutrum, due to its interference with the thought, whose foundations are constructed on the natural language, is the reason why that the manifestation of the zero degree, understood also as silence, cannot be fulfilled. Jakub Momro indicates another impossibility: that of constituting a stable neutrum; he suggests that literature in pure state cannot be observed due to the intentional work of the subject; the intentionality is the cause of the disappearance of the neutrum (2010: 125).

Nevertheless, we should move back to the question of where the neutrum manifests itself. In order to achieve the state of suspension, the neutre needs a 'space of in-betweenness,' a space that is itself suspended between the exterior and the interior. Hill proposes, similarly to Barthes, that the neutrum cannot be inscribed into the fixed frames, but exists between, yet beyond them:

> In this way, like language itself, the neutre is perhaps best understood as a movement of perpetual effacement and reinscription that is logically prior to all conceptual distinctions. It therefore cannot be subordinated to the opposition between the visible and the invisible, the present and the absent, the intelligible and the sensible, all of which it precedes, suspends and displaces. As such, it is in excess of all positionality, all principle of being (or non-being), subjectivity, or truth. (2001: 132–133)

Taking into consideration the above fragment, one may encounter an ontological problem concerning the description of the 'ideal space' within which the neutrum can be observed. Therefore, for a better understanding of Blanchot's thoughts on the notion of the 'presence,' one additional term needs to be

---

9   Roland Barthes in *Writing Degree Zero*, recognises the neutrum as the 'zero element' (1970: 76). He points out that the neutral language can exist as an alternative to two other literary categories, namely the 'singular-plural' and 'preterite-present' and calls that third category 'an amodal form.' Barthes' viewpoints on neutrum and how it can be applied to style, can be found in chapter entitled 'Writing and Silence,' pp. 74–78.

introduced, namely the 'le Dehors' (*the Outside*), especially as presented in the view of Michel Foucault (1926–1984).[10]

In *Maurice Blanchot: The Thought from Outside*[11] Foucault discusses three characteristics of the outside: philological, philosophical and metaphysical.[12] As far as the linguistic one is concerned, he suggests the difference between 'I speak' and 'I say to speak' (1987: 10). The expression 'I say to speak' refers to the communicative aspect of any language, where the relation between the object and the words that describe this object describes is safe. By safety it is meant that between the word and the object there is no place for any unpredicted obstacles,

---

10 The sources of Foucault's *le Dohors* can be traced in the philosophy of despair proposed by Lev Shestov (1866–1938) who, on the one hand characterises despair as an experience of losing everything, but on the other, he characterises the despair as the *penultimate word,* the last word that cannot be captured by any theory and cannot be said in any human language. As he later notices in his *Penultimate Words and Other Essays*, the penultimate word is an experience that not only allows us to see the horizon of despair, but also to discover what is beyond it. Shestov identifies that beyond of despair with the term faith, which inscribes in Blanchot's and Steiner's metaphysical aspect of presence:

'Ibsen and Turgenev served the same God as the swans, according to the Greek belief, the bright God of songs, Apollo. And their last songs, their *senilia*, were better than all that had gone before. In them is a bottomless depth awful to the eye, but how wonderful! There all things are different from what they are with us on the surface. Should one hearken to the temptation and go to the call of the great old men, or should he tie himself to the mast of conviction, verified by the experience of mankind, and cover his ears as once the crafty Ulysses did to save himself from the Syrens? There is a way of escape: there is a word which will destroy the enchantment. I have already uttered it: *senilia.* … What if *senilia* bring us nearer to the truth? Perhaps the soothsaying birds of Apollo grieve in unearthly anguish for another existence; perhaps their fear is not of death but of life; perhaps in Turgeniev's poems, as well as in Ibsen's last drama, are already heard, if not the last, then at least the penultimate words of mankind.' (1916: 108–109)

The traces of Shestov's philosophy on Foucault's writing can be found, for example, in: Weingrad, Michael. 'New Encounters with Shestov.' In: *The Journal of Jewish Thought and Philosophy,* 11.1/2002: 49–62.

11 The original article in French was published as 'La pensée du dehors' in: *Critique,* 229/1966: 523–546 and subsequently reprinted in *Dits et écrits I. 1954–1969.* Gallimard, Paris 1994.

12 Foucault notices that 'le Dehors' can find its origin in the mystical thinking '[t]hat has prowled the borders of Christianity since the texts of the Pseudo-Dionysus: perhaps it survived for a millennium or so in the various forms of negative theology' (1987: 16).

and the act of naming the object exhausts the whole process.[13] The function of 'I speak' is quite the opposite as it approximates us to the place beyond the language, to the place where the subject, represented by the 'I' is scattered and where the primal function of the language, namely the communication and creation of meanings, disappears:

> If the only site for language is indeed the solitary sovereignty of 'I speak' then in principle nothing can limit it – not the one to whom it is addressed, not the truth of what it says, not the values or systems of representation it utilizes. In short, it is no longer discourse and the communication of meaning, but a spreading forth of language in its raw state, an unfolding of pure exteriority. (1987: 11)

The complete dismissal of the subject from the language raises a serious philosophical question about the way of reaching the pure language without the prior infiltration through the subjectivity of 'I'. According to Foucault, the answers to this question should be searched for in the Western culture and philosophy that copes with the subject of a form of thought (1987: 15).[14] Foucault's theoretical aspect of how the thought functions within the neutral space is present both in Blanchot's definition of 'presence' and in Barthes' 'degree zero'. Among common elements one may notice both the description of the environment within which the neutrum can be observed (void, silence, suspension) and the relation between the neutral word-thought and the subject. Foucault's viewpoint adds one more vital factor to the discussion, namely the dissolution of the 'I' that is

---

13 Neither in the words in question nor in the subject that pronounces them is there an obstacle or insinuation to come between the object-proposition and the proposition that states it. It is therefore true, undeniably true, that I am speaking when I say I am speaking. (1987: 10).
14 The French philosopher's research in the matter of the history, or rather, archaeology of thought is enormous, e.g., his *The Order of Things. An Archaeology of the Human Sciences*. Foucault points out the problem of the pure representation based on Descartes' idea of cogito. He notices that the Cartesian *Cogito ergo sum* has been excluded by the modern man from the form of a 'sovereign transparency' of pure consciousness. Moreover, a 'sovereign transparency' cannot co-exist without an 'unthought', i.e. without the empirical and historical truths about who the man is:
 'The modern *cogito* does not reduce the whole being of things to
 thought without ramifying the being of thought right down to the
 inert network of what does not think.' (2002: 353)
 A detailed discussion on relations thought–language can be found in *The Order of Things*, in chapters 'The Return of Language,' 'The Analytic of Finitude' and 'The 'Cogito' and 'The Unthought.'

indispensable to reach the language-thought in a raw state. However, Foucault points out some limitations concerning his definition of the outside, noticing that his successors' aim would be to 'define the fundamental forms and categories' (1987: 16) of 'le Dehors.' He still attempts to define what the outside is as follows:

> A thought that stands outside subjectivity, setting its limits as though from without, articulating its end, making its dispersion shine forth, taking in only its invincible absence; and that at the same time stands at the threshold of all positivity, not in order to grasp its foundation or justification but in order to regain the space of its unfolding, the void serving as its site, the distance in which it is constituted and into which its immediate certainties slip the moment they are glimpsed – a thought that, in relation to the interiority of our philosophical reflection and the positivity of our knowledge, constitutes what in a word we might call 'the thought from the outside.' (1987: 15–16)

Similarly to the one proposed by Blanchot, the above definition puts the researcher of the neutrum in an apparently uncomfortable position, suggesting that the subject is not able to glimpse the moment when the pure language-thought is born. Despite the fact that Foucault's definition in this aspect is unclear,[15] it still conveys one important notion that I will adapt for my own definition of the neutrum, namely the notion of 'the threshold.' The threshold serves not as a perfect, as such a word, especially used in categories of describing space for the pure language origin cannot exist, but a sufficient word for describing the idea that stands behind the concept of the neutral space.

Before a more detailed scrutiny of the notion of 'threshold,' one final aspect that is common both for Blanchot's and Foucault's viewpoints on the neutral space, needs to be mentioned, namely the role of literature. In *The Space of Literature* Blanchot points out that the source of the neutral space is poetry, and the creator of the neutral language is the poet. The reason why poetry is the source of the neutrum is that the poetic word is contradictory both to the ordinary language and the language of thought (1989: 40). Such an effect can be achieved by completely muting the word, and what is more important, by negating the essential role that the word plays, namely the communicative one.[16] Owing to that, the

---

15 Foucault himself notices that the definition of 'the thought from the outside' has not been defined yet:
'It will one day be necessary to try to define the fundamental forms and categories of this 'thought form the outside.' It will also be necessary to try to retrace its path, to find out where it comes to us from and in what direction it is moving' (1987: 16).
16 Blanchot suggests that all goals and discourses that usually are inextricable with the function of the word should be muted and rejected:

poetic (neutral) word is a word where nobody speaks, and the work belongs to
no one; thus, the word neither plays any role nor conducts any meaning:

> From this perspective, we rediscover poetry as a powerful universe of words where relations, configurations, forces are affirmed through sound, figure, rhythmic mobility, in a unified and sovereignly autonomous space. Thus the poet produces a work of pure language, and language in this work is its return to its essence. (1989: 41)

Foucault presents a similar viewpoint on the role of literature as a neutral space. He not only points out, as it has been mentioned, that the neutral word gets rid of any discourse but also gains a possibility of self-determination that a '[l]iterary speech develops from itself' (1987: 12). Additionally, both philosophers attempt to characterise who, or what, is 'the being,' following Blanchotian terms, that speaks in the neutral language. In both cases they suggest that language speaks by itself; whereas Blanchot claims that the act of the neutral language's speaking by itself is inseparable from a continuous and never-ending work,[17] Foucault insists that the speaker of the neutral language rejects the subjectivity of the 'I say that I speak.'[18]

Having said that, we can return to the notion of the threshold that on the one hand allows us to define the neutral space (at least for Beckett's signature as well for the purpose of this thesis), and on the other to illustrate how the threshold works in the case of Beckett's work:

a) Firstly, the main purpose of the threshold is to observe the word in its pure, raw form, thus it is indispensable to get rid of the subject of 'I' that by its very presence cancels the pure word and establishes a filtered-by-subjectivity meaning. Additionally, the neutrum should, by default, reject all discourses.

b) Secondly, the 'natural' environment for the threshold should be equivalent with the state of void, permanent silence or suspension, yet this 'state zero' should convey in itself a dose of possibility.

'In poetry we are no longer referred back to the world, neither to the world as shelter nor to the world as goals. In this language the world recedes and goals cease; the world falls silent; beings with their preoccupations, their projects, their activity are no longer ultimately what speaks. Poetry expresses the fact that beings are quiet.' (1989: 41).

17 'From here on, it is not Mallarmé who speaks, but language which speaks itself: language as the work and the work as language.' (1989: 41).

18 'The "subject" of literature (what speaks in it and what it speaks about) is less language in its positivity than the void language takes as its space when it articulates itself in the nakedness of "I speak."'(1987: 12).

c) Finally, the most useful universe by which the threshold, or the neutral space, can be observed is, as Blanchot claims, the universe of poetry, or as Foucault suggests, the universe of literature in general.

4.2. The threshold of possibility

Having defined what the threshold is draws us near to a better understating what the neutrum is and how it works. However, it must be pointed out that our considerations so far have only allowed us to sketch a starting-point, a foundation for further reflections upon the concept of the neutrum. The question that should be raised at this point is as follows: if the neutral space suspends all meanings, fades all sounds, rids off all discourses and scatters the subjectivity, what role does the neutrum play in the artistic process. The above-mentioned approaches to the topic of the neutrum one may distinguish one characteristic feature that this notion conveys, a feature that has not been articulated yet, although seems to be inextricable with the concept itself. When in the fragment of *Murphy* that appears at the beginning of this section Mr. Endon mentions that he would like to commit suicide by apnoea, by saying that one can understand that the apnoea functions here as a sign of non-being, yet not of a complete cessation of being. The further part of the cited fragment presents what from Mr. Endon's point of view must be a disappointing diagnosis by Dr. Killiecrankie, who not only speaks about 'the physiological impossibility of suicide by apnoea' but predominantly suggests that cessation of one being only contributes to the appearance of another ('It was not like a real voice, one minute it said one thing and the next minute something quite different,' 2010a: 11).

The above example illustrates that even the hardest attempts of getting inside the neutral space are not only impossible due to the above-mentioned reasons, but also open a new sphere of possibilities. It turns out that even in the space of void and complete neutralisation of all meaning there may appear a different voice. The origins of that voice can be manifold, it may come from 'le Dehors,' it may have metaphysical associations – these aspects, although intriguing, will not be the core of our interests at this point. I would rather opt for Foucault's viewpoint on 'regain[ing] the space of its unfolding' (1987: 15–16), i.e., I am interested in these aspects of neutrum that depict a subject's continuous struggle to constitute the neutral space through the natural language.

These 'different voices' can be understood as possibilities, the possibilities that are not characterised and whose origin is unknown; however, they may also play an indispensable role in the creative process of getting to the essence of art. The process of getting to the neutrum as well as attempting to look out beyond the neutral space, is one of the founding elements of Samuel Beckett's artistic signature, an artistic manifesto that has been studied by the author of *Waiting for Godot* through all his artistic carrier. The thoughts on the role of the possibility can be traced in his early critical essay *Proust* (1930) where he writes as follows:

> What is common to present, and past is more essential than either taken separately. Reality, whether approached imaginatively or empirically, remains a surface, hermetic. Imagination applied – a priori – to what is absent, is exercised in vacuo and cannot tolerate the limits of the real. Nor is any direct and purely experimental contact possible between subject and object, because they are automatically separated by the subject's consciousness of perception, and the object loses its purity and becomes a mere intellectual pretext or motive. (2010c: 544)

What is surprising in the above fragment is a visible correlation with the ideas on the functioning of the neutral space and its relationship with the subject presented by both Blanchot and Foucault. It is, especially intriguing that Beckett notices that the contamination of the object by the subject's consciousness deprives the former of purity. Although, one may be tempted to juxtapose the object with the term neutrum, it should be noticed that these two terms are not synonymous, even though they are similar in the aspect of being allocated in contradiction of the subject's self-determination. The further traces of Beckett's understanding of what the object is and what role it plays should be correlated with the philosophy of Arthur Schopenhauer (1788–1860) that had a vital impact on Beckett in the 1930s, when Beckett wrote, among other texts, *Proust*.[19]

The evocation of Schopenhauer's philosophy at that point appears to be indispensable for further understanding of Beckett's deep interests in the philosophy of neutrum and how it is reflected in his art. As Pilling notices '*Proust* presents Beckett trapped between will and will not' (1997: 48), trapped between the conventional (Pilling uses the term 'demonstrative') and experimental approach towards the literary criticism. Being trapped between conventional and experimental seems to be the turning point in Beckett's understanding of the relation between the object and the subject. It has already been stated that the object should not be translated directly as the neutral space, but rather as the progenitor

---

19 Van Hulle and Nixon notice that Beckett started studying Schopenhauer in July 1930 despite '[t]he sneers from Beaufret, Péron and the other friends and colleagues at the Ecole Normale Supérieure (ENS)' (2013: 143), whereas Pilling in *Beckett Before Godot* points out that the manuscript of *Proust* was sent 'to Charles Prentice of Chatto and Windus in mid-October of 1930' (1997: 35).

for the philosophical system that eventually allows to crystallise the model of the neutrum that is presented in this thesis.[20]

From the above considerations one can draw a conclusion that possibility – which functions as the basis for the neutral space – plays an indispensable role in the artist's creative process. However, the possibility of constituting within the neutrum, or even trying to reach beyond it, is a disastrous process. Foucault's words about the outside that it is 'the never-ending struggle with unfolding the void' (1987: 15–16), may be perhaps applied to the question of possibility. Attempting to reach the 'unreachable' requires from the artist, never-ending, scrupulous work. The work of never-ending yet impossible to fulfil possibility can resemble a circle; the-always-returning-to-a-starting-point cycle that seems to be the crucial point in the artist-work relation. As Blanchot notices, when discussing Kafka's work:

> [F]rom its double aspect which Kafka expresses with too much simplicity in the sentences we ascribe to him: *Write to be able to die – Die to be able to write.* These words close us into their circular demand; they oblige us to start from what we want to find, to seek nothing but the point of departure, and thus to make this point something we approach only by quitting it. But they also authorize this hope: the hope, where the interminable emerges, of grasping the term, of bringing it forth. (1989: 93–94)

One could conclude from the above fragment in the reference to Beckett's *oeuvre* that the artist's role, is twofold: firstly, to reach an 'anchor point' in the endless void of the unknown, a point that will be both the beginning and the end that gives us the possibility or 'the hope' of revealing the unseen, and secondly to eventually reveal the world as it is in its pure form by 'bringing it forth' to us.

The next characteristic feature of the neutrum-possibility relation is, as Blanchot notices in *The Infinite Conversation*, the notion of meaning. The French philosopher suggests that the neutrum can only be fully neutral while being in the relation with meaning:

> 'Meaning would therefore only exist by way of the neutral.' – 'But insofar as the neutral would remain foreign to meaning – by which I mean, first: neutral as far as meaning is concerned; not indifferent, but haunting the possibility of meaning and non-sense by the invisible margin of a difference.' (1993: 304)

---

20 The influences of Schopenhauer's philosophy on Beckett's writing and how such a philosophy inscribes in the Irishman's signature will be evoked in the forthcoming chapters, especially the ones that deal with *Proust, Dream of Fair to Middling Women* and *Murphy*.

By introducing 'the possibility of meaning' as the very founding element of the neutrum, Blanchot cracks open the door to the 'margin of a difference' to which Beckett, eventually, is attempting to gain entry. Leslie Hill notices that '[b]y inscribing within writing the possibility of the always other word or non-word, the neutre is what turns any text – and not just Blanchot's own – into a palimpsest constantly divided from itself and dismantled from within by an alterity that it cannot internalise' (2001: 134). Such an approach can be visible in Beckett's early pieces of writing, where the words with manifold meanings are reduced to a single symbol that connotes different meanings depending on the context in which they function. The famous phrase 'womb-tomb' that appears, for instance in *Dream of Fair to Middling Women* or *Echo's Bones*[21] may serve as an example. The alterity of this phrase is an example of a non-word, a non-word that has been created as a response to the author's struggle with getting into the neutral space. The phrase can also function as the foothold that should allow the author to reveal the unseen; the 'womb-tomb' also connotes a meaning, apparently non-sensical, that allows him to constitute the neutrum by establishing the neutrum-meaning relation. For this reason that the phrase 'womb-tomb' conveys the following function: it illustrates a certain artistic process, namely Beckett's reusage of the same expressions in different works. I find that such a device inscribes in Hill's idea of the dismantled palimpsest. It means that the reoccurrence of the same expressions, in this example the 'womb-tomb,' in various contexts not only generates new meanings but also reinforces the internal communication of Beckett's texts within his semiosphere.[22]

However, the above argument on the correlation between the meaning, the possibility and the neutrum is visible in Beckett's understanding what the language is and how he uses it for his artistic purposes, suffice it to say that the author of *Molloy* uses it for the purpose of creating his own non-conceptual language, is attractive to our interpreting purposes, nevertheless its limitations need to be evoked as well. As Hill notices, despite the undeniable role the possibility

---

21 The importance of this phrase will be further elaborated in the subchapter dealing with the significance of the reduction with relation to the neutrum as well as in the chapters that are focused on the analysis of the particular Beckett's works.

22 Hill adds that in relation to Blanchot's view on the neutrum '[w]ords and names necessarily harbour within themselves the trace of their possible deletion and substitution by another name or word; by that very token, they also display in their inscription itself, and the necessary possibility of their effacement, the risk and chance of subsequent deletion, alteration, and transformation.' (2001: 135).

plays in relation to establishing the neutrum, it is the possibility that has a destructive influence on consistency, or rather the lack of the neutrum's unity:

> Words and names necessarily harbour within themselves the trace of their possible deletion and substitution by another name or word; by that very token, they also display in their inscription itself, and the necessary possibility of their effacement, the risk and chance of subsequent deletion, alteration, and transformation. (2001: 135)

At that point Hill's theory corresponds with Blanchot's viewpoint on the importance of the anchor points that words and names play in the process of regaining the neutral space, however Hill points out one of weaknesses that originates from such a viewpoint, namely that the endless transformation and alteration of meanings that derives from the very nature of the possibility, causes that the neutrum cannot be recognised as a unified entity or a total being:

> For that reason, both as logic and as name, despite the singular number of the term, the neutre cannot be subordinated to the unity or totality of being. It therefore cannot be thematised as One, but only addressed as multiple exteriority and immeasurable alterity. This explains why ultimately the neutre cannot be contained in fact within the horizon of the possible, nor can the alterity it presents to thought be thematised in relation to possibility. (2001: 135)

Hill adds that the neutrum, despite being correlated with the possibility, eventually eludes all possibility of naming and moves towards an infinite alterity beyond it. The next step in our discussion will be to examine if the infinite possibility of the neutrum conveys a certain degree of limitation.

4.3. Aporia and the limit

The term 'aporia' originates from the Greek 'impossibility of passage' ('aporos,' 'a,' 'without,' 'poros,' 'passage'), the etymology that situates, as Derval Tubridy notices, the word's topology in both spatiality and epistemology (2018: 4).[23] The function of 'aporia,' as the term used for defying the limit of the 'beyond,' will be investigated predominantly as a certain form of aesthetics used by Beckett, however philosophical assumptions of this concept will be also presented.

'Aporia' as a condition of impossibility of passage is perceived, for instance by Drucilla Cornell, as an ability of refusing silence. She suggests that to 'run into an aporia, to reach the *limit* of philosophy, is not necessarily to be paralyzed. We are

---

23 In the Greek mythology Aporia is described as a 'daimon of dearth, impediment and impotence' (Tubridy 2018: 3).

Aporia and the limit 73

only paralyzed if we think that to reach the limit of philosophy is to be silenced' (1992: 70-71). 'Aporia' in that context not only functions as a name for the 'limit of philosophy' but also, which seems more vital, as a name that attempts to tame Levinas' horror of the void caused by the pervasive silence of nothingness.[24] Moreover, Cornell raises the subject of the aporia perceived in the categories of the 'Saying,' the notion that should be used as a passage to 'the aporia of the beyond' ('the ability of traditional philosophical discourse to evoke the aporia of the beyond through the Saying of what cannot ever be said,' 1992: 71). The juxtaposition between the 'Saying' and the 'said' used by Cornell finds its sources in Levinas' theory on the nature of the otherwise.[25]

Levinas defines the 'Saying' as a pre-intentional moment that is happening in time just before its intentionalisation through the language (1991: 37). The philosopher denotes the 'Saying' with the entity that reveals transcendental connotations,[26] owing to that Levinas wants to sensitise the reader that the 'Saying' cannot be perceived solely in linguistic categories, but as 'correlative with the said' (1991: 37):

> Saying is not a game. Antecedent to the verbal sings it conjugates, to the linguistic systems and the semantic glimmerings, a foreword preceding languages, it is the proximity of one to the other, the commitments of an approach, the one for the other, the very signifyingness of signification. (1991: 5)[27]

---

24 In contradiction to Levinas' nihilistic attitude towards 'il y a' and the concept of the philosophy of the limit stands Derrida who points out that '[t]he limit challenges us to reopen the question – to think again.' (Cornell 1992: 71). Derrida's viewpoint on the 'aporia' as a possibility is presented in *Memories for Paul de Man* as follows:
'The word "aporia" recurs often in Paul de Man's last texts. I believe that we would misunderstand it if we tried to hold it to its most literal meaning: an absence of path, a paralysis before roadblocks, the immobilization of thinking, the impossibility of advancing, a barrier blocking the future. On the contrary, it seems to me that the experience of the aporia, such as de Man deciphers it, gives or promises the thinking of the path, provokes the thinking of the very possibility of what still remains unthinkable or unthought, indeed, impossible. The figures of rationality are profiled and outlined in the madness of the aporetic.' (1988: 132).
25 See Levinas, Emmanuel. *Otherwise Than Being or Beyond Essence*. Kluwer Academic Publishers, Dordrecht, 1991, pages 9-11, where Levinas indicates that the 'otherness' can be extracted from the 'time.'
26 'The saying extended toward the said and absorbed in it, correlative with it, names an entity, in the light or resonance of lived time which allows a phenomenon to appear.' (1991: 37).
27 Contrary to Levinas' idea on not recognising the 'Saying'-'Said' relation as a linguistic game stands Jean-François Lyotard's the language game theory, where he compares the

However, the concept of the 'Saying' should exclude its subordination to the realm of language, identified as the 'Said,' the failure of the 'Saying' evinces in the fact that the 'Saying' eventually 'moves into the language' (1991: 6), simultaneously becoming subordinated to the language: 'The correlation of the saying and the said, that is, the subordination of the saying to the said, to the linguistic system and to ontology, is the price that manifestation demands' (1991: 6).

The recurring return of the 'aporia' to the fabric of language, as well as the inextricability of the aporia-language relation can serve as the answer to the endless possibility. Anthony Uhlmann suggests that the core of the Beckettian speaker is 'an aporia which is at the heart of language, an aporia which, in language's efforts to unravel itself, thinking that it can, leads to confusion.' (1999: 168). On the other hand, Blanchot in *Faux Pas* describes the 'aporias of language' as a suspension between obligation and impossibility (Tubridy 2018: 3), the concept that for a writer is the source of frustrations:

> The writer finds himself in the increasingly ludicrous condition of having nothing to write, of having no means with which to write it, and of being constrained by the utter necessity of always writing it. Having nothing to express must be taken in the most literal way. Whatever he would like to say, it is nothing. (2001: 3)

The idea of saying nothing through the language correlates with the one proposed by Leslie Hill. She opts for understanding 'aporia' as an exit from language: '[c]rossing navigable verbal territory into uncharted and disorienting non-space.' (1990: 7). Hill also notices that the everlasting exiting from language becomes Beckett's method of dealing with the aporia of language:

> Beckett's work pursues one end, which is the end of language. The end of language, however, never comes. Or rather it has always already taken place. Beckett writes in the name of something which has no name, but to which he struggles to give a name. That something is what throughout this book, for my part, I have named: indifference. Yet indifference is not stasis. It is the infinity of difference, the erasure of identity and the still turbulence at the centre of language and the body .... [R]epeatedly ... the writing refuses to allow itself to be read as some form of coded message ... it does this in part by denying its own binary logic and stability. (1990: 62)

Hill's words on aporia inscribe in the theory of the neutrum. However, the above fragment equips us with an additional viewpoint on Beckett's searching of aporia, it is the recognition of aporia as the 'indifference.' Hill does not juxtapose

---

speaking process to a game and every utterance to a move that is made in this game (1984: 9–11).

the 'indifference' with such terms as apathy or impassivity, the terms that suggest the complete annihilation of the movement, but rather points out that the 'indifference' should be perceived as the infinite difference, i.e. that the term contains in itself an inexhaustible particle that pushes the subject towards the never-ending work. Nevertheless, the attempt of reaching the 'indifference' is realised by the language itself. Hill depicts that the language cannot be treated as a linguistic code that allows us to be eventually solved. Rather, it is suggested that through endless attempts of using the language to describe the 'indifference,' the language resists and refuses itself to be decoded.[28] Hill illustrates how Beckett's aporia works in practice when saying:

> In Beckett, aporia is usually signalled by devices such as the careful rhetorical balancing of contradictory periods, the repeated use of terms like 'd'un côté' or 'd'un autre côté,' 'peut-être,' and the fondness for unanswerable rhetorical questions. (1990: 62)

Hill's model of analysing Beckett's 'aporia' is based on his later works such as *Mercier and Camier* (1970) but that way of reading can be diachronically applied to his pre-war texts. In the below fragment of 'A Wet Night' from *More Pricks Than Kicks*, the unsuccessful attempts of breaking through the fabric of language to reach the 'aporia,' are illustrated by the series of rhetorical and senseless questions:

> "Ravenna!" exclaimed the Countess, memory tugging at her carefully cultivated heartstrings, "did I hear someone say Ravenna?"
> "Allow me" said the rising strumpet: "a sandwich: egg, tomato, cucumber."
> "Did you know" blundered the Man of Law "that the Swedes have no fewer than seventy varieties of Smoerrbroed?"
> The voice of the arithmomaniac was heard:
> "The arc" he said, stooping to all in the great plainness of his words, "is longer that its chord."
> "Madam knows Ravenna?" said the paleographer.
> "Do I know Ravenna!" exclaimed the Parabimbi. "Sure I know Ravenna. A sweet and noble city."
> "You know of course" said the Man of Law "that Dante died there."
> "Right" said the Parabimbi, "so he did." (2010c: 124)

---

28 Mireille Bousquet suggests a similar dependence in relation to Beckett's *oeuvre*: 'The problem here is of knowing whether it is Beckett's writing that refuses to be decoded, as if this were implicitly a function of all language, or whether we are dealing with a dubious conception of language, which the work itself criticizes.' (2015: 362).

The characteristic feature of this scene consists in the fact that it is happening at a party, where the process of uttering words, highlighted by such verbs as 'said' and 'exclaimed,' functions as an ontological attempt of constituting the subject, the method that inscribes in Beckett's later works.[29] The series of rhetorical questions inscribes in Hill's theory on Beckett's aporia in his writing, however in the above excerpt from 'A Wet Nigh,' the rhetorical questions are connected with the historical time. The conversation between the party members is aimed at speaking about Dante, one of the most important writers who had an undeniable impact on Beckett's writing.[30] The conversation finishes with a statement that Dante died in Ravenna, the statement that signalises the end of time, or the cease of being. On the other hand, Dante's *oeuvre* is still alive, even though Dante is dead. That juxtaposition connotes Heidegger's distinction between 'Time' for 'Being' and 'Time' for 'beings,'[31] thus the aspect of temporality can be applied as one of the characteristics of Beckett's way to reach the 'aporia,' an endless repetition of time through its worklessness should bring the subject nearer, even if only for a mere moment.

The second example of the struggle that one can experience while attempting to name the 'aporia' through the means of language is the continuous questioning of the idiom, namely the problem with finding the name for that what is indifferent. When the rising strumpet enumerates the apparently nonsensical sequence of nouns ('a sandwich: egg, tomato, cucumber.'), the response for that is 'that the Swedes have no fewer than seventy varieties of Smoerrbroed?,' the

---

29 Momro notices that Beckett through the act of speaking is attempting to reach the limit of the language and consciousness. Moreover, the researcher suggests that Beckett recognises the speech system as an abstract construct that through which the subject attempts to catch what is elusive, eventually reducing the act of speaking to the impossible gesture (2010: 252). Momro evokes Beckett's attempts of glimpsing the neutrum through the language on the example of *Ping* (1966):
'White ceiling never seen ping of old only just almost never one second light time white floor never seen ping of old perhaps there. Ping of old only just perhaps a meaning a nature one second almost never blue and white in the wind that much memory henceforth never. White planes no trace shining white one only shining white infinite but that known not. Light heat all known all white heart breath no sound. Head haught eyes white fixed front old ping last murmur one second perhaps not alone eye unlustrous black and white half closed long lashes imploring ping silence ping over.' (2010c: 373).
30 See: Caselli, Daniela. *Beckett's Dantes. Intertextuality in the Fiction and Criticism*. Manchester University Press, Manchester—New York 2005.
31 Heidegger, Martin. *On Time and Being*. The University of Chicago Press, Chicago, 2002.

variety of 'Smoerrbroed' can be interpreted both as the finite and infinite number of idioms that can be used for naming the unnamable. What can be additionally observed in the case of Beckett's attempts of naming either the aporia or the neutral space in general, he very often tends to a maximal reduction of the idiom.

4.4. Epochē and the reduction

All the attempts of naming and explaining what the 'aporia', the 'beyond' and the neutral space are have been based so far on language. This is exactly the element that Beckett attempts to eliminate in his writing, the attempt that I would call the project of the literature of the non-word. Thus, his research in the matter of reduction seems to be justified. Badiou notices that the method of reduction, or the 'epochē' (Greek 'suspension'), is a characteristic feature of Beckett's *oeuvre* that he attempted to fulfil through his whole artistic carrier:

> Beckett's method is precisely the opposite: it is a question of subtracting or suspending the subject so as to see what then happens to being. The hypothesis of a seeing without words will be forwarded. A hypothesis of words without seeing will also be made, together with a hypothesis of a disappearance of words. (2003: 108)

Badiou presents three qualities of the 'epochē,' namely the words without saying, the saying without words and the eventual disappearance of words. All three demands inscribe in Beckett's project but their accomplishments seem to be unreachable. The very term 'epochē' can be connoted with the philosophy of Edmund Husserl (1859–1938) and his philosophy of phenomenology. Phenomenology can be defined as 'the descriptive, non-reductive science of whatever appears, in the matter of its appearing in the *subjective* and *intersubjective* life of consciousness' (Maude-Feldman 2009: 16–17). Beckett's interests in Husserl's philosophy were motivated by his reading of Sartre between 1938 and 1939, the French philosopher very often referred to Husserl's thought in his novels, as may be illustrated by the borrowing of the terms 'noème' and 'noèse,' which mean respectively to denote the object of thought and the act of thought. Both notions were noted down by Beckett in his *'Whoroscope' Notebook* (Van Hulle—Nixon 2013: 210).[32] Moreover, Maude and Feldman suggest that Husserl's *Ideas* must

---

32 For detailed explanation of the differences between 'noème' and 'noèse' see Cerbone, David. *Understanding Phenomenology*. Acumen, Durham 2006, especially the subchapter entitled 'Noesis and noema: constitution,' pp. 28–32.

have had a vital impact on Beckett's philosophical viewpoint, even though he absorbed the ideas through the readings of Sartre.[33]

The concept of Husserlian 'epoché,' which for some time was used by the German philosopher as the synonym of the word 'reduction,' inscribes into his project of the so-called transcendental-phenomenological reduction. The term covers in itself three aspects, 'transcendental,' 'phenomenological' and the 'reduction;' 'transcendental' because it attempts to uncover the Ego[34] of all meaning and existence, 'phenomenological' refers to transforming the world into a mere phenomenon, while the 'reduction' leads the reader back to the very source of 'the meaning and existence of the experienced world, in so far as it is experienced, by uncovering intentionality' (Schmitt 1959: 240). For some time Husserl treated both terms, namely the 'epoché' and 'reduction' as synonymic, however

---

33 The appendix attached to *Samuel Beckett's Library* does not contain Husserl's *Ideas*. Yet, the German philosopher's ideas on the nature of phenomenology can be traced in Sartre's works. For instance, in *Nausea*, one of the recurring motifs of Roquentin's fight is to overcome the subject-object distinction: 'suddenly, the veil is torn away, I have understood. I have *seen*.' (1969: 126). The analogy to unrevealing the true nature of being, to overcome the mentioned subject-object distinction, can be traced in Belacqua's actions from *Dream of Fair to Middling Women* or *More Pricks Than Kicks*. The relation in the phenomenological context is presented by Husserl himself as follows: 'I obtain an original and pure descriptive knowledge of the psychical life as it is in itself, the most original information being obtained from myself, because here alone is perception the medium ... This transformation of meaning concerns myself, above all, the "I" of the psychological and subsequently transcendental inquirer for the time being ... It leads eventually to the point that I, who am here reflecting upon myself, become conscious that under a consistent and exclusive focusing of experience upon that which is purely inward, upon what is "phenomenologically" accessible to me, I possess in myself an essential individuality, self-contained, and holding well together in itself, to which all real and objectively possible experience and knowledge belongs, through whose agency the objective world is there for me with all its empirically confirmed facts ... The absolute positing means that the world is no longer "given" to me in advance, its validity that of a simple existent, but that henceforth it is exclusively my Ego that is given.' (1962: 7–8, 11)
34 The concept of the Ego is explained in detail by Husserl, for instance in *Cartesian Meditations* where one of the ego's qualities is the ability of practising 'abstention with respect to what he intuits' (1960: 20). Further Husserl's divagations on the nature of ego can be found in subchapters from *Cartesian Meditations* entitled 'The transcendental Ego inseparable from the process making up his life,' 'The Ego as identical pole of the subjective processes,' 'The Ego as substrate of habitualities,' and 'The full concretion of the Ego as monad and the problem of his self-constitution' (1960: 65–68).

in his late writings he distinguished the 'epochē' as the suspension of all-natural belief in the objects of experience, as the precondition that aims at reducing the natural world to 'a world of phenomena' (Schmitt 1959: 240).

The quality of suspension that the 'epochē' offers correlates with our understanding of what the neutrum is and how can be isolated and observed in a neutral space. Husserl adds that the 'epochē' should be understood as a method that allows the 'I' to be apprehended in a pure way, and suggests that that method allows us to reach the pure state of the Ego. Husserl's method corresponds with the Foucault's 'regain[ing] the space of its unfolding,' Barthes' 'degree zero' or Blanchot's 'presence,' namely, the author of *Cartesian Meditations* sees the sense in the apparently lost battle of reaching the state of maximal suspension and reduction:

> This universal depriving of acceptance, this 'inhibiting' or 'putting out of play' of all positions taken toward the already given Objective world and, in the first place, all existential positions (those concerning being, illusion, possible being, being likely, probable, etc.), – or, as it is also called – this 'phenomenological epochē' and 'parenthesizing' of the Objective world therefore does not leave us confronting nothing. On the contrary we gain possession of something by it; and what we (*or*, to speak more precisely, what I, the one who is meditating) acquire by it is my pure living, with all the pure subjective processes making this up, and everything meant in them, *purely as* meant in them: the universe of 'phenomena' in the (particular and also the wider) phenomenological sense. (1960: 20–21)

The way how the state of purity can be achieved is defined by Husserl as the state of continuous repetition, or rather the act of production and subsequently the reproduction of the produced structure:

> I produce a structure: a theorem or a numerical structure. Subsequently I repeat the producing, while recollecting my earlier producing. At once, and by essential necessity, an identifying synthesis takes place; furthermore, a new identifying synthesis occurs with each additional repetition (a repetition performed with a consciousness that the producing can be repeated again at will): It is identically the same proposition, identically the same numerical structure, *but repeatedly produced* or, this being equivalent, repeatedly made evident. (1960: 127)

Such a method that uses the phenomenological 'epochē' to reach the realm of 'phenomena,' or following Badiou's concept of the pre-eventual figure, corresponds in its assumptions with Blanchot's 'worklessness.' In both cases, the desperate attempt of figuring out what is located 'beyond' appears to be unable to be fulfilled. In the case of the 'epochē' that should be treated as a method that inscribes, in a broader sense, in the philosophy of Phenomenology, and that for Husserl should work as a way of discovering new foundations for all philosophy

(Cerbone 2006: 158). The project seems to be incompletable. Daniel Dennett notices that both Husserl and other thinkers who have attempted to discover the 'epochē' through the tools that phenomenology offers have 'failed to find a single, settled method that everyone could agree upon' (1991: 44).[35]

The 'epochē' although not being synonymous with the 'reduction,' is inextricably connected with that term. Before discussing in detail how Husserl's method works with Beckett's *oeuvre* on the example of *Dream of Fair to Middling Women*, the difference how the term 'reduction' functions in the writer's aesthetics needs to be indicated. Tomasz Wiśniewski notices that the same words or expressions used by Beckett twice do not reveal the same semantics. As he illustrates with multiple examples from *Waiting for Godot*, particularly with expressions connected with light and darkness, the meanings are very often contradictory.[36] Owing to that the term 'reduction' read in Beckett's aesthetic categories is not synonymous with its philosophical definition.

Husserl, as an example of phenomenological reduction, provides the description of a Japanese plum tree:

> In the reduced perception (in the phenomenologically pure mental process), we find, as indefeasibly belonging to its essence, the perceived as perceived, to be expressed as 'material thing,' 'plant,' 'tree,' 'blossoming;' and so forth. Obviously, the *inverted commas* are significant in that they express that change in sign, the correspondingly radical significational modification of the words. The *tree simpliciter*, the physical thing belonging to Nature, is nothing less than this *perceived tree as perceived* which, as perceptual sense, inseparably belongs to the perception. The tree simpliciter can burn up, be resolved into its chemical elements, etc. But the sense – the sense *of this* perception, something belonging necessarily to its essence – cannot burn up; it has no chemical elements, no forces, no real properties. (1983: 216)

When Husserl uses such words as 'plant,' 'tree' or 'blossoming,' he puts all of them in brackets purposely. The idea of the 'phenomenological reduction,' that the author of *Cartesian Meditations* also calls the 'bracketing,' is aimed at indicating that the bracketed words do not represent physical objects but are

---

35 Dennett points out that the main reason why phenomenologists could not agree upon the one, concise system for Phenomenology as the branch of science is the very nature of Phenomenology that Dennett describes as 'the things that swim in the stream of consciousness' (1991: 45).

36 In *Kształt Literacki Dramatu Samuela Becketta*, Wiśniewski indicates that the opposition of meanings derives from the way the meaning is communicated. For example, the same meanings transmitted through a theatrical communication differ from those that can be decoded in a printed text (2006: 21–46).

rather the reflection of the subject's experience of the world around him- or herself.[37] Bracketing should allow us to see the 'sense' ('Sinn'), the 'lived experience' ('Erlebnis') that can be treated as the essence of the perception (Woodruff-Smith 2013: 235). Thus, the main role of bracketing, or 'phenomenological reduction' is to shift the subject's interests to the presumed existence of objects and to concentrate on the representation of the object in one's experience, rather than focusing on the physical object that is perceived by sight. The attempt of reaching the 'sense' of the object inscribes in the search of transcendence covered in the transcendental-phenomenological reduction model, yet does not exclude the importance of the language that still functions as frames within which the 'epochē' can happen. That suspension between the transcendental 'sense' and the language understood as the tool within which the 'lived experience' can be expressed, opens the space for Beckett's reflection on the literature of the non-word. An example of such a struggle can be observed in *Dream of Fair to Middling Women*:

> The third being was the dark gulf, when the glare of the will and the hammer-strokes of the brain doomed outside to take flight from its quarry were expunged, the Limbo and the wombtomb alive with the unanxious spirits of quiet cerebration, where there was no conflict of flight and flow and Eros was as null as Anteros and Night had no daughters. He was bogged in indolence, without identity, impervious alike to its pull and goading. The cities and forests and beings were also without identity, they were shadows, they exerted neither pull nor goad. His third being was without axis or contour, its centre everywhere and periphery nowhere, an unsurveyed marsh of sloth. (2012: 121)

The above fragment encapsulates all divagations that have been presented so far in relation to the concept of the neutrum that is visible in Beckett's artistic view on that notion. The above mentioned 'third being' that anticipates with 'the third zone' from *Murphy* ('The third, the dark, was a flux of forms, a perpetual

---

37 Husserl suggests that the act of 'parenthesizing' is also correlated with the act of 'reflection,' the 'reflection' should allow us to focus more on the experience of a worldly object then on the presentation itself. Husserl adds that the 'reflection' should be recognised as the fundament of Phenomenology:
'In the phenomenological attitude in essential universality we *prevent the effecting* of all such cogitative positings, i.e., we 'parenthesize' the positings effected: for our new inquiries we do not 'participate in these positings.' Instead of living *in* them, instead of effecting *them*, we effect acts of *reflection* directed to them; and we seize upon them themselves as the *absolute* being which they are. We are now living completely in such acts of the second degree, acts the datum of which in the infinite field of absolute mental process – the fundamental *field of phenomenology*.' (Husserl 1982: 114).

coming together and falling asunder of forms,' 2010a: 70), represents a kind of pure essence, a neutral space to which Beckett, by using the series of artistic devices personified in the fictional character of Belacqua, attempts, if not to enter, then at least to glimpse at. The 'third being' is a space of complete negation, yet not complete annihilation described by such expressions as 'null' and 'Limbo' on the one hand, and 'indolence' and 'goad' on the other. The hard-to-grasp distinction between where the neutrum starts and where it ends, as discussed in e.g., Momro's and Hill's respective divagations on that matter, is expressed by Beckett as a place/ non-place without 'contour' or 'identity', adding that 'its centre [is] everywhere and periphery [is] nowhere.'

Having said that one may draw a conclusion that the daunting attempt of describing the ephemeral world of neutrum using the natural language appears almost impossible, yet, following Husserl's viewpoint in that matter, for Beckett the language is reluctant-yet-indispensable material in that process. The phrase 'womb-tomb' that appears in the above fragment of *Dream*, the phrase that recurs in many Beckett's works – to provide an example of *Echo's Bones* – illustrates the concept of 'epochē' that should allow the author of *Molloy* to enter to that elusive space. I have bracketed the compound 'womb-tomb' deliberately, following Husserl's bracketing, to indicate Beckett's artistic work in the matter of language. The juxtaposition of the 'womb' and 'tomb', which can be recognised as the maximal reduction of the human being's lifespan, serves as an example of how Beckett attempts to distillate the meaning to its 'pure' essence, and simultaneously to resign from a variety of meanings that have been cumulated through the ages of its usage. Hence, Beckett proposes not only to redefine words' meanings by using them in new contexts but also uses them for reaching the neutral space, the Husserlian 'sense.'

The 'womb-tomb' in that context functions as 'the repetition of infinite regress' (Moorjani-Veit 2001: 13), and expresses the state of suspension, the state that is neither completely alive nor dead. That phrase, the 'womb-tomb,' would have later become a *leitmotif* of Beckett's research in the maximal reduction, very often re-translated by the writer himself, for instance to the phrase 'lessness.'[38]

---

38 *Lessness* (1970/1972) echoes the indefinite realm presented in *Dream of Fair to Middling Women*, yet even more devasted by the language and time:
'Ruins true refuge long last towards which so many false time out of mind. All sides endlessness earth sky as one no sound no stir. Grey face two pale blue little body heart beating only upright. Blacked out fallen open four walls over backwards true refuge issueless.' (2010c: 375).

The language-neutrum and the language-epochē relations are strongly connected with Beckett's artistic method of using the language as the imperfect transmitter that should allow the artist to describe the unnamable. Besides the reduction of language in its physical (graphic) context, the meaning-sense relation – as the examples the abovementioned 'womb-tomb' and 'lessness' illustrate – appears to be one of the keys to decipher Beckett's thematic preoccupations, and eventually his artistic signature.[39]

Moreover, the above-mentioned notions, such as the 'epochē' or the sense, serve as tools that Beckett uses for establishing his programme and for describing his artistic method. One of the elements of that method can be found in Husserl's idea presented in *The Crisis of the European Sciences and Transcendental Phenomenology*, where the German philosopher juxtaposes the relations between the 'life-world,' i.e. the world inhabited by a subject, and the 'objective-scientific' world that he proposes to replace with the 'art-world.' Husserl notices that the relation between the 'life-world' and the 'art-world' is vague, which correlates with his struggles of explaining the fundaments of Phenomenology, however 'the contrast and inseparable union' between these two worlds is inevitable (1970: 131). John Barnett Brough in his essay 'Art and Artworld: Some Ideas for a Husserlian Aesthetic,' develops Husserl's idea in that matter:

> The artist *uses* the life-world in its fundamental perceptual sense in the making of his works. The life-world supplies him with sensible materials and with instruments for his creative activity. The work of art produced with media such as stone or wood will be just as perceptible as the stone and wood themselves before they were taken up into the work. But, again, the perceptibility of such cultural objects does not imply that they appear to us 'in the life-world like stones, houses, or trees' [132; 130]. (1988: 42)

Brough's observations depict that for both Husserl and, eventually, Beckett, the process of a piece of art creation is strictly based on the relation between the 'life-world' and the 'art-world' In the case of Beckett, we treat his attempts of describing the neutrum through the transmitters of novels, plays and poems as that process. That relation points out that the apparently disorganised 'art-world' is in fact based on structures, Husserl says about a 'purposeful structure'

---

39 Woodruff-Smith notices, after Husserl, that the relation between the meaning and the sense is focused on expressing 'an appropriate underlying act of judgement' of the sense through the meaning of a sentence (2013: 237). Husserl describes in detail the meaning-sense relations in *Logical Investigations*, especially in the parts 'Objectifying intentions and their fulfilments: knowledge as a synthesis of fulfilment and its gradations' (2001: 189–268) and 'Sense and understanding' (2001: 269–320).

reflecting a 'goal-directed life' (1970: 382, 380). These structures originate from the 'life-world,' i.e. the mediums such as wood, stone or language are used to produce art, and cultural objects are defiantly perceived through the 'life-world,' yet they originate from the 'art-world.'[40]

Coming back to *Dream of Fair to Middling Women*, the novel allows us to observe how Beckett builds the artistic structures based on Husserl's phenomenological reduction and the juxtaposition between the art and life worlds. Firstly, the author creates a 'self-enclosed world' a 'cultural space' (Husserl 1970: 379, 392) for his characters who are used for creating a world that denies any reality and subsequently he uses such characters as narrative devices for establishing a new art-reality that is more 'real' than the 'life-world:'

> What we are doing now, of course, is setting up the world for a proper swell slap-up explosion. The bang is better than the whimper. It is easier to do. It is timed for about ten or fifteen thousand words hence. (2012: 177)

> It is possible that some of our creatures will do their dope all right and give no trouble. And it is certain that others will not. Let us suppose that Nemo is one of those that will not. John, most of the parents, the Smeraldina-Rima, the Syra-Cusa, the Alba, the Mandarin, the Polar Bear, Lucien, Chas, are a few of those that will, that stand, that is, for something or can be made to stand for something. (2012: 9)

The creation of fictional systems that clash within *Dream* (Nixon calls them a 'fictional reality' – 2009: 101) is aimed at the continuous struggle between the art-world and the life-world, causing the continuous replacement of realities that results in the origin of new 'hypothetical existential models' (2009). That continuous replication may correlate with Heidegger's concepts of 'being-in-the-world' and 'being-in-the-art-world' and moreover, seems to be one of the key elements of the novel:[41]

> They are no good from the builder's point of view, firstly because they will not suffer their systems to be absorbed in the cluster of the greater system, and then, and chiefly, because they themselves tend to disappear as systems. (2012: 119)

---

40 The relation between the 'life-world' and the 'art-world' invites us to broader discussion on the separation between the life and art. Even though Beckett opted for a strong separation between these two areas, he suggested in a conversation with Lawrence Harvey that '[w]ork doesn't depend on experience; it is not a record of experience. But of course, you must use it.' (Knowlson 2006: 137).

41 Marleau-Ponty notices that the '[p]henomenological reduction belongs to existential philosophy: Heidegger's 'being-in-the-world' appears only against the background of the phenomenological reduction.' (1981: xiv).

Husserl's viewpoints on the phenomenological reduction and the 'epochē' have later been borrowed and applied by other philosophers whose interpretations in that matter allowed to enrich and broaden these notions. As far as Heidegger is concerned, he points out that the etymology of the word 'reduction' that derives from the Latin 'reducere' ('re- ', back, again, and 'ducere,' to lead) should focus our attention on something that is '[u]navailable from, or obscured by, a non-phenomenological perspective' (Cerbone 2006: 106). Heidegger is aware of Husserl's definition of the phenomenological reduction, mainly the relation between the world of things and the transcendental life of consciousness; however, he indicates one additional aspect of the phenomenological reduction, namely the apprehension:

> For us phenomenological reduction means leading phenomenological vision back from the apprehension of a being, whether may be the character of that apprehension, to the understanding of the being of this being (projecting upon the way it is unconcealed) (Heidegger 1988: 21)

The 'understanding' that Heidegger proposes should be treated as a device that allows receivers to return, rediscover and reawaken all 'invisible to the naturally oriented points of view' (Husserl 1982: 10, as cited in Cerbone 2006: 106), namely to be able to discover and comprehend original meanings. Thus, the similarities between the phenological reduction and the neutrum are visible at this point. Another viewpoint that exceeds Husserl's and Heidegger's thoughts on the phenomenological reduction was presented by Maurice Merleau-Ponty (1908–1961). In his works, especially in *Phenomenology and Perception* he adds the afore-discussed notion of possibility in the reduction by saying that '[t]he most important lesson which the reduction teaches us is the impossibility of a complete reduction' (1981: xiv). By saying that, Merleau-Ponty suggests that the fundamental task of phenomenology is to preserve the sense of openness ('I am open to the world,' 1981: xvii), the openness that is not contained by any 'explanatory hypotheses or a conception of things formed at the level of second-order expression' (Cerbone 2006: 108). Merleau-Ponty's 'openness' that can be juxtaposed with the notion of the possibility as well as Heidegger's 'apprehension' – that correlates with Husserl's apprehension of 'I' – inscribed into the transcendental-phenomenological reduction project that has been modified and applied by Beckett in his artistic systems, the systems, as it has been presented on *Dream of Fair to Middling Women* example, find their foundations in Phenomenology.

The phenomenological reduction and the 'epochē,' besides their unquestionable helpful role in decoding Beckett's oeuvre, offer other interpretational devices that allow us to decipher the third fundamental element of Beckett's artistic signature, namely the relation between time and memory. Nevertheless, before moving to these aspects of Beckett's thematic preoccupations, three additional notions that link the matters of the reduction and the memory need to be introduced, namely the 'retention' and the 'remembering'.

In *On the Phenomenology of the Consciousness of Internal Time*, Husserl juxtaposes two terms that refer to the relation between the time and memory, namely the 'retention' and the 'remembering'. The main difference between these two notions is as follows: whereas 'remembering' is more active and deliberative, thus if we are trying to call something from our memory, we are doing it actively (Cerbone 2006: 25–26), the 'retention' is a more continuous process where the 'new-points' and the 'source-points' interweave with each other creating the sense of continuity of the events that are happening, that have happened and that happened. Cerbone suggests that the process of the 'retention' is experienced '[a]s fading into the past' (2006: 26). Husserl in his definition of 'retention' refers to the category of the sound, where the already played sounds belong to the past and yet their notion still resonates in the present:

> The 'source-point' with which the 'production' of the enduring object begins is a primal impression. This consciousness is in a state of constant change: the tone-now present 'in person' continuously changes (*scil.* Consciously, 'in' consciousness) into something that has been; an always new tone-now continuously relieves the one that has been passed over onto modification.
> ...
> Accordingly, a fixed continuum of retention arises in such a way that each later point is retention for every earlier point. And each retention is already a continuum. The tone begins and 'it' steadily continues. The tone-now changes into a tone-having-been; the *impressional* consciousness, constantly flowing, passes over into ever new *retentional consciousness*. Going along the flow or with it, we have a continuous series of retentions pertaining to the beginning-point. Beyond that, however, each earlier point of this series is adumbrated *in its turn* as a now in the sense of retention. Thus, a continuity of retentional modifications attaches itself to each of these retentions, and this continuity itself is again an actually present point that is retentionally adumbrated. (1991: 30–31)

Retention presented in Husserlian way allows us to allocate, or at least attempt to allocate, the source point, the original meaning that one attempts to discover through the device that the neutrum is. In addition, the feature that distinguishes the retention, namely the sense of connection between the past and the present, will serve us in understanding how the time--memory relation, especially in the context of Henri Bergson's 'pure memory' and 'memory image' that will be further discussed in the next chapter, works.

The terms and theories presented in this subchapter have allowed us to construct the model of the neutrum, which I also call following Blanchot the 'neutral space'. That space I correlate, to some extent, with the features of the natural language and the semiosphere which we have already discussed, and which play a fundamental role in my understanding what Samuel Beckett's signature is. However, it must be indicated that I do not identify the neutrum/neutral language as the natural language but rather I can observe the vital communicational aspects that both kinds of languages share.

Moreover, I find similarities between the semiosphere and the neutrum, however one may suggest that the neutrum is rather the anti-semiosphere, or the semiosphere for the non-texts. The neutrum, in principle, is the space where on the one hand all meaning is ceased, but on the other the original meanings not infected by the natural language do exist. That paradox I recognise as beneficial for generating new associations and meanings, similarly as it is happening within the semiosphere. Before my model of Beckett's signature will be completed, the third pillar of the signature needs to be discussed, namely the correlation between the time and the memory; the subject that can be observed to be significant for young Beckett's intellectual development as well as the one that I find helpful in unifying the three pillars of my understanding what Beckett's signature is.

Chapter 5: Memory and time

The 1932 essay *Proust* reveals Beckett's interests in two notions that intermingle with each other, namely the memory and the time. In the case of this essay, the writer meditates on the notions of the 'voluntary' and 'involuntary' memory so visible in Marcel Proust's *In Search of Lost Time* and juxtaposes these notions with the time. Beckett indicates that the memory is attributed with the time, calling the latter, 'the Time cancer' (2010d: 513). The memory—time relation appears to be connected with the afore-mentioned features of the neutrum, especially in the case of searching the original meaning through Husserlian retention. The exploration how memory works and to what extent it is fallible is one of the core topics of Beckett's work, not only of the early ones, which will be explored in details in Part Two of this thesis but also in his late works.

The memory is one of the pillars of Beckett's signature because through memory he attempts to recreate something that is lost, an original memory, an original notion (it is visible both in Belacqua's attempts of recalling memories to recognise his location in *Echo's Bones* and in Krapp's attempts of recreating past memories recorded on spools in *Krapp's Last Tape*). Gontarski notices a similar connection between Proust and Henri Bergson where in both cases: 'there can be no search for lost time unless one is first convinced that what has been lost can nonetheless still be found' (2015: 10); such a belief corresponds with Beckett's signature that in general attempts at finding something that has been lost even though these attempts can end up as a failure.

Before moving to the origin of Beckett's interests in the philosophy of Henri Bergson (1859–1941), the reasons of Bergson's popularity in the English-speaking world need to be explained. Mary Ann Gillies in Henri Bergson and British Modernism indicates that the growth of interests on the British isles in the philosophy of the French philosopher can be observed between 1909–1911, predominantly due to over two hundred articles published on Bergson in English, as can be illustrated by *Time and Free Will* (1910) and *Matter and Memory* (1911) as well as due to Bergson's lectures given at the University of Oxford, University College London and the University of Birmingham in 1911 (1996: 29).

The influences of Bergson's philosophy on the British and Irish modernist writers are also unnoticed: the notion of Bergsonian intuition can be seen in

Virginia Woolf's *Mrs Dalloway* and *The Waves*,[1] Thomas Stearns Eliot's poems[2] and James Joyce's novels. As far as Joyce is concerned, knowing the fact that Beckett worked as Joyce's literary secretary, that track may seem especially interesting for the researcher of Beckett's *oeuvre*. Nevertheless, the first interests in Bergson's philosophy were injected by one of Beckett's university mentors at Trinity College in Dublin, namely by Arthur Aston Luce (1882–1977). It is generally assumed that Luce introduced young Beckett to the philosophy of George Berkeley (Gontarski 2013: 29), but in fact Luce introduced him also to the philosophy of Henri Bergson. Luce's preoccupation in Bergson's philosophy resulted in the book entitled *Bergson's Doctrine of Intuition*. The book, published in 1922, consists of the collection of lectures delivered by Luce in 1921 within the famous Donnellan lectures series at Trinity College and covers four main aspects of Bergson's philosophy: 'the method of intuition,' 'Free-Will,' 'Mind and Body,' and 'Theory of Evolution' (1922, table of contents).

Without a doubt, Luce's *Bergson's Doctrine of Intuition* must have influenced seventeen-year-old Samuel Beckett, when he enrolled in Trinity College in 1923. Suffice it to say that Luce's lectures on Bergson are not only visible in Beckett's interests from that period but also resulted in his academic and artistic work at that time. Part Three of *Bergson's Doctrine* entitled 'Mind and Body,' must have been, as Gontarski notices, 'perhaps the most important chapter in both the book and for Beckett's future' (2013: 33). In fact, in *Creative Involution: Bergson, Beckett, Deleuze*, Gontarski indicates that the relation between the mind and body seems one of the most vital interests of Beckett:

> Samuel Beckett's lifelong interest in, if not his preoccupation with, the relationship of mind to body (much generated through his interest in and critique of the work of René Descartes – his focus on, presumably, 'Descartes' errors' as well) is well if often uncritically detailed in the critical discourse. (2015: 24)

Furthermore, Gontarski in *The Edinburgh Companion to Samuel Beckett and the Arts* argues that Beckett's student interests in Bergson's have developed in his professional research:

> He [Samuel Beckett] had read Henri Bergson closely, however, since he was teaching him at Trinity College, Dublin (1930–1931), where he drew a distinction for his class

---

1 See Chapter 5 of *Henri Bergson and British Modernism* entitled 'Virginia Woolf: Bergsonian Experiments in Representation and Consciousness,' pp. 107–132). MLA?.
2 See Douglas, Paul. *Bergson, Eliot, & American Literature*. University Press of Kentucky, Lexington, 1986.

between Proust's sense of time and that of Bergson, Proust's more dualist and relative, Bergson's an absolute time, at least according to notes recorded by one of his students in that class, Rachel Burrows. (2014: 4)

The example how Luce's work has influenced Beckett's writing can be the excerpt about the 'Image.' Luce interprets Bergson's notion as follows:

> 'Image' is an existence, more than a representation and less than a thing. In a sense this is an attempt to recapture the child's view of the world before the discerns objects and names them. The intuitionist tries to imagine how men and things look to any absolutely neutral observer, say a Martian, or the Sphinx or Alexander's angel. (1922: 67)

The output of that viewpoint on the 'Image' is a reoccurring motif of Beckett's works, and in fact encapsulates in itself both the possibility and the assumption of something that exists beyond, whether we call it Husserlian 'sense' or Blanchotian 'neutrum.' That figure can be applied not only to the above-mentioned last scene of *Echo's Bones* where Belacqua is waiting for something in the coffin, as if he were trying to find out if any sign can be approached from the 'beyond,' but also to the famous opening paragraph of *Company* (1980), 'A voice comes in the dark. Imagine' (2010c: 427), the opening fragment of *Company* suggests the same assumption as the passage featuring Belacqua's.

Having mentioned Luce's viewpoint on the 'Image' and the notions of neutrality with it, Bergson's view on that matter needs to be discussed as well. In *Creative Evolution*, he says:

> At the very instant that my consciousness is extinguished, another consciousness lights up or rather, it was already alight: it had arisen the instant before, in order to witness the extinction of the first; for the first could disappear only for another and in the presence of another. I see myself annihilated only if I have already resuscitated myself by an act which is positive, however involuntary and unconscious. So, do what I will, I am always perceiving something, either from without or from within. When I no longer know anything of external objects, it is because I have taken refuge in the consciousness that I have of myself. If I abolish this inner self, its very abolition becomes an object for an imaginary self which now perceives as an external object the self that is dying away. Be it external or internal, some object there always is that my imagination is representing. My imagination, it is true, can go from one to the other, I can by turns imagine a nought of external perception or a nought of internal perception, but not both at once, for the absence of one consists, at bottom, in the exclusive presence of the other. (1941: 303)

Intriguingly, for Bergson, the category of complete nothingness, i.e. the complete annihilation of the subject, is unacceptable as he opts for a continuous presence that is the always-replacing one. Additionally, Bergson introduces the method of 'intuition' that is characterised by distinguishing two kinds of knowledge: the 'relative' one that consists in categorising the 'outside' things by intelligence, and the 'absolute' one that attempts to grasp things from the 'inside' (Scott 2013: 320). That vague description juxtaposes the metaphysical reality that is happening internally, within a living individual, and the scientific reality that is attempting to describe the presupposed reality using fixed terms. Thus, the main role of 'intuition' is to continuously question the presupposed concepts and theories covered in such fields as science or logic, which attempt to describe metaphysics from the objective, 'external' perspective. In *The Creative Mind*, he argues that the critical process must happen in the mind:

> But to do that, it must do itself violence, reverse the direction of the operation by which it ordinarily thinks, continually upsetting its categories, or rather, recasting them. In so doing it will arrive at fluid concepts, capable of following reality in all its windings and of adopting the very movement of the inner life of things. (1946: 223)

The juxtaposition between the metaphysical and scientific intuitions resembles the relation between Husserl's concepts of 'life-world' and 'objective-scientific,' or 'art-world.' In fact, the juxtaposition aims also at finding a statue of purity. While for Husserl that purity is reflected in the metaphysical 'sense,' for Bergson it is manifested in reaching the sense of 'true time' (*durée*) (Scott 2013: 321). Thus, the 'intuition' plays one of the vital aspects of catching the 'true time' in the form of 'the flow of the inner life' (Bergson, 1946: 34). Moreover, Bergson indicates that the duration (*durée*), recognised as the substantial continuity, plays an indispensable role in the act of constituting the state of being in its inner sense: '[t]o think intuitively is to think in duration' (Bergson, 1946: 37)

5.1. Body and mind

In *Matter and Memory*, Bergson asks one of the fundamental questions, namely how the two apparently separate systems, the metaphysical and the scientific, or as he calls them, the 'realistic' and the 'idealistic,' can co-exist with each other:

> How is it that the same images can belong at the same time to two different systems: one in which each image varies for itself and in the well-defined measure that it is patient of the real action of surrounding images; and another in which all images change for a single image and in the varying measure that they reflect the eventual action of this privileged image? (1991: 25)

Bergson by presenting one of the most distinguishing features of the 'image,' namely the possibility that the 'image' can exist within different 'images' and simultaneously cannot exist within the others, raises the question if the universe of images exists only in our thoughts or outside of them. That split seems to be also interesting for Beckett who in *Murphy* (1938) describes the sense of Belacqua's belonging to two separate systems as follows:

> Thus Murphy felt himself split in two, a body and a mind. They had intercourse apparently, otherwise he could not have known that they had anything in common. But he felt his mind too by bodytight and did not understand through what channel the intercourse was effected nor how the two experiences came to overlap. He was satisfied that neither followed from the other. He neither thought a kick because he felt one nor felt a kick because he thought one. Perhaps the knowledge was related to the fact of the kick as two magnitudes to a third. Perhaps there was, outside space and time, a non-mental non-physical Kick from all eternity, dimly revealed to Murphy in its correlated modes of consciousness and extension, the kick *in intellectu* and the kick *in re*. But where then was the supreme Caress? (2010c: 68)

Murphy's divagations are close to the one proposed by Bergson on the co-existence of two systems: the inner one, characterised by Murphy both as the body and as the *in re*, and the mind, or the *in intellectu*. What is more, Murphy is asking questions about the relation between the mind and the body suggesting that both cannot exist without each other, but simultaneously wondering where the 'space' is located, where these two elements meet and communicate with each other. Bergson's answer to that question assumes that if one system is put in the central role, the other is only conditioned by it and *vice versa*. For instance, if one puts the body as the central element, all systems of images are conditioned by the body, but when we want to indicate the duration of time, namely we want to connect the present with the past and the future, the body 'is obliged to abandon this central position' (1991: 26). Bergson summarises this idea of two systems accordingly: '[t]hus in idealism, as in realism, we posit one of the two systems and seek to deduce the other from it' (1991: 26).

Placing one system or the other as the central one corresponds with the theory of Lotman's semiosphere presented at the beginning of this chapter. Lotman proposes one more term that is important for his concept of semiosphere and that can be suitable for better understanding the relation between the systems of the body and the mind, namely the aforementioned term 'boundary'. In Lotman's model the 'boundary' separates the semiosphere and non-semiosphere, or the text and non-text from each other and functions as a place where the external information is recycled in order to be adapted as the one belonging to a particular semiosphere, simultaneously changing the internal structure of the latter:

> The notion of boundary is an ambivalent one: it both separates and unites. It is always the boundary of something and so belongs to both frontier cultures, to both contiguous semiospheres. The boundary is bilingual and polylingual. The boundary is a mechanism for translating texts of an alien semiotics into 'our' language, it is the place where what

is 'external' is transformed into what is 'internal,' it is a filtering membrane which so transforms foreign texts that they become part of the semiosphere's internal semiotics while still retaining their own characteristics. (1990: 136–137)

Lotman's concept of semiosphere and the boundary can be useful in decoding Bergson's duality of systems as well as Murphy's divagations upon the relation between the mind and the body, especially when Bergson suggests that when we take the idealism or the realism as the dominant system, the other loses its position. In a similar way the idea of the core of semiosphere works, where one topic becomes dominant, whereas the other is moved to the boundary and the periphery. (Lotman 1990: 123–130). Moreover, the notion of Lotman's boundary can be correlated to some extent with Bergson's body, especially when it is treated as a transmitter that allows to communicate the inner, i.e. the body with the outer, represented by the senses of smell, taste, hearing, and sight:

> They send back, then, to my body, as would a mirror, its eventual influence; they take rank in an order corresponding to the growing or decreasing powers of my body. *The objects which surround my body reflect its possible action upon them.* (Bergson 1991: 21).

The above excerpt correlates to some extent with the idea of Lotman's boundary, where the outer objects have a dose of influence on the boundary-body. Nevertheless, at that point some differences between Lotman and Bergson's theories need to be suggested. Whereas the infiltration of the non-semiosphere through the boundary into the semiosphere almost always changes the structure of the latter, especially due to 'explosions,' the two systems proposed by Bergson can function completely autonomously and the influences on each other are very weak:

> But in this deduction neither realism nor idealism can succeed, because neither of the two systems of images is implied in the other, and each of them is sufficient to itself. If you posit the system of images which has no center, and in which each element possesses its absolute dimensions and value, I see no reason why to this system should accrue a second, in which each image has an undetermined value, subject to all the vicissitudes of a central image. (1991: 27)

A similar viewpoint is presented by Murphy who at the beginning would like to believe in a '[p]rocess of supernatural determination' (2010c: 68), but finally states that:

> Any solution would do that did not clash with the feeling, growing stronger as Murphy grew older, that his mind was a closed system, subject to no principle of change but its own, self-sufficient and impermeable to the vicissitudes of the body. (2010c: 68)

By treating the mind as a 'closed system,' i.e. the one that uses the body only as a means of transport 'that the mind might move' (2010c: 69), Beckett situates the figure of Murphy in the same constellation as the characters of *Dream of Fair to Middling Women*, namely in the creation of the 'art-world' that allows the writer to create numerous worlds with its own 'reality' that is not dependent on the physical reality. The rejection of the importance of the body and its reduction to a casket whose only role is to protect and transport the brain-mind, is one of the recurring motifs of Beckett's *oeuvre*, is a case in point in the famous phrase 'We are, needless to say, in a skull,' from the short story *The Calmative* written in 1946 (2010c: 261–274). The concentration on the mind, and the diminishing role of the body is also noticed in the last scene of *Dream*, where Belacqua describes his experience connected with his hands accordingly:

> That was his hands. Now who would have thought that! He turned them this way and that, he clenched and unclenched them, keeping them on the move for the wonder of his weak eyes that were down now almost on the top of them, because he was anxious to see details. (2012: 241)

The concept of the dominance of the mind over the body is also revealed by Murphy when he talks about the 'mental non-physical Kick from all eternity.' By that the presence of the 'sense' is indicated, the presence that is more probable to be revealed by the mind than by the body. Finally, the movement of the body and its transportive function correlates with the notion of the 'memory.' As Bergson notices 'the past is only idea, the present is ideo-motor' (1991: 68), and in that statement the French philosopher encapsulates his ideas connected with the relation between the memory, time and movement.

5.2. Memory, movement, symbol

In *Time and Free Will*, Bergson points out the role that the memory plays in a conscious experience of time:

> There are, indeed, as we shall show a little later, two possible conceptions of time, the one free from all alloy, the other surreptitiously bringing in the idea of space. Pure duration is the form which the succession of our conscious states assumes when our ego lets itself *live*, when it refrains from separating its present state from its former states. (2001: 100)

Bergson assumes that the construct of the 'pure duration' functions in a similar way as the consciousness, namely the moments work as 'an organic whole' (Massey 2013: 325) rather than as separate and distinct events as in the case of the 'abstract time.' The idea of 'an organic whole' finds its results in Bergson's definition of the 'memory' that he characterises as:

a synthesis of past and present with a view to the future, in that it contracts the moments of this matter in order to use them and to manifest itself by actions which are the final aim of its union with the body. (1991: 220)

The unavoidable connection between past, present and future time and the body finds its results in Bergson's further division of the term 'memory' into the 'habit memory', the 'image memory' and the 'pure memory'. The 'habit memory' is closely related with the movement of the body; it is a body's capacity to repeat past movements mechanically.[3] The 'image memory', on the other hand, is defined by Bergson as all events of our daily life that occurred in time (1991: 81). Thus, these memories are unique and utterly personal as they refer to the subject's experience. Nevertheless, the characteristic feature of that kind of memory is its strict correlation with the body. The 'image-memories' are not recalled in order of their occurrence but they gradually create a new order, an order that is strictly correlated with the mechanisms of the body and its movements:

> But every perception is prolonged into a nascent action; and while the images are taking their place and order in this memory, the movements which continue them modify the organism and create in the body new dispositions toward action. (1991: 81)

The continuous recollection of the 'image-memories' through the movement of the body results in a paradoxical nature of these images: they are indeed the output of the past but, due to the constant body movement, they are no longer recalled but they are acted. Such an extension of the images from the past to the present causes that they can have '[t]heir useful effect into the present moment' (1991: 82). If the 'image-memories' work as a link between the past and the present, then the notion of the 'pure memory' can be recognised as the original memory, or as Bergson calls it, the virtual object (1991: 130). The 'virtual' in that context means that without the brain and the body it is hardly possible to conceptualise the 'pure memory', thus, similarly to the neutrum-language relation, the 'pure memory', without being juxtaposed with the 'image memory' and the 'perception', can exist only theoretically. Massey notices that both the 'pure memory' and the 'image memory' belong to the past, yet the 'image memory' not

---

3   'Like a habit, it is acquired by the repetition of the same effort. Like a habit, it demands first a decomposition and then a recomposition of the whole action. Lastly, like every habitual bodily exercise, it is stored up in a mechanism which is set in motion as a whole by an initial impulse, in a closed system of automatic movements which succeed each other in the same order and, together, take the same length of time.' (Bergson, 1991: 80).

only creates the link between the past and the present but also is responsible for '[a]ctualisations of the past in the present' (2013: 326).

This leads us to one of the fundamental assumptions of Bergson, namely that the memories are stored in the brain as, for instance, books on a shelf. The continuous movement of memory is described by Bergson by a 'cone of memory' diagram. The reverse cone, where its base is on top and its point is attached to the '[p]lane of experience or action' (2013: 326), represents the correlation between the memory and the movement. The point of the cone, which represents the body, is located in the present, while the base of the cone that is hovering above 'the plane of experience' stands for the 'pure memory.' The act of remembering works here as follows: it takes us back to the past, to the base of the cone that stores all memories, and brings back the more or less detailed memories that can be inserted into the present perception (Bergson 1991: 133–135). However, as it is known from the everyday experience, we are not able to recall in detail every single memory that has happened in the past, Bergson notices that the above-presented mechanism works as 'reductions of our past life' (1991: 169).

Bergson's model of the memory as the 'past-acting-in-the-present' recognises its reciprocal relation, namely the impossibility of recognising the past events without constituting the events in the present as well as the influence of the 'pure memory' and the 'image memory' on the nascence of the 'perception.' Lyotard extends that model adding that in order to apprehend the time it needs to be represented to be experienced (Connor 2014: 119):

> The constitution of the present instant ... already demands a retention, even a minimal one, of various elements together, their 'constitution,' precisely. This microscopic synthesis is already necessary for the slightest appearing. For plunging into the pure manifold and letting oneself be carried along by it would allow nothing to appear to consciousness, nor to disappear from it for that matter, appearing not even taking 'place.' This place is due to a synthesis, that of apprehension, which as it were hems the edges of the pure flow and makes discontinuous the pure continuum of the flow while making continue the pure discontinuity of its supposed elements. In short the river needs a bank if it is to flow. An immobile observatory to make the movement apparent. (Lyotard 1990: 159)

The above fragment adds two important aspects to Bergson's model of memory. Firstly, it suggests that the present is the instance that allows to observe the past memories, and works as the 'bank' for their flow. Secondly, Lyotard demands from us to insert something 'nontemporal' in the flow of time in order to be able to actually observe its passage. However, the act of time stopping should allow us to observe its flow, yet such an act excludes the process of passaging, thus it is not the static observatory that creates the passage but rather the passage creates the possibility to observe the flow of time, however that observatory cannot ever occur in the right place and time (Connor 2014: 120).

The observation of the flow of time proposed by Lyotard inscribes in Bergson's idea of the 'durée,' the idea of catching and observing the duration that should allow us to grasp the 'pure' or 'true' time. Beckett's influence under Bergson's philosophy is depicted in the former's letter to Thomas McGreevy dated 31st January 1938 where he comments on McGreevy's essay on Jack Yeats as follows:

> I think you have provided a clue that will be of great help to a lot of people, to the kind of people who in the phrase of Bergson cannot be happy till they have 'solidified the flowing,' i.e. to most people. (*Letters, Vol. I*, 599)

To 'solidif[y] the flowing' in that case correlates with Lyotard's idea of stopping the flow of time in order to observe the 'durée.' The attempts of stopping that flow of time can be illustrated by Beckett's two early short stories, 'Assumption' (1929) and 'A Case in a Thousand' (1934). In 'Assumption' the memory, especially the 'pure' memory is juxtaposed with the term silence that can be connoted with the afore-mentioned concept of the neutrum but also with Bergsonian model of the relation between the 'pure' memory, 'image' memory and representation:

> Still he fought on all day, hopelessly, mechanically, only relaxing with twilight, to listen for her coming to loosen yet another stone in the clumsy dam set up and sustained by him, frightened and corruptible. Until at last, for the first time, he was unconditioned by the Satanic dimensional Trinity, he was released, achieved, the blue flower, Vega, GOD... After a timeless parenthesis he found himself alone in his room, spent with ecstasy, torn by the bitter loathing of that which he had condemned to the humanity of silence. (2010c: 60)

The act of 'listening' to pure memories is contradicted with the mechanic memory engulfed in one's body. Intriguingly, the relation day-night is the one that also has an influence on the perception of the 'durée,' at night, when the subject is more relaxing, he is able to 'listen' intently in his mind. The correlation between the 'pure' memory and the Husserlian 'sense' is also visible in the phrase 'a timeless parenthesis,' bracketing objects in order to reach the 'beyond' is a similar process to stopping the flow of time in order to perceive its purity. A similar process can be noticed in *A Case in a Thousand*:

> He sat down on the couch, still tossed from the last patient. After a while he lay down on it. The distant furious crying of a child, the light fading and then the rain again, his heart that knocked and misfired for no reason known to the medical profession, these and a compound of minor disturbances began to exhaust his mind and senses. (2010c: 69)

Here, the process of stopping the 'durée' is pictured as difficult if not possible. The process of introducing the subject into the state of suspension represented as laying down on the couch, is constantly interrupted by the external phenomena as the rain or a cry of a child. Possibly interpreted as image-memories, these 'minor disturbances' make it impossible to completely stop the flow of time. In both cases the searching of the 'pure' time is aimed at finding its metaphysical aspects. Gontarski suggests that those people who in Bergson's phrase struggle to have 'solidified the flowing' are also the people who struggle 'to arrest the flow of durée with concepts or symbols' (2011: 65). Bergson in *The Creative Mind* points out that 'Metaphysics is therefore the science which claims to dispense with symbols' (1946: 190). Bergson contradicts the visual systems with the notions of the 'analysis' and 'translation' by claiming that the analysis reduces the object to elements that are already known. The process of analysing applies a paradoxical expression of symbols in terms of which they are not, thus the process of analysing is the process of translating a representation into symbols seen from endless points of view.[4]

What is more, the process of translation always results in the sense of dissatisfaction as the analysis 'multiplies endlessly the points of view in order to complete the ever-incomplete representation' (1946: 189). Thus, the multiplicity of the points of view, which intends to grasp the perfect view on representation, results in the multiplicity of symbols that aim at perfecting the translation. However, the multiplication of symbols is endless, all of them are aspiring to a maximal reduction, i.e. to reducing the symbols to as simple as possible (1946: 190). The examples of the 'womb-tomb' from *Dream*, the coffin from *Echo's Bones* and the rain and a child's cry from *A Case in a Thousand*, all of them function as reduced to maximum symbols of the subject's struggle with grasping the metaphysical representation, whether we call it the 'pure' memory or the neutrum or the 'sense'.

---

4 'Analysis, on the contrary, is the operation which reduces the object to elements already known, that is, common to that object and to others. Analyzing then consists in expressing a thing in terms of what is not it. All analysis is thus a translation, a development into symbols, a representation taken from successive points of view from which are noted a corresponding number of contacts between the new object under consideration and others believed to be already known.' (*The Creative Mind*, 1946: 189).

5.3. The principles of Samuel Beckett's signature

At this point the concepts that are decisive for my understanding of Samuel Beckett's signature should be succinctly summarised. The three thematic preoccupations which determine, in my opinion, the artistic signature of Samuel Beckett are: 1) the concept of language, 2) the notion of neutrum and 3) the origin and storage of the memory and its relation to the body.

I. **Language**
  a) The profound interests in foreign languages as well as in English allowed young Beckett to develop an impressive proficiency in three languages (French, Italian, German) so that he could use them with great facility.
  b) With his extensive studies in French, Italian and German literature and philosophy, Beckett was constantly exposed to the philosophy of language proposed by such scholars as Locke, Vico, Kant and Mauthner, which resulted in transferring their ideas into his own writing. On the other hand, Beckett strongly objected to the traditional cause-effect literature, represented by authors such as Honoré de Balzac, which results in his interest in literary notions such as limitation, reduction, resistance, and inconsistency, and eventually, in creating the literature of the 'non-word.'
  c) Deep studies in Fritz Mauthner's *Beiträge zu einer Kritik der Sprache* (*Contributions to a Critique of Language*) allowed Beckett to recognise the ideas of language and thought as identical, i.e. the thought as happening within language.
  d) Indebted to Vico and Mauthner, Beckett's artistic method aims at a tedious work towards the 'unknown' world, i.e. the world that is not infected by words. That never-ending process of liberation from language, which is constantly disrupted by the limitations of the tool that Beckett uses, namely the natural language, eventually leads to the notion of failure, the notion that would accompany Beckett trough all his artistic carrier.
  e) Language, besides being identical with thought, is correlated with the act of speaking. After Mauthner's 'there is no thinking without speaking,' so Beckett attempted to reduce words in his works to signs of the language failure, i.e. words that symbolise the failure of going beyond language.
  f) Thus, the notion of language in Samuel Beckett's artistic signature would be recognised in the present dissertation as the representation of thought, and the act of speaking, the two instances that are continuously trying to challenge the tyranny of language, however their attempts lead to an inevitable failure. Moreover, language would be perceived in categories

of resistance, limitation and reduction, especially in the reduction for the purpose of creating the sign of language failure, the sign that seems to be indispensable in Beckett's artistic manifesto of creating the 'non-word' literature.

II. **Neutrum**
   a) In *The Space of Literature* and elsewhere, Maurice Blanchot, calls the natural language as 'crude' and 'pure.' By that he attempts to grasp the neutral language, but also the thought, in its essential state, i.e., not contaminated by the natural language, yet. The type of thought that does not convey any meaning.
   b) Thus, the neutrum should not be perceived in categories of meaning but rather as a 'name for namelessness' or the response to everything that is 'beyond meaning' (Hill 2001: 134).
   c) The neutrum should be suspended to a state of complete purity, as Barthes calls it to 'the degree zero,' where there is no possibility for any intentional work of the subject (Momro 2010: 125).
   d) Knowing that the neutrum should be located beyond the subjectivity and it should be deprived of 'I,' the 'ideal space' for the neutrum should be stretched between Blanchotian 'presence' and 'non-presence,' in the space of Foucault's 'le Dehors' (the Outside).
   e) Even though the neutral space seems to be reduced to a complete zero point, where all meanings are suspended, the space should also offer a 'threshold of possibility,' Foucault's 'regain[ing] the space of its unfolding' (1987: 15–16), which is indispensable in the artistic process.
   f) The definition of the neutrum is not complete without the notion of the limit of the beyond. The concept of aporia is needed for the limit of the beyond that on the one hand points out the limits of philosophy but on the other tames the sense of horror that can be connected with the impenetrable void and nothingness (Levinas).
   g) The final element of the concept of the neutrum is the notion of the reduction. Husserl's 'epoché' and his transcendental-phenomenological reduction project suggests that the aim of the reduction is to lead the subject back to the very source of the existence, to the metaphysical realm of the 'sense' understood as the essence of perception.
   h) The above concept of neutrum may be recognised in Beckett's writing, especially in passages focused on identifying the end of the language. His early texts, such as *Dream of Fair to Middling Women, Murphy* or 'Echo's Bones,' convey the variety of artistic devices as repetition, substitution or reduction that reflect the searching for the neutrum. Suffice it

to say that Beckett searches for an origin of the word, analyses its nature, gives new meanings and creates new associations for artistic purposes. For instance, there can be observed a tendency of reducing his characters to symbols functioning in the 'art-world,' whose purpose is aimed at a continuous work in the fibre of the language to eventually reveal the 'pure' nature of the language. However, due to the indifferent nature of the neutrum, the struggles of describing something that has no name appear to be impossible to achieve.

III. **Memory**
   a) At the time he attended Trinity College in Dublin, philosophy of Henri Bergson offered to Beckett a vast number of tools that were to be used in the project of the non-word literature. Examples for this involve Bergson's notions on the relation between memory, body and time.
   b) The questions concerning the origin of the thought as well at the place where the memory is stored are expressed in Bergson's notions of the 'pure' memory, the 'memory-image' and the 'representation,' all of which seem to be applied by Beckett (e.g. *Murphy*).
   c) Bergson's 'durée,' the flow of time and its relation between the past and the present, as well as Lyotard's theory of stopping the time in order to be able to observe the flow of time appears attractive for Beckett's struggles with the topic of the relation between the memory and the time and finds its results in, for instance, 'Assumption' or 'A Case in a Thousand.'
   d) Gontarski's idea to 'arrest the flow of durée with concepts or symbols' and Bergson's suggestion that the metaphysics is the science based on the 'dispense with symbols' can be correlated with one of the fundamental aspects of Beckett's artistic preoccupation that depicts in his artistic signature, namely the continuous operation on symbols understood as maximally reduced equivalents of the 'image memory' that are struggling to grasp the metaphysical representation.

Part Two

Chapter 1: Early criticism in *Dante... Bruno. Vico.. Joyce.* (1929) and *Proust* (1931)

1.1. Searching for the artistic voice: *Dante... Bruno. Vico.. Joyce.*

From the very beginning, Samuel Beckett's writing attempts to depict a state of the artist's suspension between two worlds, on the one hand the artistic one and on the other the academic. Suffice it to say that Beckett originally did not plan an artistic career, however his attempts of becoming an academic scholar turned out to be rather disappointing for him. In the conversation with James Knowlson in October 1989, Beckett admitted: 'I did not intend to be a writer. That only came later when I found out that I was no good at all at teaching' (Knowlson 2006: 105). The writer's reluctance and the sense of embarrassment towards delivering lectures is visible, for instance, in Aileen Conan's memories on Beckett when he taught Modern French Literature at Trinity College Dublin between 1930 and 1931:

> He faced us all with a distracted air, or abstracted might be the better word. But one felt he did not enjoy lecturing. He did not seem to be very good, nor did he want to be, at communicating. I think he just felt that he was going to give us what he felt about these poets and writers and did not want to worry about it otherwise. At that time we were not aware that he had written anything but we did think he was brilliant. (Bair 1978: 122)

Conan's guesswork was not unjustified. In the latter dated on 19 June 1973, Beckett recalls his work as an academic lecturer accordingly: 'I did not enjoy all those women, mooning about. They were a great problem and I was sorely tempted to ask them all to get out, to leave the room' (Bair 1978: 122–123). Contrary to his own view, some Beckett's students considered him a good lecturer, Rachel Burrows' viewpoint on the writer's lectures was, in fact, positive:

> He was a very impersonal lecturer. He said what he had to say and then left the lecture room. But he was very courteous and always willing to elucidate a point, if anyone had the courage to ask him a question. I believe he considered himself a bad lecturer and that makes me sad because he was so good. (Le Juez 2009: 19)

Although Beckett appeared to detest himself in the role of a lecturer, one may observe his recurrent attempts of getting an academic position through the major part of the 1930s. Before holding a post at Trinity College, which he eventually resigned from in December 1931, Beckett held a position of the Trinity College's Exchange Lecturer with the Ecole Normale Supérieure in Paris (nominated 1927, actual post 1928–1930, Pilling 2006: 14–17). The unpleasant experiences of being an academic lecturer at Trinity College are vivid in his correspondence with Thomas McGreevy. In the letter dated 11th March 1931, Beckett writes so: 'I do not want to be a professor (it's almost a pleasure to contemplate the mess of this job)' (*Letters I*. 72), nevertheless, the writer took other attempts of getting an academic position. In the letter to McGreevy dated on 5th January 1933, he informs that he 'applied for a job in Milan' (*Letters I*, 149), moreover Knowlson notices that in the same year Beckett considered application for a position of a French lecturer at Manchester University, yet he finally resigned from this idea (Knowlson 1996: 163). His final attempt of applying for an academic post happened in 1937 when Beckett, following Professor Rudmose-Brown's advice, applied for a post of Lecturer in Italian at the University of Cape Town, South Africa. In the application dated 29th July 1937, Beckett encloses his curriculum vitae, which besides his young age of 29, indicates being a Lecturer in English at the Ecole Normale Supérieure as well as being a Lecturer in French at Trinity College. His job application also covers a list of publications, including *Proust* (1932), *Short Stories* (1934) and *Poems* (1935), as well as testimonials from Professor Rudmose-Brown, Professor Walter Starkie and Professor Robert W. Tate from Trinity College and Jean Thomas from Ecole Normale Supérieure (*Letters I*, 523–528).

The academic path of Beckett's development is inextricably connected with his struggle to become a full-time artist. In the time of holding posts at Ecole Normale Supérieure and Trinity College, the writer's first writing attempts see the light of day. At that point I would like to focus on *Dante ... Bruno. Vico.. Joyce* as an example of combining both his academic and artistic interests. Firstly, it needs to be pointed out that Beckett presented features that one may demand from a model scholar: he was well-educated and highly lettered, familiarised not only with the classics such as Plato, Dante, Vico, and Proust but also with more contemporary experimental writers and poets such as Joyce or Jules Romains. In addition, his profound knowledge of French, Italian and German allowed him to study the majority of works in original languages. Beckett was also famous for his predilection for taking notes; Le Juez notices that he had the habit of taking numerous notes that contained many observations and that were later used for Beckett's own writing (2009: 13). His ability of writing scrupulous notes can be observed in the number of comments left on the margins of the books found in his private library as well as in his notes, for example the 'Whoroscope' notebook that has been archived at Trinity College. The accounts of the people who had contact with Beckett in the late 1920s and early 1930s indicate that from the very beginning Beckett was an outstanding student and lecturer. Professor Thomas Rudmose-Brown reported that:

> Even in his first Junior Freshman year Beckett's aptitude for French and English literature, his thoughtful appreciation of the texts that they were studying and his unusual essays, as well as his silent, brooding manner, brought him to the Professor's notice. (Bair 1978: 48)

To prove that Rudmose-Brown was right about Beckett's talents, one can evoke receiving by the 21-year-old student the Large Gold Medal in Modern Literature for coming First in the First Class as well as a £50 travelling essay grant in October 1927 (Pilling 2006: 16). In addition to that, Rachel Burrows suggested one additional distinguishing feature of Beckett's work as a lecturer, namely his peculiar way of conducting classes:

> He would make long pauses between phrases, or very often pause in the wrong place, after a word which might make you lose the thread of his thought. ... In lecturing, some people like Beckett, are creating as they go along. Suddenly he would come up with something better than what he'd been going to say (Le Juez 2009: 20).

All these features that represent Beckett-scholar, namely a high level of erudition combined with an unusual way of deciphering literature, find their result in *Dante ... Bruno. Vico.. Joyce*, his first published paper in a prestigious literary magazine *transition* in June 1929. Worth mentioning is the fact that one of the figures who actively advised young Beckett which lectures he should read for the essay was James Joyce,[1] the writer who had a tremendous influence on Beckett's literary style in that period as well as a figure that introduced the young artist to the Parisian Bohemia when Beckett taught at Ecole Normale Supérieure. Début in *transition* was manifold, in the same issue besides *Dante ... Bruno. Vico.. Joyce* Beckett's short story 'Assumption' was published. In this way the young scholar debuted also as a writer. It appears to be symbolic that the dual nature of Beckett's writing, the artistic and the scientific ones, between which he was torn apart, accompanied him from the very beginning of his publishing carrier.

In fact, it appears that Beckett, contrary to what he said Knowlson about not intending to become a writer early in life, revealed his ambitions related to writing artistic texts. John Pilling in *Beckett Before Beckett* suggests that Beckett's doubts concerning his abilities were influenced by two factors: firstly his early debut in *transition* and being patronised by James Joyce, the debut which the

---

1 See letters dated on 23rd March and 26th April 1929 (*Letters I*, 7–8).

young writer was not prepared to, as he himself was not 'prepared to countenance' (1997: 11), and secondly, and this seems more vital, Beckett's recurring assumption is that becoming a writer is difficult. The doubt accompanied Beckett later in the 1930s, especially when he experienced difficulties in publishing his artistic texts. In the latter to Thomas McGreevy dated 4th August 1937, the writer explains his reasons for applying for a position of lecturer at the University of Cape Town:

> I applied last week for the Lectureship in Italian at Cape Town. It would be an excuse for taking up the subject again & people say Cape Town has its advantages. I am really indifferent about where I go or what I do, since I do not seem able or to want to write any more, or let us be modest and say for the moment. (*Letters I*, 530)

The inner struggles of finding Beckett's own artistic voice start from his very first published text, *Dante ... Bruno. Vico.. Joyce*. This observation can be used by the researcher of his work as a starting point for finding his artistic signature, especially when the work in the fabric of words is considered. In the following sections I would like to argue that the three pillars for Beckett's artistic signature as in Part One – namely: the language, neutrum and memory – can be applied to the earliest works.

1.1.1. Symbol, sign, language: 'The danger is in neatness of identifications.'

The opening sentence of *Dante ... Bruno. Vico.. Joyce*, 'The danger is in neatness of identifications' (2010c: 495), originally associated with Beckett's reluctance towards the literature of cause-effect depicted in writings of Honoré de Balzac (see Chapter 2 of Part One), can be applied to the significance of language as a fabric that is not only used for creating new worlds (e.g. in a novel), but also multiplies meanings and creates new ones in different contexts. However, the opening sentence of *Dante* depicts some interpretational problems. Firstly, the sentence appears with no particular context, the only reference available to the reader is the title that appears just before the sentence. This may suggest that one should focus more attention on the title itself. It is graphically presented in a manner that is far from the 'neatness of identifications.' Full-stops that separate the names of philosophers and writers appear to signalise the need of presenting the kind of continuation between their ideas, however the irregular usage of these full-stops only hinders from properly decoding the code.

Secondly, the opening sentence functions as an isolated statement that aims at immediately catching the reader's attention. The receiver is put *in medias res*, in the stream of the author's disquisition. Owing to that, the receiver can have

Searching for the artistic voice   109

an assumption that might have missed one of the key points at the very beginning of the story. Although, without a vivid context, the sentence 'The danger is in neatness of identifications,' which can be treated in semiotic categories as a semiosphere, begins to establish its own context, which can be seen as a static one at first, yet is subsequently being dynamised. The dynamics appears when one juxtaposes the opening sentence with the title where some concepts, on condition that the receiver possesses an appropriate set of skills to decode them, are reduced to symbols exemplified by the names of 'Dante,' 'Bruno,' 'Vico,' and 'Joyce,' the symbols that encapsulate in these names the variety of literary and philosophical traditions that these authors represent. On the one hand these symbols can be read as a relay of ideas passing through centuries (Dante to Bruno, Bruno to Vico, Vico to Joyce), on the other all of them stand for different aspects of the movement that appears in Beckett's works, e.g., Dante=verticality, horizontality, similar to the movements of characters of *Echo's Bones*, Vico=eternal return, as in the case of Belacqua's movement in 'A Wet Night' but also the unfinished cycle of *Endgame*. Owing to that context, the inner dynamics of the opening sentence is set in motion and starts to generate new meanings as well as new contexts (Lotman 1990: 127).

Thirdly, the opening sentence as well as the sentences that follow the starting one, portray a certain kind of the author's reluctance in the process of the discursive manner. The second sentence: 'The conception of Philosophy and Philology as a pair of nigger minstrels out of the Teatro dei Piccoli is soothing, like the contemplation of a careful folded ham-sandwich' (2010c: 495), besides a series of vivid comparisons, does not facilitate understanding of the point. Reluctance in proceeding with the discourse appears to be one of Beckett's discoveries of writing expression and one of the main aspects of his signature. John Pilling notices that even without a concrete 'neatness,' i.e., without the guiding topic of the discussion, '[t]he enterprise can in fact proceed nevertheless' (1997: 14). The reluctance to proceed will be accompanying Beckett through his whole writing career. Suffice it to say that in the diachronic perspective the hesitation from *Dante* can be to some degree equivalent with the statement 'you must go on, I cannot go on, I'll go on' from *The Unnamable*.

Having said that, the next step in the analysis of *Dante* should concern the importance of language understood as a transmitter for generating new meanings. Bogusław Żyłko suggests three distinguishing features of natural language that make it unique in the relation to culture, namely the pattern of systematicity, the function of a matrix, and a universal metalanguage that can be used for describing all other disciplines that are happening within the culture (2009: 109). For Beckett, in *Dante*, the natural language plays the role of such a matrix and metalanguage that allows him to gather different, sometimes apparently non-related notions, and process them further into new meanings or depriving them from their original ones. In the first paragraph of *Dante*, one may read a peculiar collection of subsequent idioms:

> And now here am I, with my handful of abstractions, among which notably: a mountain, the coincidence of contraries, the inevitability of cyclic evolution, a system of Poetics, and the prospect of self-extension in the world of Mr. Joyce's *Work in Progress* (2010c: 495)

The 'abstractions' covered in the above sentence are in fact the examples of philosophies characteristic for all main figures of the article, namely Dante, Bruno, Vico, end eventually Joyce. Each of these notions is reduced to a slogan that conveys in itself main assumptions connected with the particular philosophy; Dante is represented by his 'system of Poetics,' Bruno by 'the coincidence of contraries,' the 'cyclic evolution' stands for Vico's ideas, whereas all these notions are cumulated in Joyce's *Work in Progress*. Contrary to the title that suggests that Dante's ideas should be discussed as first, Beckett starts with Vico's viewpoint on the philosophy of eternal returns, just to present a direct allusion to Joyce's *Work in Progress*, then he devotes a minimal amount of time to mention on Bruno's coincidence of contraries, mainly in the context of Vico, and finishes the essay with the juxtaposition between the language as used by Dante and Joyce. In an interview with James Knowlson in 1989, Beckett confessed that while writing *Dante* his knowledge concerning Bruno was very limited:

> It was at his [Joyce's – R.B.] suggestion that I wrote 'Dante… Bruno. Vico.. Joyce' – because of my Italian. I spent a lot of time reading Bruno and Vico in the magnificent library, the Bibliothèque of the Ecole Normale. We must have had some talk about the 'Eternal Return,' that sort of thing. He liked the essay. But his only comment on it was that there was not enough about Bruno; he found Bruno rather neglected. They were new figures to me at the time. I had not read them. I'd worked on Dante, of course. I knew very little of them. I knew more or less what they were about. I remember reading a biography of one of them. (1996: 107)

Despite Beckett's confession on his limited knowledge in that time, especially on Bruno, the insights presented in *Dante* pivot around the topic of language, its origin and history. Starting with Vico appears to be intentional as his *Scienza Nuova* (*The First New Science*) positions the discussion and allows Beckett to further develop his ideas on the language, especially in the context of *Work in Progress*.

Vico in *Dante* is perceived in an empirical rather than mystical way. He is called '[a] practical roundheaded Nepolitan' (2010c: 495). Beckett notices that

Searching for the artistic voice 111

'[H]is (Vico's – R.B.) treatment of the origin and functions of poetry, language and myth, ... is as far removed from the mystical as it is possible to imagine.' (2010c: 496). However, the author appears to be in favour of that empirical, or we should say the natural origin of language that will be presented later, he wants to signalise the reader that in fact it does not matter as for Beckett, Vico is perceived predominantly as the 'innovator' (ibid.).[2]

One of the basic notions introduced by Vico is the notion of the 'Providence.' He defines this term as a divine architect without whom the human society cannot be formed as '[The] divine Providence, who is the architect of this world of nations. For men cannot unite in a human society unless they share a human sense that there is a divinity who sees into the depths of their hearts,' (2002: 38). Beckett in his essay quotes, in Italian, a different excerpt from *The New First Science*:

> Yet without doubt this world was created by the mind of providence, which is often different sometimes contrary, and always superior to the particular goals which people have set for themselves. Instead, to preserve the human race on the earth, providence uses people's limited goals as means of attaining greater ones. (Ghosh et al, 2009: 59)[3]

Despite a highly religious aspect that resonates from both quotations, suggesting that a God-creator is indispensable in the process of the humankind creation, it appears that for Beckett's perception of the philosophy of Vico it is more important to recognise that the language and history are bonds that create nations. There are two aspects that suggest such an idea; firstly, in the evoked fragment of *Scienza Nuova* that appears in *Dante*, there appears the expression 'the mind of providence,' which suggests that the world was created by the mind of its creator.

---

2 Joseph Mali proposes a different viewpoint on the origin of the language in Vico's philosophy. He points out that two main doctrines dominated in the eighteenth century, namely the Biblical (Platonic) one that sees the origin of language in a divine power and the conventional (Aristotelian) theory that finds the beginning of the language in human reason. Mali suggests that Vico's philosophy inscribes in the so-called Adamic-Cratylian theory that combines both some instances taken from the Bible, especially from Genesis 2: 19 where Adam is responsible for naming all living creatures – that indicates the mimetic nature of giving names based on what human beings can see, and the belief that first languages must have originated from sounds and gestures (1992: 173-14).
3 ['una mente spesso diversa e alle volte tutta contraria e sempre superior ad essi fini particolari che essi uomini si avevano proposti; dei quali fini ristretti fatti mezzi per servire a fini più ampi, gli ha sempre adoperati per conservere l'umana generazione in questa terra.'] (Beckett 2010c: 496).

Such a viewpoint correlates with Mauthner's ideas, especially with the notion that there is nothing but language, and every output of the humankind's thought is created, named and infiltrated through the language. Secondly, Beckett summarises his opinion on the given quote using the word 'utilitarian' by which he points out that the concept of the Providence conveys more practical than mystical implications – allows societies to function. It seems impossible to build a society without the language as the language is the tool that enables to set up law, culture and customs.

Subsequently, Beckett is more interested in the history of language proposed by Vico. The writer presents a correlation between the development of three stages of the human society (Theocratic, Heroic and Human) and the classification of languages that have developed in three stages as well: 'Hieroglyphic (sacred), Metaphorical (poetic), Philosophical (capable of abstraction and generalization)' (2010c: 469). The dynamics of the language development from sacred, reserved for priests and nobles, through the language of symbols, used in poetry, until the epistolary language, used in everyday life, correlates with the development of the human history.[4] Nevertheless, the theory presents one more source of influence on Beckett's writing – the development that is not constant but asymmetric, and excludes the dangers in 'neatness of identifications.'

A certain amount of asymmetricity that Vico's theory on the development of languages offers to Beckett seems especially attractive to the young writer as it correlates with his ideas against the cause—effect literature, is only one of the elements that appear to be particularly interesting for Beckett. The second one is the role of the symbol within the language, how symbols cumulate within themselves both meanings and memories. Beckett points out that before the time of hieroglyphs, language existed in the form of gestures:

> In its first dumb form, language was gesture. If a man wanted to say 'sea' he pointed to the sea. With the spread of animism this gesture was replaced by the word: 'Neptune.' He [Vico –R.B.) directs our attention to the fact that every need of life, natural, moral

---

4   Vico describes the development of the language history as follows:
'The first was a language of hieroglyphics or sacred characters, i.e. a language of the gods, of the sort that Homer said was older than his own language, a divine language that explained all things human. This is the reason for the formation of the vocabulary of Varro's thirty thousand gods among the Latin peoples. The next was a language of symbols or emblems, precisely as we have seen in the case of the heroic language of arms ... The last was an epistolary language, i.e. a language of vulgar letters and words of settled meaning, used for carrying out their final practices in everyday life.' (2002: 236).

and economic, has its verbal expression in one or other of the 30,000 Greek divinities. (2010c: 501)[5]

It is intriguing how the development of a particular word, in this case the 'sea,' has accumulated in itself not only the whole process of Vico's history of language (hieroglyphic/religious—symbolic/poetic—vulgar/abstract) but also attempts to catch the pre-lingual step of the language formation, based on gestures, or one may call it, based on nature. As it has been discussed in Chapter 3 of Part One, the examination of the pre-lingual instances, covered in the notion of the neutral language, is one of the core elements of Beckett's signature, thus it is not surprising that such interests appear in his first published text. From the diachronic perspective it is known that his advanced studies in the philosophy of language took place in the 1930s, suffice it to say that he started studying Mautner around 1932, but the origins of that interest can be traced in *Dante*.

The progression of symbols, from physical (gestures) to abstract (the 'sea') in early Beckett's view is correlated with the development of the society. As an example, he presents a sequence of words 'Forest—cabin—village—city—academy' (2010c: 501), the sequence that, besides generating new meanings and functioning in different contexts, has accumulated the meanings or functions of their predecessors. What is more, all these words have developed in the natural order in parallel to the historical development of the society in which the changes have happened. Thirdly, each of the words isolated from the sequence conveys in itself a number of expressions that allow them to create its own chain of meanings, for example, for the 'forest' it can be soil—seed—water—tree—forest. Beckett seems to be particularly interested in the process of discovering both the original meanings and the pre-lingual origins of symbols. He suggests that '[t]he root of any word whatsoever can be traced back to some prelingual symbol' (2010c: 501) and justifies that assumption on the Latin word 'Lex:'

1. Lex = Crop of acorns.
2. Ilex = Tree that produces acorns.
3. Legere = To gather.
4. Aquilex = He that gathers the waters.

---

5   Vico presents a similar correlation between words and gestures based on the word 'scythe:'
    'Hence, in such an age, since crops were undoubtedly a great discovery of human industry, men used a scythe or a scything gesture of the shoulder to indicate that they had harvested as many times as the years they wished to signify.' (2002: 179).

5. Lex = Gathering together of peoples, public assembly.
6. Lex = Law.
7. Legere = To gather together letters into a word, to read. (2010c: 501)

The scheme presented in the above example resembles the sequence 'Forest—cabin-village—city—academy' – the physical objects existing in nature ('crop,' 'tree') have accumulated more abstract meaning ('to gather'). Moreover, because of the development of the society some meanings started to function as one of the fundaments of the society ('law') and have finally evolved into the words used in everyday life ('to read'). It appears justified to assume that the attractiveness that Beckett finds in that process is a possibility to re-discover the previously cumulated meanings in particular words/symbols. The process can be also used as a tool that supposedly should allow the writer to reach the original, pre-lingual meaning. However, the pre-lingual process inscribes in the theory of the neutral language that Beckett attempted to research through all his artistic career. It needs to be stressed out that Beckett's interests in that issue presented in *Dante* concentrate more on finding the prototypes for general notions, such as law, inventor and hero rather than on more abstract Blanchotian 'name for nameless' that Beckett would be eventually exploring in his post-war texts, for example *The Unnamable*:

> The early inability to abstract the general from the particular produced the Type-names. It is the child's mind over again. The child extends the names of the first familiar objects to other strange objects in which he is conscious of some analogy. The first men, unable to conceive the abstract idea of 'poet' or 'hero,' named every hero after the first hero, every poet after the first poet. Recognizing this custom of designating a number of individuals by the names of their prototypes, we can explain various classical and mythological mysteries. Hermes is the prototype of the Egyptian inventor: so for Romulus, the great law-giver, and Hercules, the Greek hero: so for Homer. (2010c: 501)

A similar approach to reconstructing the original signs is presented in works of Vyacheslav Ivanov (1929–2017), a Russian philologist and semiotician, closely related with the Moscow-Tartu School of Semiotics. Originating in linguistic studies, he proposes a theory, in which one is able to reconstruct the primal archetypes of humans' behaviour as these archetypes have been inherited and are still visible in current generations. Ivanov suggests that the original semantics can be both forgotten and reinterpreted. For instance, for the first anthropoid apes a bucket of flowers stood for a symbol of food, whereas in the modern times it is considered a gift. Żyłko adopts Ivanov's ideas to the semiotic categories; he coins the term 'paleo-semiotics' – a device that allows to form the chain of communication, from the most primitive to the most abstract and sophisticated. Owing to that, one is able to reconstruct the whole spectrum of a particular system of signs (2009: 102). To some extent, Beckett's interests in the process of the archetype sign reconstruction correspond to Ivanov and Żyłko's semiotic postulates.

The above divagations have focused mainly on Beckett's interest in how the symbol is created, what its origins are as well as how the symbol can be used in the context of the language's development in a particular culture, since it is inseparable from the dynamic development of the history. The symbol, which we can identify with such a notion as the sign, appears to be intriguing for Beckett due to its manifold adjustments in the creative process. For example, symbols allow to cumulate and generate meanings that indicate a certain sequence of subsequent events, yet simultaneously the same symbols allow the writer to disturb the cause-effect sequence by referring to the events that took place in different time periods.

Thus, we can suggest that the model of the artistic world created in *Dante* is built of the following elements: 1) the prelingual signs that exist underneath the construction and function as archetypes for all signs that have been superstructured in the course of time; 2) the natural language(s) that play the role of the most basic ingredient in the process of creating words; and finally, 3) the symbol that is the combination of the natural language and the cumulated meanings. In *Dante*, Beckett adds one additional feature that knits together all above elements, namely the form. In the second part of the essay Beckett moves to Dante's *Divine Comedy* and Joyce's *Work in Progress* to depict a relation between the language and the form. *Work in Progress* serves here as an example of a piece of writing that eludes from any conventional understanding what the novel is and what standards should be fulfilled by a text to be treated as a novel. For Beckett, a straight line that separates the form from the content cannot be determined as in Joyce both the content and form intermingle and influence each other:

> You are not satisfied unless form is so strictly divorced from content that you can comprehend the one almost without bothering to read the other. The rapid skimming and absorption of the scant cream of sense is made possible by what I may call a continuous process of copious intellectual salivation. (2010c: 502–503)

The structure of *Work in Progress* should be perceived in the holistic way, not only as a piece of writing written in a language. Beckett notices that Joyce's novel should not be considered to be written in English or any other language, but as a piece that it perceived by all senses:

> Here form *is* content, content *is* form. You complain that this stuff is not written in English. It is not written at all. It is not to be read – or rather it is not only to be read. It is to

be looked at and listened to. His (Joyce's – R.B.) writing is not *about* something; *it is that something itself.* (2010c: 503)

Beckett's suggestion that *Work in Progress* is not written in English yet using that language for the construction of the piece of writing finds its analogy in Dante's *Divine Comedy*. The writer indicates that Dante's masterpiece was not written in any standard Italian or Latin language but was rather a mix of different dialects that were used in the thirteenth and fourteenth century Italy. The analogy between Dante and Joyce's works is as follows: they both use the language as a kind of form that determines the holistic perception of the work making that both manuscripts are written using the natural language, simultaneously denying the usage of it:

> He (Dante – R.B.) did not write in Florentine any more than in Neapolitan. He wrote a vulgar that *could* have been spoken by an ideal Italian who had assimilated what was best in all the dialects of his country, both which in fact was certainly not spoken no ever had been. (2010c: 507)

The examples of Joyce and Dante serve us to depict the language-form relation that allows to exclude the significance of the content itself. Even though both examples opt for the pure, non-contextual usage of the language, they still inscribe in Beckett's understanding of the sign. Suffice it to say that the texts written in the non-language, in fact use words that have accumulated in themselves meanings and archetypes from the past, which start to generate new contexts in their semiosphere. The cumulation of the meanings that we have evoked so many times in this subchapter leads us to the notion of the reduction that I recognise as one of the core elements of Beckett's signature. Intriguingly, this notion also appears in *Dante ... Bruno. Vico.. Joyce.*

1.1.2. The dynamic reduction: 'Church—Marriage—Burial'

So far, it has been implied that the accumulation of meanings within a single word/sign aims at generating as many notions as possible. The words put in new contexts not only implement the meanings that have already been accumulated in them but also allow to generate new meanings, subsequently causing that the artistic structure of a text not only becomes more dynamic but also paradoxically breaks off from a regular cause-effect model.[6] On the other hand, the cumulation of meanings within a single sign brings to our discussion the notion

---

6   Yet, still need to be remembered that to some extent, a certain level of sequentially still exists within signs.

of reduction. In *Dante*, Beckett brings Giordano Bruno's juxtaposition between 'maximal' and 'minimal' as a starting point for the discussion on that topic:

> The maxima and minima of particular contraries are one and indifferent. Minimal heat equals minimal cold. Consequently transmutations are circular. The principle (minimum) of one contrary takes its movement from the principle (maximum) of one another. Therefore not only do the minima coincide with the minima, the maxima with the maxima, but the minima with the maxima in the succession of transmutations. Maximal speed is a state of rest. The maximum of corruption and the minimum of generation are identical: in principle, corruption is generation. (2010c: 497)

However, the original idea that stands behind Bruno's viewpoint on the maximal-minimal relation is connected with the alchemy, which is indicated by Beckett himself while using such alchemical terms as 'transmutations' and 'circular'; the above fragment presents no explicit reference to that branch of natural philosophy.[7] Nevertheless, what seems to be most appealing for Beckett in Bruno's philosophy is the concept of the circular movement that is inextricably connected with the dynamic minimalisation and maximalisation of the object. Such an approach allows Beckett to delineate the line that connects Bruno, Vico and Joyce's philosophy, by indicating that '[t]he maximum of corruption' is reflected in Joyce's '[m]aximal compression of the word' (Kaelin 1981: 21).

That comprehension is also visible in Vico's approach to the notion of symbol. Kaelin notices that 'Vico had adopted the view of successive transformations in his account of generation and corruption of societies in history, and of signs within a language' (ibid.). Beckett refers in *Dante* to the church-marriage-burial example as a metaphor of a human being's average life span. That example is attractive not only because of accumulating in itself Bruno's 'minimal-maximal' concept, which was also modified by Vico for the purpose of his philosophy of history and providence, but predominantly Bruno's idea allows Beckett to demonstrate a straight influence on Joyce's word-comprehension philosophy of writing:

> History, then, is not the result of Fate or Chance – in both cases the individual would be separated from his product – but the result of a Necessity that is not Fate, of a Liberty that is not Chance (compare Dante's 'yoke of liberty'). This force he called Divine

---

7 Examples of the relation between Beckett writing and alchemy can be found, for example, in Okamuro, Minako. 'The Occult,' In: Uhlman, Anthony (ed.). *Beckett in Context*. Cambridge University Press, Cambridge 2013: 338–339) and Bénard, Julie. 'Dante… Bruno. Vico.. Joyce:' Samuel Beckett's 'identified contraries.' In: *E-rea*, 15.2/2018, especially the subchapter entitled 'Alchemical modernism.'

Providence, with his tongue, one feels, very much in his cheek. And it is to this Providence that we must trace the three institutions common to every society: Church, Marriage, Burial. (2010c: 498)

That triad that Beckett associates with the three ages of human history development, namely Church-Theocratic, Marriage-Heroic, Burial-Human illustrate how Beckett's ideas on the notion of the reduction could be formed. The maximal reduction applied in the case of the above example is not restricting signs, quite the opposite, the reduction is the source of generating endless meanings as well as attempting to reach the realm of pre-lingual signs, or as Blanchot suggests in his transcendental-phenomenological reduction method, to reach the very source of the existence. Beckett indicates that the Church-Marriage-Model is used by Joyce as a 'skeleton' which he applies for his writing, in the name of the content-is-form-form-is-content philosophy:

The lamp is more important than the lamp-lighter. By structural I do not only mean a bold outward division, a bare skeleton for the housing of material. I mean the endless substantial variations on these three beats, and interior intertwining of these three themes into a decoration of arabesques – decoration and more than decoration. (2010c: 498)

The dynamics that the reduction offers to Joyce can be recognised as one of the fundamental structures of his writing – the endless source of new meanings that are generated from the archetypical symbols. That dynamic, as it is depicted in *Dante*, appears to be alluring for Beckett's creation of an artistic text: without the dynamics, the generation of meanings could not take place and would result in the process of stagnation that inhibits the artistic process. In the final paragraph of the essay, the author constructs a metaphor based on *Divine Comedy*, where he compares the world to Purgatory, the place where any progress is connected with 'explosions.' That metaphor summarises the whole language model presented in the essay as well as incorporates the idea of the reduction as one of the core elements of the artistic structure that the author of *Waiting for Godot* is trying to develop:

No resistance, no eruption, and it is only in Hell and Paradise that there are no eruptions, that there can be none, need be none.
...
Then the dominant crust of the Vicious or Virtuous sets, resistance is provided, the explosion duly takes place and machine proceeds. (2010c: 510)

1.2. In search of time and memory: *Proust*

Beckett's stay at Ecole Normale Supérieure resulted in his profound study of Proust's works, predominantly because of new contacts that the author acquired in Paris, but also because of the access to new studies on Proust. Interests in Proust's *oeuvre* are especially vivid in Beckett's correspondence with Thomas McGreevy in the summer of 1929, where he expresses his fascination with the French novelist's usage of both form and unconventional narrative. However, Beckett also expresses criticism toward *Swann's Way*, finding some fragments of the novel offensive:

> I have read the first volume of 'Du Cote de chez Swann,' and find it strangely uneven. There are incomparable things – Bloch, Françoise, Tante Léonie, Legrandin, and then passages that are offensively fastidious, artificial and almost dishonest. It is hard to know what to think about him. He is so absolutely the master of his form that he becomes its slave as often as not. (*Letters I*, 11).

Even thpugh, Beckett was not fond of some qualities of Proust's writing, as in the case of his criticism of Proustian involuntary memory (Van Hulle—Nixon 2013: 74), he definitely must have been under the influence of the French novelist's writing. Suffice it to say that the Irishman was especially charmed with Proust's usage of metaphor and called it an 'explosion' of beauty ('Some of his metaphors light up a whole page like a bright explosion, and others seem ground out in the dullest desperation,' *Letters I*, 11). Thus, it is no surprise that Proust's *In Search of Lost Time* became one of essential lectures of Beckett between 1929 and 1930.

Beckett's academic engagement in Proust's *oeuvre* was only deepened when he was offered to write an essay on that topic. Richard Aldington and Nancy Cunard, novelists and publishers who sponsored a contest for a one-hundred-line poem on the subject of time, a contest that Beckett eventually won for his 'Whoroscope' in 1930, introduced the début author to Aldington's good friend, Charles Prentice, a publisher from Chatto and Windus. Aldington, passing on a suggestion from MacGreevy, implied that Beckett would be a good candidate to write an essay on Proust in the Chatto and Windus new Dolphin Books series, a suggestion that Prentice approved. For Beckett the second half of 1930 was predominantly devoted to intense studying of *In Search of Lost Time* and criticism on Proust (Knowlson 1996: 121–122). He bought the complete sixteen-volume edition of Proust's work in French (Van Hulle—Nixon 2013: 69), and delivered the full text to Chatto and Windus in London at the end of September 1930, where *Proust* was eventually published on 5th March 1931.

1.1.1. Time and sign: 'That double-headed monster of damnation and salvation'

In the previous chapter, it has been indicated that the notions of time, memory (with subdivisions to 'pure' and 'image') and the 'durée,' the flow of time, introduced and defined by Bergson with further development, for example by Lyotard, should be treated as one of the cores of Beckett's signature. The notion of time, in more general terms, appears to be understood not only as the fundament on which the whole signature is built, using such tools as the natural and neutral language that are eventually transferred into symbols, but the time plays predominantly the role of a flywheel that allows us to observe how the symbols are being created, modified, moved, and eventually stopped or ceased, as in Gontarski's suggestion 'to arrest the flow of durée with concepts or symbols' (2011: 65).

The first page of *Proust* brings Beckett's both ironical and paradoxical definition what the time is, namely '[t]hat double-headed monster of damnation and salvation' (2010c: 511). The expression 'double-headed monster' is not accidental, as Beckett further suggests that '[h]is (Proust's – R.B.) book takes form in his mind' (2010c: 512). If the mind is the vessel which all processes concerning the time and memory are taking place in, the role of the writer is, at least, to attempt to observe these processes. Beckett compares the writer's role to the profession of a translator, '[t]he duty and the task of a writer (not an artist, a writer) are those of a translator' (2010c: 549),[8] the statement that only enforces young Beckett's disambiguation between becoming a scholar and a writer (he purposely does not use the form 'an artist'), but also the statement that signalises the importance of the language as the matter that is used to tame, usually inefficiently, the flow of time.

Beckett evokes Proust's struggle with the time by quoting, in the Irishman own translation, the last sentences of the last volume of *In Search of Lost Time*, *Time Regained*:

> But were I granted time to accomplish my work, I would not fail to stamp it with the seal of that Time, now so forcibly present to my mind, and in it I would describe men, even at the risk of giving them the appearance of monstrous beings, as occupying in Time a much greater place than that so sparingly conceded to them in Space, a place indeed extended beyond measure, because, like giants plunged in the years, they touch

---

8   The given quotation is the earliest Beckett's written thought on the role of a translator, one of the most reoccurring motifs in his later work. For more, see, for example. Cordingley, Anthony (ed.). *Self-Translation. Brokering Originality in Hybrid Culture*. Bloomsbury, London 2013, 161–177.

at once those periods of their lives – separated by so many days – so far apart in Time. (2010c: 512)

Proust uses time as the device that allows him to capture characters immersed in the flow of time, not in their ideal but rather actual state. Some scholars like John Calder claim that such a level of intimacy between the reader and the writer/book had not been possible in the literature before (2001: 63–64), whereas Daniel J. Boorstin even suggests that Proust by writing *In Search of Lost Time* conquered the time (1993: 696). Beckett is not such an optimist as he calls the characters from *In Search...* the victims of time ('[v]ictims of this predominating condition and circumstance – Time,' 2010c: 512) – the victims that by having been immersed in the course of time, have been by that course both sculptured and deformed. Such a continual state of memory anchored within the flow time, understood in Bergson's the pure memory-memory image-perception, and past-acting-in-the-present models, finds their reflections in Beckett's deciphering of the last sentences of *Time Regained*:

> There is no escape from yesterday because yesterday has deformed us, or been deformed by us. The mood is of no importance. Deformation has taken place. Yesterday is not a milestone that has been passed, but a daystone on the beaten track of the years, and irremediably part of us, within us, heavy and dangerous. (2010c: 512)

Such an approach to the correlation between time and memory reveals Beckett's viewpoint on the flow of time and how the subject functions within it. Firstly, despite a certain amount of deformity that is reciprocal, i.e., that both influences on the subject and the memory, immersed in the course of time, one can still notice a continuity. This continuity is expressed by the notion of a 'daystone,' indicating that the events that happened in the past have not been finished for ever, yet, even though belonging to yesterday they still influence the subject in the present. Secondly, the notion of deformation is allocated by Beckett with the term of dislocation. He indicates that the yesterday's subject, the subject's mood to be more precise, has nothing to do with that of the present as the reference which the subject can rely on, namely the latent consciousness world, is not the same as the world within which the subject's mood took place ('Such as it was, it has been assimilated to the only world that has reality and significance, the world of our own latent consciousness, and its cosmography has suffered a dislocation.,' 2010c: 513). What is more, Beckett's divagations go even further, suggesting that the dislocation of the subject contrary to the world in which his, her or its aspirations are to be fulfilled, can be compared to continuous death of the subject:

> The aspirations of yesterday were valid for yesterday's ego, not for today's. We are disappointed at the nullity of what we are pleased to call attainment. But what is attainment?

The identification of the subject with the object of his desire. The subject has died – and perhaps many times – on the way. (2010c: 513).

From the above fragment one may notice that the constitution of the ego is inseparable with the notion of work. For Descartes, the philosopher who appears to be the most prominent for Beckett's intellectual work at the time of writing *Proust*, due to the fact of being a leitmotif of Beckett's 'Whoroscope,' the constituency of the ego is inseparable with the performance of thinking that takes place in time (Cottingham et al. 1992: 127).[9] Sartre presents similar viewpoint on the ego when he depicts that the transcendental unity of the ego consists of states and actions (2004: 12). The above viewpoint on the nature of the ego, namely its endless work within time and through time lead us to the notion of the habit, a habit that plays a crucial role *In Search of Lost Time* and that is called by Beckett in *Proust* as '[t]he ballast that chains the dog to his vomit.' (2010c: 515).

So far, I have indicated the dual nature of habit presented by Beckett in *Proust*, namely the repetitive chain of actions that eventually leads the subjectivity to the annihilation and simultaneously the never-ending process that allows the subjectivity to re-constitute it in relation with the surrounding world. In *Swann's Way*, Proust presents similar qualities of what the habit is:

> Habit! That skilful but slow-moving arranger who begins by letting our minds suffer for weeks on end in temporary quarters, but whom our minds are none the less only too happy to discover at last, for without it, reduced to their own devices, they would be powerless to make any room seem habitable. (1992: 8-9)

---

9   Beckett's dislocation and deformation can correspond with René Descartes' philosophy on the nature of the human mind, such as the French philosopher's divagations that appears in his *Meditations*, especially in the 'Second Meditation,' where the philosopher points out the deceptive nature of memory:
'I therefore suppose that all I see is false; I believe that none of those things represented by my deceitful memory has ever existed; in fact I have no senses at all; body, shape, extension in space, motion, and place itself are all illusions. What truth then is left? Perhaps this alone, that nothing is certain.' (2008: 17-18)
The relation between Beckett and Descartes' philosophy has been researched thoroughly, e.g., Morot-Sir, Edouard. 'Samuel Beckett and Cartesian Emblems.' In: *Samuel Beckett and the Art of Rhetoric*. University of North Carolina 1976: 25-104, Scruton, Roger. 'Beckett and the Cartesian Soul.' In: *The Aesthetic Understanding: Essays in the philosophy of Art and Culture*. Carcanet Press, Manchester 1983, 222-241 and Feldman, Matthew. 'René Descartes and Samuel Beckett.' In: *Beckett's Books: A Cultural History of Samuel Beckett's 'Interwar Notes.'* Continuum, London 2008, 41-57.

Beckett also indicates another crucial role that the habit plays in the matter of time and memory, namely that its role is to hide the true essence, the preconceptual idea: 'Habit has laid its veto on this form of perception, its action being precisely to hide the essence—the Idea—of the object in the haze of conception—preconception' (2010c: 517). At that point the device that should, at least theoretically, allow us to get through the matter of the habit is a sign. Gilles Deleuze (1925–1995) in *Proust and Signs* juxtaposes two terms: the 'search' and the 'sign'. For him, the 'search' should be understood not as a mere effort of exploring the memory but predominantly as the strong desire of searching for truth (2000: 3). On the other hand, the 'sign' is perceived by Deleuze as '[t]he object of a temporal apprenticeship, not of an abstract knowledge' (ibid.), the object that aims both at implicating, implying and unfolding or even explaining something (Bogue 1989: 38). These two notions, namely the 'search' and 'signs' are cooperating with each other as the 'search' explores the worlds of signs, the worlds that, according to Deleuze, are organised in '[c]ircles and intersect at certain points, for the signs are specific and constitute the substance of one world or another.' (2000: 4). Before further discussion of Deleuze's divagations on the nature of signs, two important qualities of the sign need to be evoked. Firstly, Lotman's understanding of the sign is not only the generator of new meanings but also '[a] condenser of cultural memory' (2009: 18). Secondly Roman Jakobson's notion of the 'diachrony in synchrony' indicates that the sign, despite its present usage, has also accumulated the memory of its previous uses (Jakobson 1962).

Lotman and Jakobson's ideas that enhance the role of the time and memory within signs can be further developed in Deleuze's typology of signs. It has been mentioned that the signs are organised in the world of signs, in fact Deleuze proposes four categories of signs that are called as follows: 1) the signs of art, 2) sense experience, 3) involuntary memory, love, and 4) worldliness. In his hierarchy, the signs of art are at the top of the hierarchy as they aim at expressing a meaning that is an essence. Below them are the signs of sense experience that offer an imitation of existence of essences and pure time. The next in the hierarchy are the signs of involuntary memory, i.e., the ones that reveal the existence of both the essence and the pure time, but their true nature cannot be fully revealed as they are confined to an intransigent matter (Bogue 1989: 41–43).[10]

---

10 Intriguingly the signs of involuntary memory are depicted by Beckett in *Proust* as the '[e]cho of a past sensation,' whereas the instance that is responsible for their confinement is the intellect:
'The most successful evocative experiment can only project the echo of a past sensation, because, being an act of in intellection, it is conditioned by the prejudices of the

The signs of love are deceptive and tend to unfold the hidden worlds, Deleuze indicates that one of their features is that '[t]hey are not empty signs, standing for thought and action' (2000: 9), thus the signs of love can only address us by concealing what they express. It indicates that the signs of love should be treated in more material categories where their contact with the essence is only general and obscure. Finally, the signs of worldliness, or the worldly signs, serve as the 'replacement of an action or a thought' (2000: 6), the worldly signs are perceived by Deleuze as disappointing or even cruel as they do not refer to something else but are trying to usurp the 'supposed value of meaning' (ibid.).

For Beckett, the signs of involuntary memory appear to be the most appealing as he is trying to analyse that kind of memory based on *In Search of Lost Time*. The involuntary memory, which is associated with Bergson's spontaneous recollection defined as a 'perfect from the outset; time can add nothing to its image without disfiguring it; it retains in memory its place and date' (1991: 83) contrary to either learned or habit memory that 'passes out of time' (ibid.). The involuntary memory encapsulated by Proust in his famous madeleine is called by Beckett as a 'fugitive salvation in the midst of life' (2010c: 524). For our purposes of deciphering the Beckett's signature, Deleuze's definition of signs of involuntary memory correlates with the features of the neutral language that I have characterised as one of the fundaments of Beckett's signature. Although Deleuze indicates that the involuntary memory signs may reveal the true nature of essence and pure time, it is not possible due to the signs' confinement to the intransigent matter, Beckett's understanding is close to Blanchot's viewpoint on the pure language or Bergson's idea of pure memory. Thus, in *Proust* Beckett's work on the signs of involuntary memory indirectly covers the matter of signs (language), memory and neutrum:

1. The Madelaine steeped in an infusion of tea.
   (*Du Côté de Chez Swann*, i. 69–73.)
2. The steeples of Martinville, seen from Dr. Percepied's trap.
   (Ibid., 258–262.)
3. A musty smell in a public lavatory in the Champs-Elysées.
   (A l'Ombre des Jeunes Filles en Fleur, i. 90.)

---

intelligence which abstracts from any given sensation, as being illogical and insignificant, a discordant and frivolous intruder, whatever word or gesture, sound or perfume, cannot be fitted into the puzzle of a concept.' (2010c: 543).

4. The three trees, seen near Balbec from the carriage of Mme. De Villeparisis. (Ibid., ii. 161.)
5. The hedge of hawthorn near Balbec. (Ibid., iii. 215.)
6. He stoops to unbutton his boots on the occasion of his second visit to the Grand Hotel at Balbec. (*Sodome et Gomorrhe*, ii. 176.)
7. Uneven cobbles in the courtyard of the Guermantes Hotel. (*Le Temps Retrouvé*, ii. 7.)
8. The noise of a spoon against a plate. (Ibid., 9.)
9. He wipes his mouth with a napkin. (Ibid., 10.)
10. The noise of water in the pipes. (Ibid., 18.)
11. George Sand's *François le Champi*. (Ibid., 30.) (2010c: 524–525)

The above collection of signs can be used as an example of how the involuntary memory, following Bergson's theory of retaining memories, may allow us, on the one hand, to reach the essence, the pure memory that we can attempt to observe by slowing down the memories and observe its durée, and on the other hand, the symbols of involuntary memory can serve as the reduced objects that reflect the life's span. Beckett suggests that the sequence cobbles—spoon—plate—napkin—water in the pipes – *François le Champi* can serve as the key to Proust's life and work (2010c: 525). However, these sequences of signs, which Beckett used from the very beginning of his writing, should be perceived as passkeys which the author of *Happy Days* correlates and reorders in so as to reach the realm of neutral language. The process echoes the sequence of signs presented in *Proust* works, the 'womb-tomb' from *Dream of Fair to Middling Women*, and the sequence church—marriage—burial from *Dante ... Bruno. Vico.. Joyce*. The above examples of sequences indicate that the work on signs as well as building the literary worlds based on the matter of signs play a significant role in Beckett's artistic *oeuvre*.

Moreover, in *Proust* Beckett correlates the signs not only with the involuntary memory, but also with the work of memory in general. The essay ends with the word 'defunctus' (2010c: 554), which means in Latin *have done something, perform, finish*. The word also refers to Schopenhauer's statement: 'life is a pensum to be worked off: in that sense 'defunctus' is a fine expression' (Pothast 2008: 15).[11] The continuous work of memory, the work it has to do, is in fact not

---

11 The word 'pensum' plays an important role in Beckett's universe as well. He divides the world into two fundamental sections; the world of 'reality' or 'pensum' that can be called a slave labour world, and the world of a fragile, but blissful freedom. Both in

finished, it is more about to be finished yet it fails at the very end, nevertheless the 'defunctus' cannot be just eradicated. Because even though the realms of reality and, as Beckett calls it, the 'invisible reality' run apparently in parallel, the precious moments when the synthesis of these two realities takes place, it opens for a very short moment an ephemeral space where the essence, Deleuzian signs of art, can be observed.

Proust and *Murphy* the world of 'pensum' is the world of the body on the earth (Pothast 2008: 148).

Chapter 2: *More Pricks Than Kicks* (1934)

2.1. *More Pricks Than Kicks*: the young artist's 'intricate festoons of words'

In this chapter our main task will be to demonstrate how Beckett uses symbols, which I have defined as the reduced forms of the natural language, based on the example of some short stories from the collection *More Pricks Than Kicks*. The multitude of functions that the symbols play in the stories are aimed at indicating how through the matter of the natural language, the author attempts to explore the topics of the neutrum and aporia. Moreover, the natural language is used in reference to such devices as Lotman's 'asymmetry', where the symbols taken from the works of other writers (Dante, Shakespeare) are artistically translated by Beckett into his stories. Such a technique results in not only building their worlds that can find its roots in different authors' texts but predominantly in using them as a material for exploring such significant themes for Beckett's works as naming the nameless and the eternal returns but also the self-referentiality that internally strengthens Beckett's texts.

A series of promising publications at the beginning of Beckett's artistic career, for example, his double début in *transition* in June 1929 through the acclaimed poem 'Whoroscope' in 1930 and finishing with the publication of *Proust* by Chatto and Windus in 1931 suggested a rapid development in the author's career. However, especially between 1931 and 1933, Beckett started to confront a sense of creative powerlessness that soon became a source of frustration to him. It is vital to delineate a genealogy of works that were written in that period. One can divide them into three categories: 1) those that were published; 2) those that were not sent to publication and yet appeared in some modified way in other works; and 3) those that were dismissed by publishers.

The first category would include the poems 'Alba,' published in *Dublin Magazine* (1931), 'The Possessed' that appeared anonymously in *T.C.D.: A College Miscellany* (1931), 'Yoke of Liberty' (originally entitled 'Moly'), 'Hell Crane to Starling,' 'Casket of Pralinen for a Daughter of a Dissipated Mandarin,' and 'Text,' which all appeared in *The European Caravan: An Anthology of the New Spirit in European Literature*, 1931 (Knowlson 1996: 130) as well as a short story *Sedendo et Quiescendo* that appeared in *transition* in 1932. Moreover, it is worth adding that the opening story from *More Pricks Than Pricks*, 'Dante and the Lobster' was originally published in *This Quarter* in 1932.

The second category is represented by the short story *The Smeraldina's Billet-Doux* (1931) and the poem 'Enueg II' (1931), whereas the third category, i.e., the works dismissed by publishers are represented, for instance, by the poems 'Enueg I'(1931) and 'Dortmunder' (1932). However, the most powerful episode that resulted in Beckett's doubt in his artistic work was the rejection of the novel *Dream of Fair to Middling Women*, written in 1932 and eventually published posthumously in 1992.

The series of rejections of *Dream* by subsequent publishers, such as Chatto and Windus, Hogarth Press, Cape, and Grayson in 1932 and Titus in 1933 (*Letters, Vol. I*, 103–104, 147) as well as inimical reviews of the novel resulted in the author's pessimistic view on his further artistic carrier. Such a mixture of uncertainty and resignation is depicted in Beckett's letters to Thomas McGreevy, for instance, the letter dated 13th September 1932:

> No news from Grayson, and I hesitate to write them a stinger. But now it is a good three weeks since they promised me their decision immediately. Rickword never acknowledged the poems. Nothing seems to come off. I made a desperate effort to get something started on Gide but failed again. (*Letters, Vol. I*, 121)

Confronted with such publication difficulties, the author started to incorporate fragments of modified versions of his works into others. That strategy is especially intriguing for the researcher of Beckett's *oeuvre*, who can now observe the development of the creative process, sketch the genealogy of works, their origin, evolution and the final form. Lotman in *Culture and Explosion* indicates that the dynamics of culture cannot be both isolated and passive (2009: 133). The dynamism of culture eventually results in the collisions between the spheres that he calls 'external' and 'internal,' where by the spheres he understands different cultural systems (e.g., the Holy Roman Empire and the barbaric kings).

The infiltration of the 'external' into 'internal' causes tensions that contribute to creating new names, Lotman calls this process 'renaming' (2009: 133). I recognise the dynamics of culture as a similar process that takes place within the semiosphere of Beckett's works. Here, the collision of names and notions is depicted by the juxtaposition of different works of the same author, however the process follows the same principles as in Lotman's internal-external relation, including the semiosphere's dynamism, self-development and collision.

The way in which the above-mentioned processes work in the case of *Dream* will not be analysed in detail. Yet, to prove that such measures do exist it is worth evoking some titles of other works by Beckett that appear in his first unpublished novel. In *A Beckett Canon* Ruby Cohn suggests that the phrases, images and ideas of at least six Beckett's poems overlap in *Dream*, namely 'Sanies II,' 'Alba,' 'Enueg

I,' 'Enueg II.' 'Dortmunder,' and 'Text' (2005: 40). In the novel, one can also find the modified versions of 'The Smeraldina's Billet-Doux' and 'A Wet Night,' a short story that was finally published in *More Pricks Than Kicks*. That blend of different pieces of writing emphasises, on the one hand, the continuous artistic ferment but, on the other, can be deciphered as a desperate attempt of fulfilling a young artist's ambitions.

An example of Beckett's high expectations towards his works was his reserved reaction when he received the information that Chatto and Windus agreed to publish his first artistic book in September 1933. *More Pricks Than Kicks* is a collection of ten short stories linked by the character of Belacqua Shuah, a protagonist that appears at first in 'Sedendo et Quiescendo,' then is the protagonist of *Dream of Fair to Middling Women*, and of a short story *Echo's Bones*. Belacqua is frequently identified with Beckett himself and recognised as his alter ego; however, it is worth indicating that the Belacquas from the above works are not identical; they are rather avatars of Belaqua that share some common features yet do not constitute the same character.

In *Dream* Belacqua plays a metafictional role: he is not only a fictional character, which is particularly visible in chapters 'Two' and 'Three,' but also a narrator who expresses a certain degree of metafictional awareness. In chapter 'Two' the narrator suggests that 'we' are 'concensus, here and hereafter, of me' (2012: 5). In the chapter 'Und' Belacqua is described by the narrator from a third person perspective that 'he [Belacqua-R.B.] was bogged in indolence, without identity, impervious alike to its pull and goading' (2012: 121). Belacqua, by being characterised as without identity, plays his role. In the opening scene of *Dream*, the reader encounters Belacqua on the Carlyle Pier where the protagonists divagates on the doubtful beauty of his girlfriend Smeraldina-Rima ('[i]n the mizzle in love from the girdle up with a slob of a girl called Smeraldina-Rima,' 2012: 3). In a short story 'Fingal' from *More Pricks Than Kicks*, Belacqua is accompanied by his different girlfriend, Winnie Coates in the Hill of Feltrim (2010d: 91), whereas in 'Walking Out' also from *More Prics*, we find Belacqua in the scene of walking out a dog and getting to know that the protagonist is already engaged to his fiancée Lucy (2010d: 152).

All above examples share some common features, namely all of them present Belacqua's love affairs with different women, however the surroundings in which the scenes take place are different. Moreover, in all above examples the reader does not know much about Belacqua's background, where he comes from, what his profession is, why he finds himself in such surroundings as the Carlyle Pier or the Hill of Feltrim.

Beckett's reserved attitude towards the publication of *More Pricks Than Kicks* derives from the fact of being somehow forced to combine different short stories into one collection. Similarly to *Dream of Fair to Middling Women*, where other published and dismissed pieces were incorporated, Beckett applied a similar measure in *More Pricks*. It was partially forced by Charles Prentice, a publisher from Chatto and Windus, who suggested Beckett should incorporate the already published short story 'Dante and the Lobster' at the beginning of the collection (Knowlson 1996: 168). Moreover, Beckett himself incorporated fragments of *Dream* into *More Pricks*, probably recognising it as the only opportunity of publishing at least parts of *Dream*. This is why in *More Pricks...* there appeared two stories: 'The Smeraldina's Billet-Doux' and 'A Wet Night.'

The other reason for Beckett's mixed feelings towards the publication of *More Pricks* was a fear of how his family will react on the book. As Knowlson suggests in *Damned to Fame*:

> Beckett's feelings about the publication of the stories were highly ambivalent; they included excitement at the prospect of seeing his first volume of creative writing appear in print, and hope that this might well lead to other commissioned work – but also worry that the stories would offend relatives and friends (1996: 176)

The author's suppositions turned out to be well justified. When the book was finally published on 24th May 1934, Beckett's mother, May Beckett completely ignored it; the book appeared in the Becketts' house in Foxrock several months after publication. Moreover, *More Pricks...* turned out to be a mediocre financial success. Despite many enthusiastic reviews in press, for instance, in *Times Literary Supplement*,[1] critics described Beckett's works as 'a define fresh talent at work in it, though it is a talent not yet quite sure of itself' (Knowlson 1996: 177). Moreover, Charles Prentice could not sell the stories to an American publisher. Another aspect of the criticism of *More Pricks...* focused on the similarity of the text to the style of James Joyce. In a review for *John O'London Weekly* one may read that 'Mr. Beckett has imitated everything in James Joyce – except the verbal magic and the inspiration' (ibid.).

More Pricks Than Kicks consists of ten short stories: 'Dante and the Lobster,' 'Fingal,' 'Ding-Dong,' 'A Wet Night,' 'Love and Leathe,' 'Walking Out,' 'What a Misfortune,' 'The Smeraldina's Billet Doux,' 'Yellow,' and 'Draff.' For the purposes of examining how the principles of Samuel Beckett's artistic signature can be applied to the author's *oeuvre*, I examine two stories, namely 'Dante and the

---

1   *The Times Literary Supplement*, 26th July 1934.

Lobster' and 'Ding-Dong.' These two texts should allow us to observe how Beckett's signature is constructed within the structure of a text. In addition, such a selection should enable us to capture another characteristic feature of Beckett's writing, namely the dialogue of the texts within the borders of that signature; we can also see how that dialogue – or a self-referential use of the same idioms, motifs and themes from different Beckett's works, is used in the course of the creative process.

2.2. 'Dante and the Lobster:' The space of 'somewhere else'

In *Beckett Writing Beckett: The Author in the Autograph* H. Porter Abbott, suggests that the fundamental feature of Beckett's writing is the act of reinvention. The scholar claims that 'by repeating names, images, and motifs from one work to another – sufficiently developed to be recognisable, insufficiently developed to connect – Beckett was constantly reinventing his entire oeuvre' (1996: 20). However, the above statement is beneficial for our further analysis of Beckett's works and will be eventually applied to prove one's argumentation, a weak point of that theory needs to be pointed out. Porter Abbott's statement implies a certain degree of intentionality in the creative process, exploring Beckett's *oeuvre* form the perspective of the author's late work, *Company* (1980), where, as he proves, the sense of intentionality and the writer's artistic self-reference is intermingled with the notions of autobiography and autography.[2]

Nevertheless, if '[t]he greatest influence on the texts of Samuel Beckett are the texts of Samuel Beckett' (Caselli 2005: 58), one needs to examine if such a statement can be applied in the case of 'Dante and the Lobster.' The opening sentence of the story equips the reader with a collection of symbols, themes and motifs:

> It was morning and Belacqua was stuck in the first of canti in the moon. He was so bogged that he could move neither backward nor forward. Blissful Beatrice was there, Dante also, and she explained the spots on the moon to him. (2010d: 77)

In the sentence one can notice a multitude of symbols that refer to Dante's work (Belacqua, Beatrice, Dante, 'the first canti in the moon'), however the

---

[2] Porter Abbott claims that 'if Beckett's postwar endeavor is not conventional autobiography it is nonetheless best understood not as fiction but as a species of autography (self-writing).' (1996: 2). A useful study on the notion of autobiography within a literary text as well as on the author—subject—voice relation can be found in Czermińska, Małgorzata, *The Autobiographical Triangle. Witness. Confession. Challenge.* Peter Lang, Berlin 2019.

Beckettian translation of the passage from Dante's *Purgatorio* cannot be read as the solely source of inspiration. Belacqua, as presented in 'Dante and the Lobster,' shares some similar features as Dantean one, such as indulgence and unwillingness to take any action, however the character of Beckett's story, when read in the context of the whole *Divine Comedy*, represents a different type of allegory. Sam Slote notices that the main difference between Dante's pilgrim and Beckett's Belacqua is situated in the contrast progress-aporia (2010: 16). He notices that the pilgrim's travel is aimed at a spiritual journey, whereas Belacqua is 'stuck in the first of canti in the moon' (ibid.).

The reinvention of Dante's story that is happening in 'Dante and the Lobster' indicates an asymmetry in which I find the sources of Belacqua from the story in other Beckett's texts rather than in Dante's. Caselli suggests that the origin of the text '[i]s always somewhere else, in unlocatable spaces which nevertheless belong to other Beckett works' (2005: 59). To illustrate how Ceselli's statement works in practice one needs to examine features of Belacqua-symbol presented in the story. Belacqua by being stuck in the canti of the Moon is physically stuck in the surface of that celestial body.

While Dantean pilgrim's being stuck in the Moon means his progress towards God, for Belacqua getting stuck means only an impossibility to move, to make any progress (Slote 2010: 16). That metonymy of aporia is also expressed in the sentence 'He was so bogged that he could move neither backward nor forward,' both examples reinforce Belacqua's aporia and draw our attention to search for other sources, not only Dantean, of that symbol.

In my view, similar features of Belacqua from 'Dante and the Lobster' may be found in Beckett's other texts, for example in *Dream of Fair to Middling Women* Belacqua's aporia is expressed by finding him 'sat on the stanchion at the end of the Carlyle Pier,' (2012: 3) and in *Echo's Bones* where Belacqua is sitting on a fence and is not sure whether to jump off it or not (2014: 3). The statement on Beckett's text belonging to 'somewhere else' can be also visible if one juxtaposes the opening sentence of 'Dante and the Lobster' with the opening lines of the poem 'Alba:'

before morning you shall be here
and Dante and the Logos and all strata and mysteries
and the branded moon
beyond the white plane of music
that you shall establish here before morning... (2010d: 16)

The similarity that can be evoked both in 'Dante and the Lobster' and 'Alba' is a collection of symbols, Dante—moon—morning. The triad of symbols applied in both texts functions as a series of events that aim at constituting the texts' worlds through the work of signs. I recognise that work as a dynamic process of a continuous work of the symbol. That work is also revealed by the reciprocal communication of the used signs between different texts from Beckett's universe. In the cases of 'Dante and the Lobster' and 'Alba', the signs establish the worlds, however they do not indicate any particular point of origin. On the contrary, the reader is rather put in *medias res* of that process and can observe its constituency intermingled with the world's indeterminacy.

Having said that, one can depict the principles of Beckett's signature in the opening incipit of 'Dante and the Lobster.' Firstly, the culture is the source of all symbols, motifs and ideas that are established within the mind, in the case of the story one can correlate the space where the story is taking place with the reader's mind. Secondly, the instability of the world in-progress as well as a certain level of in-betweenness ('He was so bogged that he could move neither backward nor forward,' 2010d: 77) connotes with the notions of neutrum, possibility and reduction. Finally, the role of symbols used in that constituting process is to, if not arrest, then at least attempt to slow down the flow of memory, of the durée.

Furthermore, the principles applied in the opening sentence of 'Dante and the Lobster' can be recognised as a recurring pattern that is visible in other stories from *More Pricks Than Kicks* that we will discuss later, i.e., 'Ding-Dong' and 'A Wet Night.' What is more, it is visible that reinvention was further developed by Beckett in his post-war works, yet in the extremely reduced way. For example, the opening quote of *Waiting for Godot* (1952) expressed by Estragon says 'Nothing to be done' (2010c: 3), in *The Unnamable* (1953) it is 'Where now? Who now? Unquestioning. I say I' (2012: 32), in *How It Is* (1961) 'how it was I quote before Pim with Pim after Pim how it is three parts I say it as I hear it' (2010b: 411).

The central role in 'Dante and the Lobster' is played by Belacqua, the protagonist of all stories from *More Pricks Then Kicks* as well as the main character in *Dream of Fair to Middling Women*. The paradox of that character is twofold, since Belacqua is the source of the story's origin as well as the story's incoherent reality of the novel.[3] The name Belacqua connotes with the character from Dante's *Divine Comedy*, who appears in 'Canto IV' of the *Purgatory* part:

---

3   The incoherence of the world of the novel is expressed by Belacqua in the chapter 'Und' of *Dream of Fair to Middling Women*, when he decides to switch from the role of the narrator to the writer. He projects the assumptions of his novel as based on the experience of silence ('The experience of my reader shall be between the phrases, in the silence,' 2012: 138). Further Belacqua mocks his own intentions as well as other

I came to him he hardly raised his head,
Saying: 'Hast thou seen clearly how the sun
O'er thy left shoulder drives his chariot?'

His sluggish attitude and his curt words
A little unto laughter moved my lips
Then I began: 'Belacqua, I grieve not

For thee henceforth; but tell me, wherefore seated
In this place art thou? Waitest thou an escort?
Or has thy usual habit seized upon thee?'

And he: 'O brother, what's the use of climbing?
Since to my torment would not let me go
The Angel of God, who sitteth at the gate. (2019: 23-24)

Dantean Belacqua is a background character that Dante meets during his travel through the Purgatory; Belacqua epitomises inanition and lazy spirits. The same features – apathy or laziness – are visible in Beckettian Belacqua as well. The central role of the story is depicted in the number three: in the opening scene Dante's reference is repeated three times, Dante—Beatrice—Belacqua, and reinforced by the information that the opening meditations of '[t]he spots on the moon' derive from Beckettian Belacqua's study of *The Divine Comedy* ('He scooped his fingers under the book and shovelled it back till it lay wholly on his palms. The *Divine Comedy* face upward on the lectern of his palms,' 2010d: 77–78). Number three occurs through the whole story as it divides the plot into

---

artists like Hölderin and 'Beethofen' claiming that 'I think of his [Beethoven's—R.B.] earlier compositions where into the body of the musical statement he incorporates a punctuation of dehiscence, flottements, the coherence gone to pieces, the continuity bitched to hell because the units of continuity have abdicated their unity,' 2012: 139). Belacqua's vision of the literature is then based on splitting the story's coherence into the smallest possible pieces ('unprevisable atom,' 2012: 139), the method that should allow to create a ramshackle book. Eventually, Belacqua's divagations in that matter are disrupted in an omnipotence voice that claims that Belacqua's intentions are wrong ('But there he was probably wrong,' 2012: 140), after that utterance Belacqua abandons his literary theories and starts doing other actions (steeping a ladder). Taking into account the metafictional nature of the chapter 'Und,' Belacqua's attitude towards being a writer depicts the novel's incoherence. From setting up a cohesive model of literature expressed through Belacqua-writer, the disruption of the voice completely diminishes that model, moving Belacqua-writer back to Belacqua-character that populates the literary world of the novel.

a triptych 'What did matter was: one, lunch; two the lobster; three, the Italian lesson' (2010d: 78).

All these symbols play the purpose of decoding the central theme of the story, namely the impossibility of reconciling divine justice and mercy in this world (Cohn 2005: 43). That theme derives once again from Dante's *The Divine Comedy* and is depicted by the phrase that appears in 'Canto XX' of the *Inferno* part: 'qui vive la pietà quando e ben morta' [here pity lives the best when it is dead]. The same superb pun' is evoked" by Belacqua from 'Dante and the Lobster' during his Italian lesson with Mrs. Ottolenghi:

> "I recall one superb pun anyway: qui vive la pietà quando e ben morta.."
> She said nothing.
> "Is it not a great phrase?" he gushed.
> She said nothing.
> "Now" he said like a fool "I wonder how you could translate that?"
> She still said nothing. Then:
> "Do you think" she murmured "it is absolutely necessary to translate it?" (2010d: 85)

The three main milestones of the story, namely the lunch, picking up the lobster from the grocery store for dinner and the Italian lesson, the apparently trivial task to by fulfilled by Belacqua, serve as the background for meditation on the themes of death, pity and God's mercy. Another characteristic feature of the world created in 'Dante and the Lobster' is the act of superimposing Dantean Italy on modern Dublin. The reader does not know when the action of the story is taking place, the narrator, who is not identified with Belacqua as he presents him in the third person narrative, appears to be constructing the time of the story during its durée. Finally, the narrator proposes that the action takes place during the winter claiming: 'let us call it Winter, that dusk may fall now and a moon rise' (2010d: 86). Owing to such suggestions in the text itself, one can observe a visible dynamism in the processes of establishing the world of the story. The process of decoding and encoding the semiotic space of 'Dante and the Lobster' by Beckett through Dante's *The Divine Comedy* is similar to the process Dante used to encode *The Ulysses* in *The Divine Comedy*. Lotman in *Universe of the Mind* indicates that the author takes the role of the creator who rather than playing the role of the receiver, takes the role of the transmitter:

> If the world is like a vast missive from the Creator then there is a mysterious message encoded in the language of its spatial structure. Dante deciphers this message by recreating this world for a second time in his text; he thereby adopts the position of a transmitter of the message rather than its receiver, and the poetics of *the La Divina Commedia* is thus oriented towards enciphering. (1990: 177)

Taking the role of the transmitter allows Beckett to encode symbols and themes through the motifs of external texts (*The Divine Comedy, The Bible*), through the matter of language as well as through the symbols that are getting new meanings within the semiosphere of the short story. To illustrate that measure, let us concentrate on the subjects of death, pity and God's mercy that are the *leitmotif* of the story. Intriguingly, these motifs occur in accompaniment of the four milestones of the story, namely the lunch, the visit at the grocery's, the Italian lesson, and the diner during which the lobster plays the role of the main course. However, the topic of death appears to be the source of Belacqua's serious moral divagations, the references to that topic are only shattered and signalised though the story.

When Belacqua prepares the meal, he glimpses at the newspaper where the face of McCabe, a murderer to be sentenced to death, is visible: 'He deployed an old *Harald* and smoothed it out on the table. The rather handsome face of McCabe the assassin stared up at him' (2010d: 78). The usage of that figure seems to be intentional. McCabe, the murderer sentenced to death on 9th December 1926, was accused for murdering six people and arson, however to the very end the claimed to be innocent (Cohn 2005: 47). The moral aspect between crime and punishment was certainly registered by young Beckett, who during McCabe's execution was a student at Trinity College, thus it seems intentional to use his name as the symbol of death and pity. Another reason that stands behind using the murderer's name is the juxtaposition of the surname McCabe with the names of Cain and Abel. In fact the name Cain appears when Belacqua cooks his lunch on the grill. When he uses the tiller he notices that 'the spots were Cain with his truss of thorns, dispossessed, cursed from the earth, fugitive and vagabond.' (2010d: 79)

In neither case Belacqua displays any signs of pity, after glancing at McCabe's photo he lit 'the gas-ring and unhooked the square flat toaster' (2010d: 79) whereas his thoughts on Cain end up with divagations, but on the condition of the tiller ('it had been good enough for his mother, it was good enough for him,' 2010d: 79). The third symbol representing death and pity is the lobster. Belacqua collects the creature from the grocery's and at the beginning is not aware that lobsters are boiled alive. The process is suggestive that is happening when Belacqua discovers the lobster's destiny. From the very beginning of the story the theme of death is only accompanying other everyday situations yet they do not trigger any deeper thoughts in Belacqua's mind. Until the end of the story he declares no statement towards Cain's death, contrary to McCabe's and the lobster's.

The starting point of Belacqua's moral thoughts is the Italian lesson during which Mll. Glain, the French teacher asks about the parcel in the hall, a parcel in which Belacqua keeps the lobster. In that conversation, one can observe an intriguing shift in the relations of the meanings that results in redirecting Belacqua's thought into moral aspects of the pity seen from the Christian perspective. Because Mll. Glain asks about the parcel in French and Belacqua does not know how to say the lobster in French, he claims that in the parcel is fish. That semiotic transformation from the lobster into the fish connotes in Belacqua's mind the reference to Jesus's last supper during which Christ was offered fish as well ('He did not know the French for lobster. Fish would do very well. Fish had been good enough for Jesus Christ, Son of God, Saviour. It was good enough for Mll. Glain,' 2010d: 86). Moreover, when Belacqua wants to return to the Italian lesson with the question 'where were we?,' Mrs. Ottolenghi answers mysteriously 'where we were, as we were.' (ibid.)

The teacher's question works as an 'explosion' that is redirecting Belacqua's mind into the topic of pity. The thought is only reinforced by the number of symbols that the protagonist encounters while going from the lesson to his aunt's house. He sees a man sitting on a down horse's head and '[a] poorly dressed couple stood in the bay' (ibid.), he also asks Mrs. Ottolenghi's question in his mind answering 'why not piety and pity both, even down below?' (2010d: 867), Belacqua's answer is ambiguous as it may relate both to the moral aspects but also to proper translation of Dante's sentence from *The Divine Comedy*.

The protagonist's switched viewpoint is directed towards McCabe's death where Belacqua starts to pity his destiny:

> Why not mercy and Godliness together? A little mercy in the stress of sacrifice, a little mercy to rejoice against judgement. He thought of Jonah and the gourd and the pity of a jealous God on Nineveh. And poor McCabe, he would get it in the neck at dawn. What was he doing now, how was he feeling? He would relish one more meal, one more night.' (2010d: 87)

From now on the topic of death is correlated with the symbol of the last supper, the meal that will occur the last for the lobster as well. When Belacqua finds out from his aunt that the lobster is to be boiled alive, he is terrified but his aunt assures him that the lobsters 'feel nothing' (2010d: 86). When finally, the creature is put to the boiling water, Belacqua's hope, expressed by the narrator, that the animal's death is going to be quick, is disrupted by an unknown voice with a statement 'it is not' (2010d: 88).

Finally, one more characteristic way of the symbols' functioning in the story needs to be highlighted. The chain of meanings cumulated in 'the lobster' that I have presented so far, namely the lobster-lunch-pity-mercy-quick-death should be also equipped with two additional, namely the neutrum and the reduction. During the story the lobster is described as a neuter creature that, as Belacqua originally thought, is not alive. However, later he claims that 'suddenly he saw the creature move, this neuter creature. Definitely it changed its position. His hand flew to his mouth.' (2010d: 87). The creature's movement epitomises the principles of the neutrum that we have defined in Chapter 1 as well as they correspond with Lotman's theory of semiotic explosion. It can be depicted that a small change in the movement of the creature, which accelerates the vector from the position of in-betweenness or suspension to the act of generating new meanings.

The second aspect concerns the act of reduction that can be illustrated in the case of the lobster. Through the whole story the creature serves as an object that accumulated meanings only in the context of other symbols (the lunch, the grocery's). However, at the end of the story, when the accumulation of meanings is spreading, the lobster starts to function as the generator of meanings itself. The narrator shares with the reader the lobster's story, the story that can epitomise the condition of the human's worldly life:

> In the depths of the sea, it had crept into cruel pot. For hours, in the midst of its enemies, it had breathed secretly. It had survived the Frenchwoman's cat and his witless clutch. Now it was going alive into scalding water. It had to. Take into the air my quiet breath. (2010d: 88)

The fragment that summarises the lobster's existence in the story epitomises several aspects of my reading of Beckett's signature. The word 'lobster' at the beginning of the story is a neutral expression that accompanies other apparently meaningless ones (the lunch, the lobster, the Italian lesson). However, through the course of the story 'the lobster' starts functioning as a symbol associated with manifold meanings (e.g., a religious one—Jesus Christ, fish and an epitome of neutrum—the animal's change of the position). The shift of the meaning that the word lobster conveys from a name of the animal to the symbol of neutrum can be also noticed in the following metonymies, namely 'it had breathed secretly' and 'my quiet breath.' Both examples represent the symbol's intentions towards the neutrum.

Nevertheless, the work of the word is eventually diminished; the symbol is ceased by 'going alive into scalding water,' the other metonymy that I recognise as the sign of the language failure. The second aspect of Beckett's signature that has been depicted in 'Dante and the Lobster' is his self-reference and the dialogue of the author's different texts that reinforce the internal structure of the signature. Such a self-referentiality can be observed in a short story 'Ding-Dong.'

2.3. 'Ding-Dong:' The spherical journey into the mind

Similarly to 'Dante and the Lobster,' 'Ding-Dong,' the third story in the collection, portrays the above-mentioned movement of Beckett's texts towards his other texts as well as Beckett's movement towards the texts of other authors. In the case of the first story the vector moves towards *The Divine Comedy*, in 'Ding-Dong,' the movement is directed towards Shakespeare's *The Tempest*, where the onomatopoeic expression that imitates the bell sound is juxtaposed with Ferdinand's memory of his apparently drown father:

> *Ariel (sings)*: Full fathom five thy father lies,
> ...
>
> *(burden: Ding-dong)*
>
> Hark now I hear them, ding-dong, bell.
> *Ferdinand*: The ditty does remember my drowned
> father.
> This is no mortal business, nor no sound
> That the earth owes. I hear it now above me. (2006: 34–35)

At that point the main topic of 'Ding-Dong,' what will be visible later, communicates with 'Dante and the Lobster,' however is achieved not through Dante's but Shakespeare's work. The theme of cruelty will be the dominant for 'Ding-Dong,' the theme only reinforced by the symbols that occur later in the narrative. But before examining these symbols in detail, one needs to concentrate on the relation between Belacqua and the narrator.

Contrary to 'Dante and the Lobster,' where the reader knows nothing about the narrator, in 'Ding-Dong' we are assured that both subjects know each other in person. The narrator even calls Belacqua his 'sometime friend.' In the opening phrase the narrator describes Belacqua's relation with solipsism and the importance of movement:

> My sometime friend Belacqua enlivened the last phase of his solipsism, before he toed the line and began to relish the world, with the belief that the best thing he had to do was to move constantly from place to place (2010d: 99).

To make his acquaintance more probable, the narrator starts using the first person singular while describing Belacqua's favourite pastime, namely boomeranging: 'We were Pylades and Orestes,' 'I have witnessed every stage of the exercise,' 'I have had glimpses of him enjoying his little trajectory' (2010d: 100). However, the narrator is omniscient and we get to know from the beginning of the text that he or she is not a friend with Belacqua any more: 'He was impossible person in the end. I gave him up in the end because he was not *serious*' (ibid.). Two aspects are intriguing at that point: firstly the usage of the pronoun 'I' and secondly the description of Belacqua as an 'impossible' person.

Besides 'The Smeraldina's Billet Doux', which is written in the epistolary way and was incorporated into *More Pricks Than Kicks* from *Dream of Fair to Middling Women*, 'Ding-Dong' is the only one of Beckett's early stories where the narrator lapses into the first-person pronoun (Cohn 2005: 50). Following Foucault's theory of 'I speak' described in detail in Chapter 4 of Part One, the usage of such a pronoun can suggest that the protagonist is the language construct, i.e., he exists within the language, is defined by the language, and if he is not speaking, is located beyond the language. That statement is only reinforced by the narrator's opinion on Belacqua's state of being an 'impossible' person. In the opening scene of the story we receive the information that Belacqua has to be in constant movement and his interests in boomeranging, the play that consists in eternal returns of an object to the same point corresponds with signs' dynamics within the semiosphere.

What is more, such a character's construct can be also related to the notion of the possibility that the pure language offers, on condition that such a language is not contaminated by the natural language. The neutrum-language relation is also visible in the description of what is happening with Belacqua when he does not play boomerang or move; the narrator describes that '[h]e lived a Beethoven pause' (2010d: 100), the phrase that can be understood as the state of silence. The above relation between movement and silence implies that, a conclusion can be drawn that Belacqua as a linguistic figure epitomises the assumptions of our theory of Beckett's signature, where the movement is correlated with generating meanings through the language, yet the impossible expression of the neutral language can be only expressed by the state of silence, by the non-language.

The theme of cruelty in 'Ding-Dong' is examined in a similar way as in 'Dante and the Lobster', the symbols of that cruelty accompany Belacqua through his travel through Dublin; however, they do not become the central points of the story until the final scene. Belacqua's awareness of the importance of symbols which serve as the basic fabric for the constructed world is intriguing. Belacquian Dublin is sketched on these symbols and despite the fact that the names of the streets and places that appear in the story are real (the Park Gate, College Street, the Liffey, Pearse Street, 2010d: 101–102), it can be pointed out that the map on which Belacqua is moving in multiple directions serves the role of a vehicle that lets him enter into his inner self rather as the background scenery for the plot of the story. That awareness is visible when the narrator sketches Belacquian Dublin as follows:

> There were signs on all hands. There was the big Bovril sign to begin with, flaring beyond the Green. But it was useless. Faith, Hope and – what was it? — Love, Eden missed, every ebb derided, all the tides ebbing from the shingle of Ego Maximus, little me. Itself it went nowhere, only round and round, like the spheres, but mutely. (2010d: 101)

The construction of Dublin is definitely spherical, the movement of the character aims at going round and round whereas the dynamics of other symbols within that space is different. Some symbols such as the Bovril sign attempt to communicate something towards Belacqua yet for him their announcement is 'useless.' Belacqua ignores some symbols simultaneously paying attention to others. That switch in the character's interests is especially vital for understanding how the cumulation of meanings works in Beckett's works. Here the subject disregards one symbol, 'the Bovril sign,' but pays attention to the other the 'Faith.' That switch results in a chain of new symbols generated from the 'Faith,' namely 'Hope,' 'Love,' and 'Eden' that eventually influenced the further course of the story. Contrary to that, the symbol of 'the Bovril sign' also started generating its own chain of symbols 'flaring,' 'Green,' however that process turned out to be too weak to draw Belacqua's attention. Both examples depict that signs in Beckett's signature carry a certain amount of possibility that, following Attridge's observation on 'singularity,' cannot be constituted in advance, but requires the author, his or her signature and the reader to be initiated (2004: 64).

Moreover, the sound-silence juxtaposition also revels the other layer of Belacqua's journey. On the one hand, he wants to separate his mind from the cacophony of Dublin's streets that are filled with '[a] tumult of bushes, red and blue and silver' (2010d: 102) by travelling into the inner, mute realm that his mind offers. On the other, the events that are happening around him are the significant trigger for his divagations on the topic of cruelty. While walking through Dublin he sees 'the blind paralytic who sat all day near to the corner of Fleet Street' (2010d: 102), Belacqua is also the witness of a little girl run down by a bus as well as a woman who has stolen the dead girl's loaf of bread ('only one girl, debauched in appearance and swathed in a black blanket, fell out near the sting of the queue and secured the loaf,' 2010d: 103).

Despite being the witness of such horrific events, Belacqua, as in 'Dante and the Lobster,' does not comment on them. His spherical journey ends in the place that he patronises often, namely in the public house. The place full of 'dockers, railwaymen and vague joxers on the dole' (2010d: 103) serves for the protagonist as the harbour where he experiences art and love. The symbolic entrance from the cruel street of Dublin into a questionable space of the public house, the space that works on reversed rules, resembles the infiltration through Lotmanian boundary. Namely, the symbol that functions within one semiospheric space (the streets of Dublin) start to adopt to the other (the public house), however the process of such an adaptation is enhanced by the generation of new meanings (the public house as the space of art and love).

The space of the public house also functions as Belacqua's 'Beethoven pause.' It is the place where the protagonist wants to be suspended and immersed in the silence, the place where he 'wait[s] for a sign' (2010d: 105). The paradox of that situation is that public houses in general are the places full of noise and music, thus they appear the least suitable choice for such a meditation. Belacqua's state in the public house can be translated into one of the principles of the neutral language, namely the 'degree zero' state. This is the state where no work of the subject's consciousness should be observed. However, Belacqua's mind appears to be aware of the possibility that the external sounds that surround him, such as whisperers of other guests or sounds of bottles, can foster the work of his consciousness, on condition that he allows the external sounds to infect his internal silence. The external sounds experienced in the pub are not the type of music connoted with pleasant melodies. They are rather unnoticed at first sight sounds of clicking bottles, broken glass and twinkling sounds of the cask. Surprisingly, for Belacqua all these sounds could be used by Beethoven himself in his symphonies:

> A great major symphony of supply and demand, effect and cause, fulcrate on the middle C of the counter and waxing, as it proceeded, in the charming harmonics of blasphemy and broken glass and all the aliquots of fatigue and ebriety. So that he would say that the only place where he could come to anchor and be happy was a low public-house, and that all the wearisome tactics of gress and dud Beethoven would be done away with if only he could spend his life in such a place. (2010d: 104)

The figure of Belacqua in the public house from 'Ding-Dong' corresponds with the lobster from 'Dante and the Lobster.' They are both symbols of suspended consciousness that while being triggered by a movement towards the external world of signs, move from the states of suspension and possibility into the process of creating meanings in the story. In the case of 'Dante and the Lobster,' it is the change of the position of the creature, in 'Ding-Dong' such a change appears at the end of the story when a 'hatless woman' (2010d: 105) approaches Belacqua that immediately awakes him from the state of suspension. Here, Caselli's suggestion that the action in Beckett's works always takes place in his other works should be evoked once again. The moment a woman approaches Belacqua in 'Ding-Dong' is similar to the scene from 'Assumption.' The unknown protagonist of Beckett's first published short story is also awaiting for a sign that is marked by the appearance of a woman in the protagonist's room: 'Still he was silent, in silence listening for the first murmur of the torrent that must destroy him. At this moment the Woman came to him' (2010d: 59)

The woman from the pub is an old beggar who is selling 'seats in heaven' (2010d: 106). She is probably either drunk or lunatic and yet, Belacqua is fascinated with the woman's face 'full of light' and her 'white voice' (2010d: 105,107). The woman offers Belacqua four seats for the price of three, since a tanner is sixpence. In this example, the act of Lotman's asymmetry can be depicted. The old woman from a public house is presented as an 'angel,' mainly due to her 'face' and 'voice' (2010d: 105). The example of the public house that is correlated with the symbols of 'love' and 'art' (2010d: 106) works in a similar way.[4] The woman's speech is expressed in the Irish accent ('tuppence apiece, four fer a tanner,' 2010d: 106, 'yer da, yer ma an' yer motte, fur fer a tanner,' 2010d: 107), moreover she is persistent to Belacqua's refusals and eventually forces him to buy the 'seats in heaven.'

The woman's speech also corresponds with the Dublin Bovril sign that goes 'round and round, like the spheres' through Dublin. She claims that 'Heaven goes rowan an' rowan' (2010d: 107): these two statements work as buckles for 'Ding-Dong' and reinforce internally the fabric of the story. Going round and round is also visible in Belacqua's movement through Dublin, the city where the sacrum juxtaposes with the profane, the theme that is depicted in the last part of the story. After thanking the woman for a blessing by saying 'Amen,' Belacqua departs the pub '[f]or Railway Street, beyond the river' (2010d: 107), the red lantern district.

To conclude, Beckett extracts motifs, characters and certain phrases from other texts such as Dante's *The Divine Comedy* and Shakespeare's *The Tempest* in order to translate them into his own language. Such a language that is still

---

4 The term 'Asymmetry' appears here one purpose and refers to Lotman's definition of that notion from *Universe and the Mind*. Lotman notices that 'the structure of the semiosphere is asymmetrical' (1990: 127). Since the majority of languages that appears in the semiosphere, in the case of the above example the notions of the public-house, love, the old woman and the angel play the role of such languages, do not share semantic correspondences, the translations between them are asymmetrical. Because, as Lotman suggests the translation is '[a] primary mechanism of consciousness' (1990: 127), the languages that build the fabric of the semiosphere, due to their lack of possibility to be semantically translated, can be perceived as a generator of information and meanings. Thus, the asymmetry in the translation of languages within the semiosphere like the public-house into the place of love serves as the example of how the meanings within 'Ding-Dong' are generated.

immersed both in the cultural inheritance and the principles of the natural language is eventually used by Beckett to create a unique language of intertextual elements. Such a measure is called by Lotman the 'renaming' and by Abbott the 'reinvention.' The symbols that the author uses in his stories, such as 'Dante and the Lobster' and 'Ding-Dong,' work continuous within the fabric of the text, and additionally are involved in an endless dialogue between the external texts (Dante, Shakespeare) and the texts within Beckett's semiosphere ('Alba,' *Dream of Fair to Middling Women*). The continuous work in the matter of symbols by reducing such ideas as love, death and a human's lifespan into single words and expressions like 'Alba,' 'graveyard' and 'womb-tomb,' implies the process of that can be characterised as the neutrum.

In order to illustrate how such work functions in practice the example of the word 'lobster' has been used. The movement of the animal in the story, from a complete motionless (the animal is in the neutral position and does not move) towards a certain degree of dynamism (Belacqua glimpses a minute move of the animal, the move results in generating in Belacqua's head meanings such as religious associations to the Last Supper). Finally, the dynamism moves again towards motionless (the animal does not move any more), however with a certain degree of possibility that the movement can occur again (the lobster is eventually boiled alive, however contrary to what Belacqua thinks, the animal can feel the pain yet cannot express it in sound; such a situation does not exclude the chance that the animal starts moving in the pot).

In a similar manner the symbol of Dublin from 'Ding-Dong' works. Hence, the spherical travel of Belacqua through the streets of the city is juxtaposed with the continuous attempts of intertextual elements to communicate messages towards the protagonist (the Bovril sign, the bus that run down the girl). All these exercises in the language, and through the language should, possibly lead the author to the neutrum, such an attempt is also observed in 'Ding-Dong,' where the first-person pronoun 'I' appears to indicate that the narrator is located beyond the language.

Finally, the self-referentiality of symbols within Beckett's semiosphere, the symbols that have originally been borrowed from the external texts of other authors, functions as a vital element of constructing and internally reinforcing the fibre of Beckett's *oeuvre*. Self-referentiality on the one hand indicates that Beckett's symbols frequently occur in his other texts, usually generating different meanings (for example 'Belacqua' in *Dream of Fair to Middling Women* and in *More Pricks Than Kicks* is not the same construct). On the other hand, the existence of similar-yet-different symbols in texts allows the author to explore the limits of language through the matter of the natural language.

Chapter 3: *Murphy* (1938)

3.1. Between pain and persistence

The aim of the chapter is to present how symbols are used to construct one concise system, called by Murphy, the main protagonist of the self-titled novel, the 'closed' one. The features of such a system correspond with principles of Beckett's signature, namely the fundaments of such a system are constructed on the signs that derive from the natural language. However, in the case of *Murphy* the signs echo the principles employed in *More Pricks Than Kicks*, namely the encapsulation of a variety of external notions such as psychology (the MMM, a mental hospital) or Democritus' atomistic theory of the universe's construction, the difference is in the way other signs communicate towards the primary symbol of the novel, Murphy himself. The metatextual allusions from the text suggest that Murphy is a dominant sign towards which other symbols of the novel, called the 'puppets' such as the kite, the gas, Celia, Mr. Endon, and Mr. Kelly communicate.

Nevertheless, Murphy's greatest desire is to get rid of the external signs, called the outer (big) world to construct his own inner (little) world. The ideal inner world is the one where no external signs have access to, which means that any external communication is ceased, which resembles the neutral space. Finally, Chapter 6 of the novel suggests that the ideal space for the closed system would be Murphy's mind. However, an encounter with Mr. Endon, who according to Murphy entered his own closed system, results in Murphy's revelation that due to being anchored to the external signs, e.g., a romantic relation with Celia, the protagonist will never be able to create a closed system.

The acceptance of *More Pricks Than Kicks* for publication correlated with a devastating event in Samuel Beckett's private life, namely the death of his father, William. Beckett senior died due to a heart attack on 26th June 1933. Father's death devastated the young writer to such an extent that he demonstrated health problems. Knowlson notices that Beckett experienced a cyst that was growing on his palm as well as night sweats and attacks of panic (1996: 167). Besides the physical symptoms, the playwright's mental health was not in a good condition either. Beckett remembers this period as follows:

> After my father's death I had trouble psychologically. The bad years were between when I had to crawl home in 1932 and after my father's death in 1933. I'll tell you how it was. I was walking down Dawson Street. And I felt I could not go on. It was a strange experience I cannot really describe. I found I could not go on moving. So I went into the nearest pub and got a drink just to stay still. And I felt I needed help. (Knowlson 1996: 167)

Beckett received help from Geoffrey Thompson, his friend and doctor, who proposed the writer to try psychoanalysis. However, in order to apply that method of treatment, Beckett had to leave Dublin as psychoanalysis was illegal in Ireland at the time. Because of that Beckett moved to London where he started intensive psychoanalysis in December 1933. In London, Beckett attended the Tavistock Clinic on Malet Place where he was assigned to Dr. Wilfred Ruprecht Bion on the advance of Thompson (Knowlson 1996: 169). The importance of the relocation to London, which resulted in several subsequent travels from Dublin to London between 1933 and 1935 as well as deep friendship that was born between Beckett and Bion (the result of which can be observed in the growth of Beckett's interests in psychology) can be traced in *Murphy*, a novel written between 26th August 1935 and 27th June 1936, and eventually published on 7th March 1938 (*Letters I*, 577).

In September 1934 Beckett moved to a new room at 34 Gertrude Street in Chelsea, the place that he rented from Mr. and Mrs. Frost. London became a huge inspiration in the creative process of *Murphy*. Beckett started to write the narrative, originally entitled 'Sasha Murphy,' at Gertrude Street on 20th August 1935 (Knowlson 1996: 193). The year before he started writing *Murphy*, i.e., between September 1934 and August 1935, had a vital impact on the shape of the novel. Beckett attended the sessions with Bion three times a week and the rest of the time he shared between visiting galleries, reading books and going to the concerts. Knowlson notices that during that period Beckett was especially gripped by philosophical ideas, the ideas that are visible in the fabric of the novel (1996: 191). In addition, Anthony Cronin suggests that Beckett himself felt the intellectual ferment in his head as the playwright described the state of his mind from that period '[a]s though the brain were full of milk that the least act of interested thinking brought to the boil' (1999: 217).

The problems that Beckett encountered with *Murphy* were of a similar nature as those with *Dream of Fair to Middling Women*, namely he could not find a publisher to accept the novel. In June 1936 he sent the manuscript to Chatto and Windus, the publisher that accepted *Proust* and *More Pricks Than Kicks*; however, the firm dismissed the novel. Harold Raymond, a partner at Chatto and Windus, in a letter to Richard Church of 19th January 1937 expresses his concerns about the commercial potential of *Murphy*:

> I agree with much that you say about this book I certainly do not feel happy at letting go of Samuel Beckett. Yet I feel pretty confident that the recondite nature of so much of his writing would prevent this book from selling more than a few hundred copies, and if we are right, the loss involved would be a high price to pay for an option on his next work. (Knowlson 1996: 268)

Disappointed as he was, Beckett continued attempts to publish the novel. After numerous rejections – such as those by Simon and Schuster from New York in October 1936 (*Letters I*, 292), Constable and Doubleday Doran (*Letters I*, 418) – the artist felt more and more resigned. He even offered the book to a literary agent George Reavey, however the list of publishers that rejected the novel was getting longer and longer (Knowlson 1996: 268). The situation changed due to Jack Yeats, an Irish painter and Beckett's friend who recommended *Murphy* to Routledge:

> A friend of mine, Sam Beckett, has the manuscript of a novel 'Murphy' which is to be submitted to your firm. I have not seen it, but his other novel [*More Pricks Thank Kicks*] I read and I thought it the real thing. There was inspiration in it. It was published a year or two ago and I daresay by now the public readers have crept under its inspiration. ... I write to ask you, if you cannot read Beckett's Ms yourself just now, to give it to some very open minded reader. (Knowlson 1996: 268).

The novel sent to Routledge by Reavey was accepted by T.M. Ragg, a partner at Routledge who appreciated the novel simultaneously pointing out that '[i]t is far too good to be a big popular or commercial success' (Knowlson 1996: 268). The novel was accepted on 9th December 1937 and eventually published on 7th March 1938 (*Letters I*, 577). Ragg's forecast about the financial results came true, as for the second instalment of the novel Beckett received £16 2s 8d. in March 1938 (Pilling 2006: 76).

3.2. Constructing the fundamentals: The kite, the horoscope and the Mental Hospital

If one would like to define the pillars of the novel – the cores which the structure is built on – three should be paid special attention to: the kite, the horoscope and the Mental Hospital called in the book the Magdalen Mental Mercyseat. These three symbols not only pivot around the character of Murphy, who can be treated as a core of the story but predominantly they are a starting point for initiating the book's main motifs, namely the relations between the mind and the body, the inner and outside world and the search for self-inversion, silence and solitude. In order to build such a binary world, the author uses a vast number of philosophical, literary and medical references that allow him to create a huge number of characters that populate this world. In the following section we concentrate on these three 'pillars' that subsequently should allow us to decipher other pillars of the system based on which the structure of the novel is constructed.

According to the Beckett's letter to Thomas McGreevy dated 8th September 1935, the kite became one of the direct inspirations for the former to write the novel. The writer correlates the toy with a shabby but respectable man whose hobby was flying kites by the Round Pond in Kensington Gardens:

> The little shabby respectable old men you see on Saturday afternoon and Sunday, pottering about doing odd jobs in the garden, or flying kites immense distances at the Round Pond, Kensington. Yesterday there was a regular club of the latter, with a sprinkling of grandchildren, sitting in a crescent waiting for a wind. The kites lying in the grass with their long tails beautifully cared for, all assembled and ready. For they bring them in separate pieces, the sticks and tail rolled up in the canvas and a huge spool of string. Some have boats as well, but not the real enthusiasts. (*Letters I*, 274)

Moreover, the writer appears to be fascinated by the old man's behaviour when the kites are high above in the air so the people from the earth can hardly see them. In that period of pause '[w]hen the string is run out they simply sit there watching them, chucking at the string, the way coachmen do at a reins, presumably to keep them from losing height' (*Letters I*, 274). Beckett finds something alluring that does not allow him to simply walk away. In the letter to McGreevy the other vital aspect for the construction of *Murphy* is depicted, namely the division of the world into the outer and the inner world: 'My next old man, or old young man, not of the big world but of the little world, must be a kite-flyer.' (*Letters I*, 274). The division into the little world, the one that would be understood in the novel as the inner space of Murphy's mind and the big world, a huge space populated by manifold characters and sketched on the triangle Dublin-Cork-London (Cohn 2005: 75–76) that serves as a diorama for Murphy's actions.

Both 'a kite-flyer' and the 'old man,' appear in the novel, the first one is depicted in the character of Mr. Willoughby Kelly, the other is called 'the old boy,' a mysterious Murphy's flat-mate who never leaves his room and who ends up found undead with cut throat (2010a: 81–82). The characters as well as others that appear in the novel correspond, or rather reflect Murphy's crave for leaving the wide-world and move to the inner one, the crave that eventually cannot be fulfilled due to Murphy's death.

As a symbol, the kite points out the relation between Murphy and the sky, or rather the relation between seen-unseen and willingness-will-lessness (Mooney 1982: 227–228); these two pairs of notions function as the central elements of the novel. Moreover, the way in which they are incorporated in the story corresponds with our principles of Beckett's signature, especially in encapsulating a wide range of ideas into a single sign. The atomistic theory of Democritus serves as such an example. Democritus claims that the matter consists of atoms and the void. The atoms are 'ultimate indivisible entities' that are permanent and unchangeable (Whyte 1961: 41). The atoms move within the void, the infinite space that can be juxtaposed with Cosmos, thus the relation atoms (seen)—the void (unseen) is reflected in the symbols used in the novel.

The seen—unseen relation can be also deciphered as a relation physical—transcendental, where the physical atoms prove the existence of the transcendental void as it is pointed out by Anaxagoras in his statement '[v]isible existences are a sight of the unseen' (Freeman 1948: 83). The atomistic features of Murphy will be discussed further in this chapter, however at that point I would like to concentrate on the word 'speck' that Murphy is defined by (2010a: 150). Murphy's atomic feature is juxtaposed with Mr. Endon's 'unseen' stare while the characters look at each other after a chess game. Thus, the number of symbols that correspond with Murphy such as Celia, the rocking chair and the kite can be deciphered as atoms belonging to the realm of 'seen.' Furthermore, the kite is also descried as 'a speck in the glades' (2010a: 167) that only strengths the atomic nature of that symbol. When Celia throws the kite into the sky, the object is gradually changing its position so Mr. Kelly cannot '[m]easure the distance from the unseen to the seen' (2010a: 167).

The kite is then the sign of belonging to the 'in-betweenness' where the reality intermingles with transcendence following Democritus' theory. The work on signs that repeatedly accumulate in themselves, (e.g., philosophic or artistic ideas) is also seen in the relation of other characters of *Murphy*. The pair willingness-will-lessness is epitomised in names of Mr. Willoughby Kelly's name (Latin *caelum* means the sky) who is juxtaposed with Will-less Murphy. The willlessness is also epitomised in the old boy who is described by Miss Carridge as a 'never still' who '[d]id spend a great deal of his time ranging his room in every direction' (2010a: 44). Both characters serve as the vector direction for Murphy himself, i.e., the vertical relation Murphy-sky or seen-unseen and the external-internal movement of the outer-inner worlds.

The second source of inspiration can be found in horoscopes and astrology in general. Beckett's interests in that topic can be detected in his psychoanalysis with Wilfred Bion who evinced interests in horoscopes, probably due to the fact of using horoscopes in the patient treatment by Carl Gustav Jung.[1] In October 1935 Beckett, alongside with Bion, attended Jung's Tavistock Institute lecture (Pilling 2006: 54). After that, one may assume that Bion asked Beckett to prepare

---

1 In the letter to Thomas McGreevy dated on 8th October 1935, Beckett informs that during the lecture Jung usually demands from patients their horoscope casts (*Letters I*, 282).

his own horoscopes as the examples of one can be found in Beckett's famous notebook called 'Whoroscope' (Knowlson 1996: 197).

Robert Harrison in *Samuel Beckett's Murphy: A Critical Excursion* suggests that the role of astrology in the novel is only reduced to the way of structing the novel (1968: 71, 76–77); however, that interpretation should be broadened as the only structural aspect of the story does not fulfil the role that astrology plays. We opt more for the conception of Sighle Kennedy who suggests that the role of astrology in *Murphy* should be diminished to the novel's overall concern with the notion of time (1971: 249, 259). The very opening scene of the novel depicts the astrological relations to the sun, '[t]he poor old sun in the Virgin again for the billionth time' (2010a: 3). The references to the Virgin in that excerpt can be correlated both with the astrological constellation of Virgo, which the sun occupies from 24th August to 22nd September (Kiely 2017: 63) and with the affirmation of inevitable that hints '[a]t the redemption of time' (Ackerley 2010: 29).

The references to horoscope and astrology interweave through the novel, however they are never called by the proper name of the actual thing. Celia refers to the horoscope as 'it,' which is even noticed by Mr. Kelly who asks her '[a]re you afraid to call it by its name?' (2010a: 16), whereas the narrator describes the horoscope cruelty as '[a] fake jossy's sixpenny writ to success and prosperity' (2010a: 19). Murphy mocks the horoscope calling it 'my life-warrant' (2010a: 22). The other example of mocking horoscope prospects is the diagram that appears in the novel that includes such prophets for Murphy's fate as: 'Lucky Gems. Amethyst and Diamond. To ensure Success the Native should sport,' 'Lucky Days. Sunday. To attract the maximum Success the Native should begin new ventures.' 'Lucky Number 4. The Native should commerce new enterprises, for in so doing lies just difference between Success and Calamity,' and 'Lucky Years. 1936 and 1990. Successful and prosperous, though not without calamities and setbacks' (2010a: 23–23).

The comic sound of these ideas, especially of those that refer to financial prosperity and the lucky year 1936, the year when Murphy dies an accidental death, indeed interweave the subject of astrology with the course of time; however, the letter does not blindly follow the rules of the horoscope.[2] What is more, Celia

---

2   Ackerley notices that Murphy's model of horoscope can be traced in the one presented in the *British Journal of Astrology*, April 1935, where four principles of creating a horoscope were listed:
   1. The personal nature, or the disposition, life, character and mind of the subject.
   2. The physical nature, temporal and physical conditions, health, disease, and death.

brings Murphy the diagram on purpose to encourage him to find a job, however in the protagonist's view this is a blackmail on her part. Murphy is strongly against working for living, he is an idle person who craves for entering the little world of suspension, thus the act of working that has been imposed on his by the astrological diagram appears for him comical. In *The Stars Down to Earth*, Adorno notices an intriguing correlation between the astrology and obedience:

> Moreover, by strengthening the sense of fatality, dependence and obedience, it paralyzes the will to change objective conditions in any respect and relegates all worries to a private plane promising a cure-all by the very same compliance which prevents a change of conditions. It can easily be seen how well this suits the over-all purpose of the prevailing ideology of today's cultural industry; to reproduce the status quo within the mind of the people. (2001: 164)

However, while Adorno writes these words in the context of the society-authority relation, blaming astrology for encouraging deference towards authority, the state of preventing 'a change of conditions' may appeal to be attractive for Murphy who wants to leave the big world epitomised in the notion of working, to the little world of willing-less. Similar thoughts on astrology were written by Beckett in his 'Whoroscope' notebook, where he noticed '[n]o longer a guide to be consulted but a force to be obeyed' (Knowlson 1996: 197).

The temptation of following the fate may appear to be alluring for Murphy at first sight as the fate would allow the protagonist to forgo his responsibility on his life, the notion that corresponds with his viewpoint on the role of work. However, through the course of the story it is indicated that he, rather than the faith registered in the stars is the core of the system built in the novel. The dominant relation of Murphy on the world is suggested in the text when the protagonist says 'I hate the charVenus and her sausage and mash sex' (2010a: 26). The prefix *chare* refers to a chore, an odd job and used to refer to form words that distinguish those who do cleaning work such as a charboy or a charmaid (Kiely 2017: 68). By using the form charVenus, Murphy suggests that the stars are obedient for him not *vice versa*. In fact, they work in his system, thus the horoscope is no longer in power.[3]

---

3. The worldly position, relating to all temporal and material conditions of life, such as finance, marriage, profession, etc.
4. The progress of the life, particulars of good and bad fortune as shown by the directions operating after birth. (2010: 61).
3   Murphy's revelation on himself as 'the prior system' which the stars are subordinated to is expressed Chapter 9 during his stay at the MMM:

The third inspiration is the Bethlem Royal Hospital in Beckenham, the hospital which Geoffrey Thompson started to work at as a senior house physician in February 1935. In the period of February to October Beckett visited Thompson several times. It is worth mentioning that the doctor allowed the writer to walk corridors of the hospital (Knowlson 1996: 197–198). The Magdalen Mental Mercyseat that represents Bethlem in the novel derives his name from the Ark of the Tabernacle that with its mercyseat of pure gold, whence God would commune to Moses[4] (Ackerley 2010: 146). O'Hara notices that for Murphy the hospital replaces the rocking chair (1997: 48), the object that represents his little world that is 'his own' (2010a: 3).

The Magdalen Mental Mercyseat, also referred in the novel as MMM, plays the role of an asylum, not only for its patients, but for Murphy himself. The protagonist, who paradoxically starts working in the MMM, tries to find the system of the little world. However, Murphy describes himself as '[a] creature without initiative' (2010a: 96), his relation with the hospital workers is similar to his relation with the starts, namely he does not subordinate to the workers' instructions:

'Are they all certified?' said Murphy.
'That is not your business,' said Bim. 'You are not paid to take an interest in the patients, but to fetch for them, carry for them and clean up after them. All you know about them is the work they give you to do. Make no mistake about it.' (2010a: 97)

Bim who epitomises here the wide-world attempts to impose on Murphy its dominant role, however the very next sentence suggests that Murphy is the character who owns and creates, at least at that point, the system:

Murphy learned that about 15 per cent of the patients were certified, a little band select only in name, treated with exactly the same sanguine punctilio as the 85 per cent that were not certified. For the M.M.M. was a sanatorium, not a madhouse nor a home for defectives... (2010a: 97)

Murphy was revolted by Suk's attribution of this strange talent solely to the moon in the Serpent at the hour of his birth. The more his own system closed round him, the less he could tolerate its being subordinated to any other. Between him and his stars no doubt there was correspondence, but not in Suk's sense. They were *his* stars, he was the prior system. He had been projected, larval and dark, on the sky of that regrettable hour as on a screen, magnified and clarified into his own meaning. But it was *his* meaning. The moon in the serpent was no more than an image, a fragment of vitagraph. (2010c: 110).

4 See Exodus 25: 17–22.

The MMM patients serve for Murphy as a key to a micro-world. Due to their mental problems that result in focusing on the mind, not on the body, the patients' condition is far closer to Murphy's viewpoint then the point of view offered by the big-world characters like Celia. Moreover, the isolation of the hospital from the outer world of the city also depicts its role as a symbol of the little world.[5] Murphy identifies the patients far more similar to himself. What is more, he does not fear them, as a healthy part of society would ("They caused Murphy no horror," 2010a: 102). In addition, the protagonist reveals extensive knowledge on the patients' symptoms and disorders, thus in that fragment an omniscient perspective of the world's creator is once again revealed:

> Melancholics, motionless and brooding, holding their heads or bellies according to type. Paranoids, feverishly covering sheets of paper with complains against their treatment or verbatim reports of their inner voices. A hebephrenic playing the piano intently. A hypomanic teaching slosh to Korsakow's syndrome. An emaciated schizoid petrified in a toppling attitude as though condemned to an eternal tableau vivant, his left hand rhetorically extended holding a cigarette half smoked and out, his right, quivering and rigid, pointing upwards. (2010a: 102)

Although both the hospital and its patients are the closest to the system of the little world, Murphy finally finds out that he is not able to live both in the wide world and Murphy's surroundings. We have mentioned so far two characters that correlated with Murphy's idea of the little world, Mr. Kelly and the old boy. The third one, who appears to be the protagonist's untouchable inspiration is Mr. Endon, a patient who suffers from apnoea and is voted 'the most biddable little gaga in the entire institution' (2010a: 143). Due to the chess match with Mr. Endon (Greek *within*), Murphy realises that he is not able to reach the full state of the little world. However, before the match he boasts 'I am not of the big world, I am of the little world' (2010a: 107), Murphy surrenders the duel and dies short after. Leslie Hill notices that '[a]sylum is precisely what Murphy does not find in the asylum' (1990: 15)

The above symbols, namely the kite, the horoscope and the MMM represent the fundaments of the system presented in *Murphy*, nevertheless it must be pointed out that also other topics play a vital role in the plot. Ruby Cohn defines four strands that play the principal components of the story, namely Murphy,

---

5   The building of MMM is characterised by the protagonist as an epitome of a little world: 'Within the narrow limits of domestic architecture he had never been able to imagine a more credible representation of what he kept on calling, indefatigably, the little world.' (2010c: 109).

Celia, the Irish posse, and the Mercyseat population (2005: 74). For our purpose of examining how the structure of Beckett's signature is reflected in the system of the novel, I would like to focus on the character of Murphy with his relations to the mind, will-lessness, nothingness, and in-betweenness, i.e., all the notions that belong to the microcosm, and juxtapose that with the protagonist's relations with the outer world, represented by the other characters.

Having said that the sign of 'Murphy' will be used in the following subchapters as a transmitter of Beckett's artistic signature principles. The main focus pivots around the reduction of Murphy to a single atom, the atom that cannot be further reduced following Democritus' theory. The relation of 'Murphy,' the sign with other signs withing the system of the novel will be aimed at generating meanings, however almost always through Murphy these mutual relations Murphy—other signs will be eventually used to explore the topic of the memory, depicted in Chapter 6 of the book.

3.3. Murphy, 'the puppets' and the system

To begin with defining who Murphy is and what role he plays in the system of the novel, one needs to start with decoding his name. Ackerley provides us with the most exhausting origins of that name, finding its origin in Joyce's *Ulysses* (Stephen Dedalus notices that 'Shakespeares were as common as Murphies,' 578) – that suggests that 'Murphy' is a very common Irish surname. The researcher also finds the name's roots in the Cork stout or Murphy's Law, the law that suggests the inevitability of an event that will happen anyway (2010: 28). The other root of the name Murphy, which is also noticed by Cohn, Ackerley finds in the Greek word 'morphe,' meaning form (2010: 28. Cohn 2005: 73). Such a meaning allows us to indicate that form is sought both by the protagonist and by the novel itself. Additionally, Murphy's name, which will be further indicated in the novel, finds its roots in Democritus' 'atomic figure.' John Beare, following Democritus' theory, suggests that 'the atomic shapes ... generate *all* objects of sense' (1906: 163), in a similar way Murphy resonates on all characters of the novel.

Similarly to Belacqua from *More Pricks Thank Kicks*, the reader knows hardly anything about Murphy: he is rather perceived as a generator of objects through which the characters are constituted. The questions that a reader would like to ask are articulated by Mr. Kelly, however not towards Murphy himself, but towards his granddaughter Celia:

> 'Who is this Murphy,' he cried, 'for whom you have been neglecting your work, as I presume? What is he? Where does he come from? What is his family? What does he do?

Has he any money? Has he any prospects? Has he any retrospects? Is he, has he, anything at all?' (2010a: 13)

Celia's answer is simple 'Murphy was Murphy.' The only information she provides Mr. Kelly and the reader with is that Murphy is from Dublin and that he belongs to '[n]o profession or trade.' His way of earning money is summed up to 'small charitable sums' that the protagonist lives on. (2010a: 13). Murphy's atomic nature is also expressed in calling him a 'speck' ('Mr. Murphy is a speck in Mr. Endon's unseen.,' 2010a: 150). His atomistic features are also expressed by the recurrent motifs of gas, perception, and unseen epitomised in the last scene with the kite.

The notion of gas appears at least several times through the course of the story. For example, in the conversation with Ticklepenny at the MMM, Murphy investigates the source of the smell of gas that Ticklepenny notices ('You speak of gas' said Murphy, 'but I smell no gas,' 2010a: 104), which turns out to be a radiator. After having investigated the source of the gas, Murphy asks a philosophical question 'What was the etymology of gas?' (2010a: 106), which leads him to a sequence of generated symbols that connote Biblical relations ('The Chaos and Waters Facilities Act. The Chaos, Light and Coke Co. Hell. Heaven. Helen. Celia.,' 2010a: 106). Finally, the gas is the cause of Murphy's death ('the gas went on in w.c., excellent gas, superfine chaos. Soon his body was quiet.,' 2010a: 151). It is worth pointing out how Murphy's existence is correlated with the gas; at the beginning he is not able to smell the odour of gas at all, contrary to Ticklepenny, after that the gas becomes a pretext to consider Murphy's origin. Finally, the protagonist dies because of the gas, or at least his body part dies, whereas his mind travels vertically, towards the sky, similarly as the gas particles do.

The atomistic nature of Murphy can find its roots in Berkley's *esse est percipi*. After the chess match with Mr. Endon, Murphy's perception abilities degrade:

Then this also faded and Murphy began to see nothing, that colourlessness which is such a rare postnatal treat, being the absence (to abuse a nice distinction) not of *percipere* but of *percipi*. (2010a: 147)

The sense of not being perceived not only in Murphy's eyes but in Mr. Endon's as well ('The last Mr. Murphy saw of Mr. Endon was Mr. Murphy unseen by Mr. Endon. This was also the last Murphy saw of Murphy,' 2010a: 150) corresponds with the symbol of atom, i.e., a particle that cannot be grasped with the naked eye. That nature of Murphy is also indicated in the final part of the story, where after the protagonist's death, Mr. Kelly and Celia fly a kite, unfortunately the string breaks and the kite flies away so the characters are unable to see it. The disability of perceiving the kite, which symbolises the perception of a particle, is cumulated in the very last sentence of the novel where Celia closes her eyes and the story ends with a blunt 'all out' (2010a: 168); when Murphy is not perceived any more, the world of the novel ceases to exist as well.

To indicate Murphy's creator role in the story, one important sentence needs to be evoked, namely: 'All the puppets in this book whinge sooner or later, except Murphy, who is not a puppet' (2010a: 76). It has already been depicted that other characters in the novel serve as subordinated to Murphy. All their actions are condensed to populate the big world and, by interacting with Murphy, to build its structure. To illustrate that one needs to evince that all the characters' names are meaningful, William Tritt groups the names of sixteen characters (1976: 202–203), the characters are also grouped in the novel itself. We have already indicated the etymologies of Mr. Willoughby Kelly and Celia, both names correlated with the sky, and reduced to the symbols of the kite and the horoscope-star.

The Irish posse consists of Neary, Murphy's teacher form gymnasium and Wylie, who is Neary's student. The pair Neary-Wyllie corresponds with the space-time relation (near and while, Cohn 2005: 74). There is also the Irish waitress Cathleen na Hennessey, who claims that Murphy is her lover. Her name phonetically corresponds with William Butler Yeats' Cathleen ni Houlihan, the allegory of Ireland. Moreover, there is also Cooper, an agent sent by Cathleen to find Murphy in London, and whose name corresponds with Greek *copros*, the body. The MMM is also populated with characters who co-exist in pairs, for instance, the twins and the male nurses Thomas Clinch ('Bim') and Timothy Clinch ('Bom').[6] The relations which link characters into pairs work by chance, for example Murphy and Celia meet by chance as well as Neary and Wylie or Murphy and Ticklepenny (Cohn 2005: 74) however, the dominant agent is Murphy's atom:

> Both these lines led to Murphy (everything led to Murphy), but so diversely, the one from a larval experience to a person of fantasy, the other from a complete experience to a person of fact, that only a woman and one so... intact as Celia could have given them equal value. (2010a: 43)

---

6   Ruby Cohn in *Just Play* notices that the usage of names Bim and Bom, whose names can be correlated with a pair of Russian clowns, are used by Beckett as a symbol of cruelty:
    'From the time of his collection of stories *More Pricks than Kicks*, written over two decades earlier, Bim and Bom recur sporadically in Beckett's work. Russian clowns whose comic routines contained—and were allowed to contain— criticism of the Soviet regime, they became for Beckett emblems of human cruelty, disguised under a comic garb.' (1980: 177).

Besides the puppets, who are observed by an omniscient narrator, the novel is also populated with the references to poets, psychologists, painters and scientists (Tritt indicates at least ninety-nine figures), whose ideas, similarly to Murphy-puppets relations, allow to construct the body-mind/outer-inner world system. The references to Geulincx's *ubi nihil vales ibi nihil velis* (2010a: 107, Berkley's *esse est percipi* (2010a: 147) or Pre-Socratic 'nothing is more real than nothing' ('Abderite naught is more real,' 2010a: 148) can be recognised as vehicles that enact the philosophical mind, or a philosophical journey (Anderson 2013: 76).

All the above devices used by Murphy are aimed, as it has been mentioned, at entering into an inner world. However, it needs to be precised that the ideal system of the inner world is a closed one. The ideal inner word is epitomised in the figure of Mr. Endon, the world which Murphy does not have access to. While Murphy tries to see something in Mr. Endon's eyes, all what he sees is his own reflection. The inability of first creating and second entering into the closed system derives from being anchored into the outer world that is especially seen in Murphy's romantic relation with Celia. Whereas Mr. Endon has abandoned any communication with external signs, Murphy is unable to do that. The crave for a closed world is reinforced by manifold repetitions that appear through the story, for example 'the horse leech's daughter was a closed system' (2010a: 72) or '[t]he more his own system closed round him, the less he could tolerate its being subordinated to any other.'(2010a: 110). However, through the whole story Murphy appears to be close to the little world, epitomised by the MMM, the chess game and Mr. Endon's mind, the complete closure is the factor that causes Murphy's failure.

The key to Murphy's mind is Chapter 6 of the story in which he presents his principles of the closed system based on three pillars: light, half-light and dark. Before discussing these principles in detail, one needs to define the principles of the world model presented in *Murphy*. Ackerley proposes the following division of the world represented in the novel:

1) Murphy's mind: Light (actual), Half-light (actual⊠virtual), Dark (virtual),
2) Greek thought: Socrates, Plato and Aristotle, Pre-Socratic (Pythagoreans), Atomism (Democritus),
3) Western thought: Cartesian realism, Christian mysticism, Non-Newtonian motion,
4) Psychology: Conscious, Pre-conscious, Unconscious (2010: 117).

Our conception, besides covering Ackerley's philosophical threads that correlate with the notion of the philosophical journey, will be more systematic:

1) Fundaments: the kite, the horoscope, the MMM recognised as symbols which both reduce and multiplicate meanings connected vertically with the pair seen-unseen and horizontally with the closed system of the inner world.
2) The vertical vector: the line on which there are located: the outer world—Murphy—the inner world that correlate with the triplet Light—Half-light—Dark.
3) Murphy as the core of the system (semiosphere) that gets into interactions with other characters (puppets). The bilateral relations with the puppets trigger the body—mind/outer world—inner world relations that are emphasised through the device that the philosophy used in the novel offers.
4) Repetitions: the re-occurrent appearance of the same or similar phrases of events reinforces the structure of the system and its solipsistic construction. Moreover, the repetitions are the vehicle that allow to create quasi-closed (the MMM, the chess game) or closed (Mr. Endon's mind) systems within Murphy's system.

The above principles of the so-called closed system find its appliance in Beckett's signature. Firstly, the search for a perfectly closed space that does not intermingle or communicate with the external world corresponds with the neutral space. The means that is used for reaching the neutrum is the natural language reduced to symbols such as the kite or the horoscope. Secondly, the signs used in the construction of the closed system encapsulate in themselves, as in the above example, the broad philosophical notion of Democritus' seen-unseen relation, such a reduction of philosophical ideas is characteristic for Beckett's signature and his way of working on symbols. Thus, unremarkable symbols such as the kite carry in themselves not only highly complex ideas but with relation to other symbols start generating the new ones. Moreover, in the construction of the closed system one dominant sign, i.e., 'Murphy' is noticed, all other signs are called 'puppets' in the novel. The 'puppets' enter into the relation with Murphy who through them reveals his suspension between the outer and the inner world, or the external, physical and internal, virtual world.

Owing to that one can say that the system is constructed both on vertical and horizontal levels, vertical because Murphy finds himself half way through between the outer and inner world; the construction that is reinforced in the novel by the signs of Light, Half-light and Dark. The horizontal line indicates Murphy's relation with the 'puppets,' i.e., the signs such as Celia, Mr. Endon, Mr. Kelly, the kite, the MMM or the gas. Finally, the signs used in the novel serve as a vehicle to reflect the processes that are taking place in the mind, Chapter 6 is all about what is happening in Murphy's head, and through the reciprocate work of symbols such a process is aimed at being revealed.

3.4. The mind-body split

Chapter 6 divides the novel into almost equal halves (the total number of chapters is thirteen) and bluntly distracts a sequence of events of the plot.[7] Chapter 5 ends with the suspense ('a shocking thing had happened,' 2010a: 65), but that 'shocking thing' is not revealed until Chapter 8 where the reader finds about the old boy's death. Chapter 6, contrary to the old boy's plot which appears to follow the rules of a thriller and combines the subsequent sections of the novel, seems to be added out of context as if it had been written not on the purpose of the novel but as a separate work. In this short chapter there are presented the principles of Murphy's mind, his understanding of what the closed system is and how that system is divided into three zones, namely light, half-light and dark.

The chapter starts with a sentence 'Amor intellectualis quo Murphy se ipsum amat' ['the intellectual love with which Murphy loves himself'] (2010a: 67), which is a variation on Spinoza's Ethica 'Deus se ipsum amore intellectuali infinito amat' ['God loves himself with an infinite intellectual love'] (Ackerley 2010: 116). Such a reference to Spinoza's quotation indicates two important features that the field of associations constructed on the sign of Murphy stands in the novel. Firstly, the replacement of 'Deus' by 'Murphy' indicates a god-like nature of the latter, which has already been partially indicated by placing the character as the central one of the novel. Secondly, 'Murphy' is juxtaposed with the adjective 'intellectual,' the suggestion that the figure of God should be read in intellectual, not metaphysical categories. On the other hand, both Ackerley (2010: 122) and Kiely (2017: 63) indicate that the place of an absent God has been taken by the astrology. All three symbols, namely the 'intellect,' the 'metaphysics' and the 'astrology' are reflected in Murphy, who both plays a god-like role as other signs communicate towards him and is simultaneously subordinated to the rules of the astrology that appear to be the word of the novel's determent.

Moreover, 'God' as a symbol can be also juxtaposed, in the context of the novel, with the sign of the 'mind.' In *Creative Evolution*, Bergson takes the definition of God from Leibniz as 'the substance that has no point of view' (1941: 382). If one compares that definition with Murphy's definition of mind, i.e., the '[m]

---

7   Jacek Gutorow calls Chapter 6 that divides the novel as a 'quasi-notional treatise' (2019: 112).

ind pictured itself as a large hollow sphere, hermetically closed to the universe without' (2010a: 67), one can notice similarities. Leibniz's God (mind), due to the lack of any point of view, stays constant and immovable – without any point of reference there is no possibility to change the view. Ideally, Murphy's closed system should also work without any interactions with the external world. In addition, Murphy suggests a self-efficiency of the closed system that 'excluded nothing that it did not itself contain' (2010a: 68), all past, present and future actions and memories are already happening within the mind and do not need any external reference:

> Nothing ever had been, was or would be in the universe outside it but was already present as virtual, or actual, or virtual rising into actual, or actual falling into virtual, in the universe inside it. (2010a: 67)

That idea of the simultaneous past-present-future nature of memory corresponds with Bergson's notions of *pure memory*, *memory-image* and *perception* as well as the cone model of memory from the philosopher *Matter and Memory* that we have already discussed in Chapter 5 of Part One, however it is worth to juxtapose that model with Murphy's ideal memory.

Despite the fact that Murphy claims to have achieved the ability of entering into the hermetically closed space of his inner world, we have already proved that he is not able to completely leave the outer world. The protagonist seems to be aware of it as he '[f]elt himself split in two, a body and mind' (2010a: 68). Here appears the highest dilemma of Murphy's theory, namely the juxtaposition between the virtual and the actual. Virtually, he would like to be hermetically closed so all his actions would be occurring without the external context, actually if his mind did not intercourse with his body, he would not know that they had anything in common (Cornwell 1973: 42). Being aware that the mind is tight to the body, Murphy suggests that there must be a space between virtual and actual, yet he does not have access to that space as he is not able to articulate it. Thus, he proposes that his body-mind model consists of three spaces: 'there were the three zones, light, half light, dark each with its speciality.' (2010a: 69)

The first zone can be compared with the body:

> In the first were the forms with parallel, a radiant abstract of the dog's life, the elements of physical experience for a new arrangement. Here the pleasure was reprisal, the pleasure of reversing the physical experience. (2010a: 69)

The light zone can be traced in *Murphy* in the protagonist's relations with puppets. The most vivid example is Murphy-Celia relation that is driven by the sexual factor. Celia works as a prostitute, whereas Murphy's interest in her is condensed to the physical aspects. In Chapter 2, Celia is described by her physical attributes, e.g., 'Eyes. Green.,' 'Hair. Yellow.,' Wrist. 6."' Bust. 34' (2010a: 9).[8] The other mind-body relations are epitomised in the pair Murphy-Cooper. While Murphy craves for will-lessness, Cooper is constantly in movement ('It was true that Cooper never sat, his acathisia was deep-seated and of long standing,' 2010a: 74). Moreover, Cooper is the one who is looking for Murphy in London, the symbol that encapsulates the aforementioned virtual-actual relation.

However, Murphy cannot eventually escape from the body—mind relation, it is not suggested that he has not tried, however his attempts did not succeed. At one point of the novel he evokes Arnold Geulincx's axiom:

> How should he tolerate, let alone cultivate, the occasions of fiasco, having once beheld the beatific idols of his cave? In the beautiful Belgo-Latin of Arnold Geulincx: *Ubi nihil vales, ibi nihil velis*. (2010a: 107)

Murphy raises here the recurring theme that will be visible in Beckett's latter oeuvre, namely the attempt of naming the unnamable, the continuous work of the agent despite of being aware of the inevitable failure. The theme is epitomised in a famous excerpt from *Worstward Ho* (1983): 'Ever tried. Ever failed. No matter. Try again. Fail again. Fail better.' (2010c: 471). In Murphy's case the fiasco apparently derives from the mind's interaction with the body, namely once Murphy hears the noises of the external world, the whole construction of the closed system of his mind collapses, however Geulincx's axiom is to reverse that understanding. 'Ubi nihil vales, ibi nihil velis' can be translated as 'where you are worth nothing, there you should want nothing.'

The Belgian philosopher suggests in his *Ethica* (1665) that the true end of Reason takes place when the love of God appears. That thought was further developed into the mind—body separation. David Hesla juxtaposes the world of 'I' that does not enter into the external world as well as the external world of things that is not affected by the 'I'. Owing to that '[t]he world of things does not affect and is not affected by the I. If the world is worth nothing, it is not worth being desired. Ubi nihil vales, ibi nihil velis.' (1971: 38). Such a theory corresponds with Murphy's attempt of escaping from the external world of the body into the inner world, and Geulincx's work is incorporated into the text's fabric as the reduced symbol of the protagonist's crave.

---

8 Murphy–Celia relations is asymmetrically translated from Ben Jonson's *Volpone*, where Volpone, similarly to Murphy expresses sexual desires towards her. Jonson's Celia is good and innocent, whereas Beckett's Celia expresses love towards Murphy.

The second zone called 'half light' is described as the bliss of contemplation:

> In the second were the forms without parallel. Here the pleasure was contemplation. This system had no other mode in which to be out of joint and therefore did not need to be put right in this. Here was the Belacqua bliss and others scarcely less precise. (2010a: 69)

Paradoxically the way to enter into the half-light zone, which we can call the quasi-hermetic system, leads through the body. Murphy uses for that the rocking chair in which he rocks until his body is virtually numb. Only after that when '[h]is body was appeased that he could come alive in his mind, as described in section six' (2010a: 4). In that scene there is no information that Murphy sits in light nor that he is in the darkness. As we know that in his room there is only one window, we can assume that he finds his contemplation in the half-light. The light-half-light pair is juxtaposed in a parallel scene when Celia sits in the same rocking chair, here her face is in the light ('[s]he spent sitting in the rocking-chair with her face to the light,' 2010a: 43), that juxtaposition indicates that Celia, as a puppet, cannot enter into Murphy's mind, thus belongs to the world of body.

Another intriguing element that appears in the definition of the second zone is the 'Belacqua bliss' (2010d: 69). The self-reference to Belacqua from *More Pricks Than Kicks* and *Dream of Fair to Middling Women* only reinforces the body-mind dualism that Belacqua(s) is/are looking for in 'Dante and the Lobster' and 'Ding-Dong.' It is worth noticing that both Belacqua and Murphy fail in entering the microcosm, however Murphy appears to be closer to the aim than Belacqua. For instance in 'Dante and the Lobster,' he attempts to reach the state of bliss through Dante's *Divine Comedy*, i.e., through the external factor (similar to the horoscope in *Murphy*); the state that through the course of the story cannot be defined as a closed system as is based on an internal dialogue both with the *Divine Comedy* and the Bible. On the other hand, the microcosm in *Murphy* is the central topic. The microcosm of Murphy is also depicted in the name of the novel itself, Cohn notices that the novel bears Murphy's name, when it does not happen in the case of *More Pricks* or *Dream* (2005: 73).

The third zone is connotated with the dark: '[t]he third, the dark, was a flux of forms, a perpetual coming together and falling asunder of forms' (2010a: 70). The dark zone we can correlate with the realm of neutrum that I defined in Chapter 4 of Part One. In the case of the novel, Murphy appears to be closest to the dark zone at his appointment with Mr. Endon. During the chess match, there appears a vast number of expressions that can be referred to the state of neutrum, where Murphy is completely reduced through his disability of being heard and perceived:

Mr. Endon's, seeing himself stigmatised in those eyes that did not see him, Murphy heard words demanding so strongly to be spoken that he spoke them, right into Mr. Endon's face, Murphy who did not speak at all in the ordinary way unless spoken to, and not always even then.
> 'the last at last seen of him
> Himself unseen by him
> And of himself' (2010a: 149-150)

The disability of the subject to enter the third zone, is pictured in the scene when Cooper finally finds Murphy, apparently the dead one. The protagonist is cremated and his ashes are given to Cooper to take them back to Ireland. Nevertheless, Cooper who also epitomises dishonesty and uncertainty, loses the bag of Murphy's ashes in the saloon. Here the ideas that have constituted his existence, namely the body, the mind and the soul, are diminished by the interference of the sounds and objects that reach Murphy's hearing and sight. Owing to that the protagonist's work to get rid of any external stimuli appears to have been done in vain. However, in a different point of reference, the symbols start the working process from the beginning:

> By closing time the body, mind and soul of Murphy were freely distributed over the floor of the saloon; and before another dayspring greyened the earth had been swept away with the sand, the beer, the butts, the glass, the matches, the spits, the vomit. (2010a: 164)

In conclusion, the function that signs play in *Murphy* illustrates how Beckett uses symbols for constructing the fabric of the text. Similarly to *More Pricks Than Kicks*, where the reference to external texts is visible, in the case of *Murphy* it is Democritus' atomic theory, however the gradation of signs is different than in other works. As the name of the novel suggests, Murphy is the central figure, a core sign that communicates both internally and externally. Using the principles of Democritus, Murphy is recognised as a 'speck' an unchangeable atom, that builds the world of the text. Every other external sign that communicates with Murphy, for example Celia, Mr. Kelly, the MMM, the kite, or the gas, plays a utilitarian function, without Murphy they are needless signs whose only role is to support the core sign in constructing the world. The utilitarian aspect of these signs is highlighted in the plot of the novel, when Murphy dies, the story moves towards the end, the kite flies away into the sky and Celia ends the story with a short phrase 'all out.'

Murphy, as his name suggests referring to 'morphe,' is a transmitter of several philosophic concepts, he can be treated as a 'God,' but also the opposite, as a Democritus' atom, the seen, which is juxtaposed with the transcendence of the void, the unseen. Through the field of associations that is created upon the sign of 'Murphy,' Beckett makes an attempt to construct the world that in its principles resembles a neutral space, the closed system where the subject does not communicate with the external, outer world. Murphy's world is definitely not only internal, which is proved once he meets Mr. Endon who has entered the true inner world to which Murphy does not have access. On the other hand, the world is not completely external, he is split between the mind and the body, as it is suggested in a metatextual Chapter 6 of the novel.

The endless suspension between inner and outer worlds results in creating a second one, a world of half-light. It is a world of 'Belacqua bliss' devoted for contemplation. That state of contemplation can function as a synonym to another important sign in Becketts's universe, namely the 'womb-tomb,' i.e., the sign that signalises the subject's craving for being in a state of continuous suspension, in 'in-betweenness.' Murphy claims that he can achieve the state of complete contemplation, however he is unable to prove this statement. Albeit, the never-ending work of external signs, such as in the above fragment 'the sand,' 'the beer' or 'the vomit,' result in demolishing the closed system that Murphy is trying to create. Thus, the example of *Murphy* illustrates Beckett's endless struggle with the matter of the natural language that he uses for describing the neutrum or that what he will later call the 'unnamable.'

Chapter 4: 'Echo's Bones:' A short story (wr. 1933 – publ. 2014)

4.1. A connector between early and post-war texts: 'Echo's Bones'

Contrary to the previous chapter, Chapter 3, where the main focus of my divagations was devoted to the construction of the 'closed' system in Beckett's text through the work of symbols, Chapter 4 will concentrate on the semi-closed qualities of the world built in a short story 'Echo's Bones.' By a semi-closed system, I understand the definition of the phrase as presented in *Murphy* and called a 'half-light zone' or 'Belacqua bliss,' i.e., the state where the subject aims at constructing a completely separated system from external texts, the texts which can be characterised as external stimuli like voices, sounds and physical objects. Unfortunately, the never-ending infiltration by external symbols results in failing the subject, in this case Murphy, to establish a closed system. The signs in 'Echo's Bones' – from Belacqua, the protagonist, through Lord Gall and the Alba, the characters that appear in other Beckett's pre-war texts such as *Murphy* and *More Pricks Than Kicks*, and ending on the stone, the urn and the lantern – function as, following Tomasz Wiśniewski's nomenclature, 'atomistic compositional units' (2010: 53). Such an understanding of the signs' role will allow us to indicate that the world construction of the short story is not a closed space but is constantly in the process of being rebuilt through the signs taken from Beckett's other texts.

Such a process indicates that the world of 'Echo's Bones' is in the state of permanent in-betweenness, the state that is reinforced by the plot of the story. Belacqua finds himself in the realm that resembles a Biblical Purgatory or Dantean Limbo. Similarly to 'Dante and the Lobster' and *Murphy*, Beckett constructs the story referring to literary tradition, in the case of 'Echo's Bones' it is Ovid's *Metamorphoses*, especially the myth of Echo. The title itself as well as the signs used in the text such as 'the stone,' 'the voice,' 'the lantern' but also 'the womb-tomb' are used not only in aesthetic categories but also as the vehicles of constructing the neutrum.

The history of the story 'Echo's Bones' (not to be confused with the same-titled poem) allows us to look at Beckett's early texts from a distant perspective. Similarly to *Dream of Fair to Middling Women* that was published in 1992, the short story was published posthumously in a critical edition by Mark Nixon in 2014. In the case of Beckett's universe, the text offers a two-fold interpretative perspective, namely it can be read both in comparison to other texts that were written at the pre-war period such as *Dream*, *Murphy* and *More Pricks Than Kicks* and diachronically in the perspective of the whole *oeuvre*. Both directions can allow the researcher of Beckett's text to analyse how certain subjects and motifs have evolved through the artistic carreer of Samuel Beckett.

On 25th September 1933, the publishing house Chatto and Windus accepted *More Pricks Than Kicks* to be published. The short story collection consists of ten stories, where in the ninth one entitled 'Yellow,' Belacqua dies. Even though, the main protagonist of the collection dies, Charles Prentice, the Chatto's editor proposed Beckett to write the eleventh short story which could help the book '[b]y bulking up the content' (Nixon 2014: viii). The idea of resurrecting Belacqua, one of the main themes of the story, was expressed by Beckett in a letter to Thomas McGreevy from 9th October 1933: 'I have to do another story for More Pricks. Belacqua redivivus, and I am as stupid as a goat' (*Letters I*, 167). Beckett delivered the story in November 1933, as Prentice acknowledged receipt on 10th November (Nixon 2014: xii); however, on 13th November the publisher informed Beckett that the story would not be accepted:

> It is a nightmare. Just too terribly persuasive. It gives me the jim-jams. The same horrible and immediate switches of the focus, and the same wild unfathomable energy of the population. There are chunks I do not connect with. I am so sorry to feel like this. Perhaps it is only over the details, and I may have a correct inkling of the main impression. I am sorry, for I hate to be dense, but I hope I am not altogether insensitive. 'Echo's Bones' certainly did land on me with a wallop.

> Do you mind if we leave it out of the book – that is, publish 'More Pricks than Kicks' in the original form in which you sent it in? Though it's on the short side, we'll still be able to price it at 7/6d. 'Echo's Bones' would, I am sure, lose the book a great many readers. People will shudder and be puzzled and confused; and they won't be keen on analysing the shudder. I am certain that 'Echo's Bones' would depress the sales very considerably. (Nixon 2014: xii)

Prentice's opinion on 'Echo's Bones' was certainly not encouraging to Beckett. In a letter to McGreevy of 6th December 1933, he wrote: 'I have not been doing anything. Charles's fouting à la porte of 'Echo's Bones,' the last story, into which I put all I knew and plenty that I was better still aware of, discouraged me profoundly' (*Letters I*, 171). Beckett's reaction on the rejection of the story was similar to the one he experienced while he was having problem with publishing *Dream*, namely the self-doubt and resignation. On the other hand, the letter to McGreevy reveals two aspects that will be significant for the writer's further development.

Firstly, Beckett appears not to resign easily from publishing 'Echo's Bones.' In the letter, the writer includes a poem that will be later entitled 'Echo's Bones' and eventually will become the title of a poem collection *Echo's Bones and Other Precipitates* published in December 1935 (*Letters I*, 238). Beckett in that matter applied a technique that he did in the case of *Dream*: he used a part of the story and artistically recycled some motifs in a new work. The second, more intriguing aspect is the writer's confession of putting everything that he knew in the short story. Indeed, the density of motifs, quotations and intertextual references to literature, culture and philosophy is very high in the case of 'Echo's Bones.' Such a density must have been the reason of its rejection. Rubin Rabinovitz notices that: 'it is easy to imagine why Beckett's editor – no doubt motivated by the best intentions – found the story objectionable. The setting is unrealistic, the plot improbable, the characters bizarre' (1984: 55).

Moreover, Mark Nixon suggests that the multiplicity of references and motifs to other texts by Beckett written in the 1930s, should locate 'Echo's Bones' nearer *Dream of Fair to Middling Women* and *Murphy* than to *More Pricks than Kicks* (2010: 93, 99). Owing to that, one should not be surprised that, in Prentice's eyes, the story appeared to be odd and not compatible with other stories of *More Pricks*.[1] José Francisco Fernández also evinces that the structural construction of the plot in 'Echo's Bones' is closer to *Dream* then *More Pricks*. He points out that through the whole short story collection one is able to observe a certain degree, however sometimes naïve (as in 'Dante and the Lobster'), of Belacqua's inner development that links all stories. In the case of 'Echo's Bones,' the author appears to reject a coherent narration and focuses on '[t]he narrator's textual games' (2009: 6). Cohn adds that 'nowhere in the published *Pricks* is the narrator quite so ubiquitous as in the unpublished 'Echo's Bones"' (2005: 59).

Nixon, similarly to Fernández, also suggests close relations between *Dream* and 'Echo's Bones,' especially in the story's self-awareness and fragmentation (2010: 99). He refers to Beckett's letter to McGreevy and recognises the author's declaration of putting his entire knowledge in the story as the evidence of the change that was happening in Beckett's writing process. Joyce's influences are

---

1 The opposite argument is claimed by Rabinovitz who finds the key to combine *More Pricks* and *Echo's Bones* in synthesising Belacqua's relations with women. Suffice it to say that both works share such characters as the Alba, Caleken Frika or Parambini. Rabinovitz suggests that 'without 'Echo's Bones' an essential part of the novel's complex structure is lost ... *More Pricks than Kicks* is subtle, intricate, brilliant work; the removal of 'Echo's Bones' has made it needlessly obscure' (1984: 61).

quite vivid in the short story, however the author of *The Unnamable* appears to start searching for his own style. Such predictions can trace its evidences in the story itself. The prediction to abandon English for French is expressed by Lord Gall in a conversation with Belacqua: "'Cut out the style" shouted Lord Gall, "how often must I tell you?'" (2014: 28). As far as self-awareness is concerned, the text expresses the author's self-consciousness about the density of intertextual references: "'My ideas!' exclaimed Belacqua. "Really, my Lord, you forget that I am a postwar degenerate. We have our faults, but ideas is not one of them.'" (2014: 26).

The manuscript of 'Echo's Bones' survived in two copies; the one that Beckett offered to his friend A.J. Leventhal and in this way contributed to the Leventhal collection located at the Harry Ransom Center in Austin. The second typescript was provided to Laurence Harvey and can be found at Dartmouth College Library. The copies are identical, yet they differ in marginal corrections (Nixon 2010: 39). The print version of the story, with Nixon's critical notes, was published by Faber & Faber in 2014. Owing to limited access to the manuscripts, the text has received little critical attention so far.[2]

4.2. The story's construction: 'This little triptych'

The title of 'Echo's Bones' takes its roots in Ovid's *Metamorphoses*, especially in the myth of Narcissus and Echo. Echo was a nymph who fell in love with Narcissus; however, due to the curse cast by Juno, the nymph could not express her feelings towards Narcissus as she could not speak, yet only repeat the lover's words. The reference to the ancient literary tradition as the main theme of the story correlates with a similar measure that Beckett applied in *More Pricks, Dream* and *Murphy*; however, in the case of the previous works they were constructed as references to the works of Dante and to the Bible.

Building the structure of 'Echo's Bones' on Ovid's poem shares intelligible similarities as in both cases the theme of the stories pivots around the topic of

---

2   In this chapter, I will refer, for example, to Julie Campbell, 'Echo's Bones and Beckett's Disembodied Voices.' In: *Samuel Beckett Today/Aujourd'hui*, 11/2001, 454–60 as well as to Fernández, José Francisco "Echo's Bones: Samuel Beckett's Lost Story of Afterlife." In: *Journal of the Short Story in English* 52/2009, 115–24. The author of this thesis covered the analysis of Beckett's signature based on *Echo's Bones* in the book: Borkowski, Rafał. 'Beckett przed Beckettem? Poszukiwania początków sygnatury Beckettowskiej na przykładzie opowiadania 'Echo's Bones.' In: Wiśniewski, Tomasz (ed). *Beckett w XXI. Wieku. Rozpoznanie.* Gdańsk University Press, 2017, 87–104.

death. For the story's construction, the writer uses the pair echo–bone or rather bone—rock, such a pair allows to encode the main topic into a reduced symbol that through the course of the story generates and multiplies meanings. Such an encoding of an external text, especially the texts that originate from Judeo-Christian literary traditions and have already been evoked in the previous chapters for example, Dante's *The Divine Comedy* in 'Dante and the Lobster' and Democritus in *Murphy*. That tendency is sustained in 'Echo's Bones,' where Ovid uses the transformation of 'bones' into 'rocks' to illustrate a process of a deceased body which is interwoven with the topic of melancholy. Similarly, Beckett uses indicators of an inaudible voice ('do not hear,' 'speak up,' 2014: 5) to eventually refer to Ovid's melancholy through the symbol of the voice ('I find your voice'... 'something more than a roaring-meg against melancholy,' 2014: 6). The shift from the signs of the 'voice' to the 'stone' is depicted at the end of the story where Belacqua is surrounded by such symbols as the 'tombstones' and 'stones' (2014: 51), thus Beckett's work on the artistically recycled symbols appears visible in the case of 'Echo's Bones.' The stone as a symbol of death, grief or non-being is evoked not only by the title itself and its literary reference but also by the objects that appear in the story, especially in their third part where Belacqua appears in the graveyard surrounded by stone graves. The 'echo—stone' transition from *Metamorphoses* finds its symmetry in Beckett's voice (language)—stone (getting rid of langue towards neutralisation of the subject) as well as the asymmetry of reinterpreting Echo's story:

> To feed her love on melancholy sorrow
> Which, sleepless, turned her body to a shade,
> First pale and wrinkled, then a sheet of air,
> Then bones, which some say turned to thin-worn rocks;
> And last her Voice remained. Vanished in forest,
> Far from her usual walks on hills and valleys,
> She's heard by all who call; her voice has life. (1958: 76)

Incidentally, the juxtaposition death--stone can be also traced in Beckett's biography. Gottfried Büttner notices that the writer as a child very often played with stones that latter resulted in adding that topic to his creative works:

> Beckett's relationship to stones, which he called 'almost a love relationship,' was associated by Beckett himself with death ... As a child he frequently picked up stones from the beach and carried them home, where he built nests for them and put them in trees to protect them from the waves and other dangers. On the same occasion, Beckett mentioned Sigmund Freud, who had once written that man carried with him a kind of congenital yearning for the mineral kingdom. (1984: 163)

The motif of stones is a recurring element in Beckett's post-war works – for instance, *Malone Dies* (1951) and Malone's imaginary play space with stones or *Molloy* (1951) and a famous scene of sucking pebbles. Moreover, one can notice a correlation between Ovid's Echo whose voice emanates from her bones, the voice that can be decoded as the symbol of being simultaneously dead and alive with the significance that the voice plays in *The Unnamable* (1953) (Campbell 2001: 458–459).[3] As we would like to predominantly read the symbol of stone and echo in 'Echo's Bones,' the above examples of re-using such symbols in later works are aimed at showing a link between the pre- and post-war period. Such examples signalise that the motifs, albeit artistically recycled, remained a vital point of Beckett's oeuvre.

Moreover, Nixon observes the other vital interpretational element covered in the title of the story namely the echoing of multitude references to other works and authors as well as self-references that build the fabric of 'Echo's Bones'(2010: 98–99). The self-referential figure that links the previous works with the story is Belacqua, who similarly to the measures used in other texts by Beckett, is not the same figure but an echoing symbol that shares some motifs. Belacqua in 'Echo's Bones' finds himself in the afterlife, which links the story with *More Pricks Than Kicks*, where Belacqua dies in the story 'Yellow.' In addition, Belacqua from 'Echo's Bones' depicts, to some extent, the sense of humour presented in *More Pricks*, yet the light attitude towards the topic of death and purgatory from the story lacks a characteristic quality of darkness and seriousness ("Echo's Bones' treats death and purgatory with such lightness – more so than anywhere else in Beckett – that it would perhaps have given the volume of stories too bathetic a conclusion.', Campbell 2001: 456).

The structure of the space in 'Echo's Bones' sets Belacqua in the state of in-betweenness, he is neither passive nor active, neither inward nor outward. That state of suspension is signalised in the text itself, when we encounter Belacqua in the realm of afterlife, '[i]n the dust of the world' (2014: 3), he is sitting on a fence smoking cigars ('It occurred to him on day as he sat bent double on a fence like a case-poitrine in delicious reverie and puffed away at his Romeo and Juliet,'

---

3   The features of the disembodied voice from *The Unnamable* evoke similarities with Echo, especially its repetitive qualities, for example 'I must speak, with this voice that is not mine' (2012: 45),' [n]o words but the words of others (2012: 50), 'I'm in words, made of words, others' words' (2012: 111). The echo-repetition relations in Beckett's works are discussed in detail in Hunkeler, Tomas. *Echos de l'Ego dans l'Oeuvre de Samuel Beckett*. Editions L'Harmattan. 1998.

2014: 3), the significance of the fence as a symbol of being both inside and outside is strengthened by the first character that he meets in the afterlife namely Miss Zaborovna Privet, a prostitute whose first name in Russian means a 'fence' whereas the last name 'hello' (2014: 5–7). On the other hand, it is suggested that Belacqua is not a human in flesh but a ghost as he, contrary to the fence and Zaborovna, cannot cast his shade ('But her first impression was confirmed by the absence of any shadow but the fence's and her own,' 2014: 7).

The being of Belacqua in the afterlife locates him somewhere between human, ghost and even an echo that resonates with thoughts and symbols from the past. In that sense, the character generates and recycles the motif of Ovid's work, his function is to repeat phrases heard somewhere else in the space of that unidentified realm. Owing to that the references to the previous life expressed in the space of the afterlife appear non-contextual, yet they often refer to the signs that appear further in the story. For instance, 'My soul begins to be idly goaded and recked' (2014: 5) is a quotation from Augustine's *Confessions* (1991: 128), '[a]n ego jam sedeo?' ('am I now sat?,' 2014: 27) refers to Seneca's quotation that conveys Belacqua's mocking allusion that even in the afterlife Latin is needed ('The rags of Latin flogged into us at school, in afterlife they stand to us well.,' 2014: 27), Belacqua also quotes Jonathan Swift's love poem 'Cadenus and Vanessa:'[4] "*A dog, a parrot or an ape… / Engross the fancies of the fair*" (2014: 12).

The above examples illustrate how the echoing of the external texts simultaneously reinforces the signs used in 'Echo's Bones,' namely Adeodatus, the fence, the Alba correspond with Saint Augustine, sitting and Vanessa. Moreover, the echoic nature of Belacqua is reinforced in the first part of the story where in the conversation with Zborovna he uses such expressions as 'I do not hear what you say' (2014: 5), 'I like the way you speak very much' (2014: 6); intriguingly Zaborovna will also answer with an echoic 'The way I speak' (2014: 6).[5]

---

4   Jonathan Swift wrote the poem for Esther Vanhomrigh who was passionately in love with him. Such a reference in context of the Alba's abandonment of Belacqua in the last scene of 'Echo's Bones' appears to be ironical.

5   The importance of voice and repetition on the example of *Molloy, Malone Dies* and *The Unnamable* have been analysed by Rabinovitz in the article 'Repetition and Underlying Meanings in Samuel Beckett's Trilogy.' In: St John Butler, Lance, Davis, Robin, J. (ed). *Rethinking Beckett*. The Macmillan Press, New York 1990: 31–67. Rabinovitz notices that in example of Molloy and Moran, however these observations can be also applied to Belacqua, the protagonists use internal voices as the source of messages they are looking in themselves. These voices play the role of a transmitter for these messages (1990: 56). In 'Echo's Bones,' the symbol of voice on the one hand attempts to locate the

Here we arrive at the next vital aspect of the realm presented in 'Echo's Bones,' namely the shift of Belacqua from the external into the internal world. The already presented qualities of the space of 'Echo's Bones,' namely the state of in-betweenness where the subjects are not willing to make any move resemble Dantean Limbo. Dante describes this space as the first Circle of Hell where the condemned souls find themselves in a state of suspension (*Inferno*, 'Canto IV'). The resemblance between the Limbo and the space of 'Echo's Bones' is depicted by a number of symbols that appear in the first part of the short story. The suspension has already been depicted in the symbol of Belacqua sitting on a fence who cannot make his mind whether to move or not; the similar indecisiveness of the protagonist's state of being is expressed in his description as a human who is 'dead and buried' (2014: 4) yet still alive.

The second similarity between Dante's Limbo and the space of 'Echo's Bones' can be traced in their infernal nature. Belacqua does not find himself in a completely neutral space, it means that he can feel pain. While sitting on the fence he is '[s]uffering greatly from the exposure' (2014: 4) and his only past-time is to smoke cigars. Moreover, Belacqua wishes that he had been burned rather than buried so he would not find himself in the present condition. Here one can observe some symbols that encapsulate a hint of the infernal nature of the space, namely the cigar that produces the fume and the urn that should be used to hold Belacqua's ashes (2014: 3–4). Owing to that, one can suggest equivalence between Dantean Limbo (the space that is between the Hell and the Purgatory) and the space of 'Echo's Bones' (the space beyond which subjects are suspended, however they can experience pain and the sense of eternal fiasco).

Moreover, the Limbo of 'Echo's Bones' can share some similarities with the second and third zones from *Murphy*, and the public house from 'Ding-Dong.' The third zone was defined by Murphy as a closed system without states or elements but a place of pure forms '[b]ecoming and crumbling into the fragments of a new becoming' (2010d: 70), the space of neutrum where the external world does not have access to. The second zone, on the other hand, was defined in *Murphy* as a half-light zone, where one can find Belacqua's bliss, i.e., it is the space of Belacqua/Murphy's contemplation where the impulses of the external world arrive however the protagonist attempts to ignore them. Such an example of the second zone is the public house where Belacqua attempts to find a bliss of contemplation

---

subject in the space that he present, on the other, the voices correlate with the structural construction of the story and corresponds with Ovid's *Metamorphoses*.

yet external impulses such as the old woman's speech prevent Belacqua from achieving his 'bliss' (see Chapter 3 of Part Two).

Belacqua from 'Echo's Bones' finds himself between the second and third zones. On the one hand there is a suggestion that both the external and internal worlds are in fact the one closed system of Belacqua's mind, the suggestion that is encapsulated by the symbol of a dream: '[h]e sometimes wondered if his lifeless condition were not all a dream and if on the whole he had not been a great deal deader before then after his formal departure,' (2014: 3). On the other hand, the vast number of external signs that continuously communicate towards Belacqua such as Zaborovna, Lord Gall but also Doyle and the Alba, (the last two characters originate from the external world of *More Pricks Than Kicks*) are the reason that the system is not completely closed. In other words, Belacqua is still searching for a space for contemplation: Belacqua's sitting on a fence corresponds with Murphy's rocking in the chair, in both cases these symbols serve as vehicles to achieve the 'bliss.' Moreover, Belacqua's attempt of abandoning everything that belongs to the human world in 'Echo's Bones,' i.e., the world of liberation from any desires, reason and problems (Fernández 2009: 5), or in general the third zone, is also presented in *Dream of Fair to Middling Women*:

> The third being was the dark gulf, when the glare of the will and the hammer-strokes of the brain doomed outside to take flight from its quarry were expunged, the limbo and the womb-tomb alive with the unanxious spirits of quiet celebration, where there was no conflict of flight and flow and Eros was as null as Anteros and Night had no daughters ... The cities and forests and beings were also without identity, they were shadows, they exerted neither pull nor goad. His third being was without axis or contour, its centre everywhere and periphery nowhere, an unsurveyed marsh of sloth. (2012: 121)

The set of motifs and symbols used in the fragment of *Dream* are similar to the one from 'Echo's Bones.' In both cases there are references to the Ancient literature, both realms are undefined space: the limbo, the world inhabited by spirits, echoes and shadows. The symbol that summarises and defines the third zone is the phrase 'womb-tomb,' the phrase is echoed in Beckett's late texts such as *Molloy* or *The Unnamable* where the subjects want to fall into the state of non-existence and descend into the 'womb-tomb.' The expression also appears in 'Echo's Bones' and is used to describe Belacqua's emotional status: '[h]e felt himself nodding in the grey shoals of angels, his co-departed, that thronged the womb-tomb' (2014: 4–5). Campbell recognises in the phrase womb-tomb the 'skullscapes,' an empty cave to which Echo withdraws. That empty cave she further juxtaposes with the voices that can be heard and echoed in the space, a space that can be identified with protagonists' heads of such texts as *The Unnamable* and *Texts for Nothing* (2001: 457–458). On the other hand, Angela Moorjani recognises the womb-tomb space as '[t]he tomblike womb and the womblike tomb in the darkness of the mind in which the living are unborn and the dead do not die' (1990: 21), such a definition is close to the realm presented in 'Echo's Bones' as approaches the reader to the zone of darkness where all movement and action is suspended, the realm of neutrum. Moreover, one can indeed recognise in the phrase the attempt of reducing one's existence to maximum, to neutralise the role of the language simultaneously leaving a hidden possibility of generating new meanings; on condition that the symbol womb-tomb will be juxtaposed with other symbolic units.[6]

Besides the literary references to Ovid's *Metamorphoses*, 'Echo's Bones' displays some allusions to Dante's *The Divine Comedy* as well. The opening scene of the story describes how the undead enter the realm of limbo. The description of the path that the dead need to go through resembles more a Biblical purgatory than a paradise:

> The dead die hard, they are trespassers on the beyond, they must take the place as they find it, the shafts and manholes back into the muck, till such time as the lord of the manor incurs through his long acquiescence a duty of care in respect of them. Then they are free among the dead by all means, then their troubles are over, their natural troubles. But the debt of nature, the scandalous post-obit on one's estate, can no more be discharged by the mere fact of kicking the bucket than descent can be made into the same stream twice. This is a true saying. (2014: 3)

It is worth noticing that in this fragment Beckett attempts to combine several literary registers, namely a Biblical tone ('This is a true saying,' 'the lord of the manor'), a Dantean guide's perspective of what can be found in the Purgatory and how to get there ('they find it, the shafts and manholes back into the muck') and an ironic register that is expressed by using the colloquial language

---

6 The author of this thesis also recognises the stylistic function of the womb-tomb and its correlation with the Anglo-Saxon tradition of kennings. The construction used by bards in the early Medieval era was aimed at expressing certain phrases indirectly yet in an understandable way for the receiver, for example the whale's path could mean the sea (see Borkowski 2017: 97–98). Such a stylistic function of not expressing certain notions directly can be noticed for example in a short story 'Assumption.' Namely, some of the expressions concerning sound-silence relation are named in a kenning tradition, e.g., 'sea of silence,' 'driblets of sound,' 'boiling an egg,' or 'cry of the sea' (2010a: 57–60). In 'Echo's Bones' the example of kenning is included in the description of Lord Gall who is described as a one with 'the Saint's Paul skull' (2014: 15), which means that Lord Gall is bald.

('the mere fact of kicking the bucket'). However, the appearance of a mysterious lord of the manor, who is later recognised as Lord Gall and plays a vital part in the central part of the story, and the visible reference to Dante's work may raise questions about the figure of God. In this sense, the space of 'Echo's Bones' is similar to the one from *Waiting for Godot*; God, if exists, is definitely not present in that world:

> 'No crows where I come from' he said, 'God be praised'
> 'Ah' said Zaborovna. 'Then there is a God after all?'
> 'Presumably' said Belacqua. 'I know no more than I did.' (2014: 9–10)

The combination of symbols such as the echo, stone and voice appear to be the fundaments of Belacqua's construction. In a notebook dated 1926, so three years before his first official publication in *transition*, Beckett writes about Belacqua as follows:

> … and while they continue their discourse a voice addresses them, at which they turn, and find several spirits (I neglegenti) behind the rock, & amongst them one named Belacqua, a Florentine and known to Dante, & who tells that he is doomed to linger there outside the gates of Purgatory for a period the equivalent of his life on earth, on account of his having delayed his repentance to the last. (Engelberts 2006: 45)

The above fragment proves that the symbols, though used in a different context, accompany Beckett in his further literary texts. The comparison of 'Echo's Bones' in manifold contexts with other Beckett's works (*Dream,, More Pricks, Murphy*, but also *The Unnamable* and *Molloy*) can reveal how the multitude of symbols and motifs used in the short story resonate and echo with the symbols used in other texts. That assumption will be diagnosed in detail, on the example of the central and third part of the short story. Similarly to 'Dante and the Lobster' where we have the triplet alliteration lunch-lesson-lobster, or in *Murphy*'s kite-horoscope-mental hospital, 'Echo's Bones' is also divided into three parts ('[t]he least presentable, aspect of his cruel reversion, three scenes from which, the first, the central and the last, we make bold solicit as likely material for this fagpiece, this little triptych,' 2014: 4). These three scenes are the above discussed scene of Belacqua's appearance in the limbo and the meeting with Zaborovna, the central scene of Belacqua's meeting with Lord Gall of Wormwood, and the final scene on the graveyard where the protagonist meets Doyle, the groundsman.

4.3. A system of structural relations: 'A classic-romantic corpse'

So far in our discussion on the structure of 'Echo's Bones' we have depicted how the multitude of motifs, references and symbols, juxtaposed with other Beckett's texts, construct the space of the story as well as highlight the characteristic features of the writer's artistic signature, such as the body-mind relations and the search for a neutral space. At that point, one needs to investigate how the fabric of the story is constructed on the most elementary level, namely the compositional unit.

Tomasz Wiśniewski notices that a characteristic feature of Beckett's writing in the atomised compositional units that can be found in details and marginalia, the units that aim at generating semiotic relations with all compositional units, not only with the analogous ones. It means that a single word can multiplicate its meanings not only in relation with the neighbouring words but paragraphs, sentences or even other Beckett's texts (2010: 53). Moreover, Lotman notices that such units are the basic ones in the process of constructing an artistic text, they not only form the organisation of the text but also create structural relations between the text's levels such as grammatical, phonological or semantical. (1977: 53).[7] Both scholars' viewpoints on the functions of compositional units correspond with our understanding how signs are used in Beckett's works. Lotman depicts one more important factor of the semiosphere's structure, namely once an external text crosses the boundary of the semiosphere, the internal organisation of the latter transforms the external text '[o]n the syntagmatic level' (1977: 53).

To analyse how external compositional units work in the space of 'Echo's Bones,' one can take scene where Lord Gall presents Belacqua the content of his slide-box. Among objects that one can find inside the box are 'an ale of hellebore' and 'photographs of Fräulein Dietrich gushed forth with a piercing vagitus' (2014: 18–19). The external signs of the hellebore, photographs of Marlene Dietrich and the vagitus only apparently do not correspond with the plot of the

---

7 'This is likewise manifested in the artistic text, which is constructed as a form of organization, as a system of relations between constituent material units. Correspondingly, additional structural bonds—relations between system types can be established between the various levels of the text. A text is divided into subtexts (the phonological level, the grammatical level, and so on) each of which can be viewed as an independently organized text. Structural relations between these levels become a specification of the text as a whole.' (1977: 53).

story. As it will be further discussed, the central part of 'Echo's Bones' pivots around the impossibility of Lord Gall to father a heir. The above signs inscribe in, following Lotman, the internal organisation of the text. 'A vagitus' is a medical term meaning the cry of a new-born baby, Lord Gall's greatest desire, 'the hellebore' is a plant that can be used as a poison, whereas the appearance of photographs of Marlene Dietrich refers to the relation between Lord Gall, Lady Gall and Baron Extravas.[8] All three units by being apparently irrelevant and out of context, through the meaning that they carry and incorporate to the text of 'Echo's Bones' start adjusting to the structure of the text.

Beckett seems to be aware of the significance of the basic compositional unit of the text which can be even further subdivided from words or signs to letters, units without which no text could be established. One of the fragments of 'Echo's Bones' suggests such awareness:

> But these women, positively it was scarcely an exaggeration to say that the four and twenty letters made no more and no more capricious variety of words in as many languages than they, their jigsaw souls, foisted on them that they might be damned, diversity of moods. (2014: 13)

Beckett depicts that the fundament of the text finds its source in the natural language, the same language that he also tries to get rid of through his whole artistic carrier. The combination of twenty-four letters derives from natural languages, in Beckett's case English, French, German, and Italian, which is visible in the story as words from all these languages appear in 'Echo's Bones.' A number of sufficient examples for the above assumption can be found in the central part of the story, where Belacqua meets Lord Gall.

Contrary to the opening scene, which combines Dante's purgatory with late Beckett's realm of nowhere, the register of the central part resembles a mixture of myth and a fable. Belacqua finds himself suddenly in a realm that he calls 'the

---

8   Lord Gall is afraid that Lady Gall has a romance with Baron Extravas, the relation that may end up in delivering an illegitimate heir. The asymmetrical situation takes place in a 1930 movie *The Blue Angel* where Marlene Dietrich plays the main role of Lola Lola, a dancer in a local cabaret who is in a relation with the movie protagonist, Immanuel Rath. In the course of the plot it turns out that Lola Lola has an affair with Mazeppa, a strongman (Nixon 2014: 79). The affair ends up tragically for Rath who eventually dies humiliated in solitude. Intriguingly, 'Mazeppa,' as the reference to Byron's poem appears in 'Echo's Bones' as well, thus it can be indicated that the relation of several external units incorporated in the text of the short story starts generating new meanings assigned to the internal organisation of the text.

Bayswater of Elysium' (2014: 14). The name of the place refers to the realm of happy souls from the Greek mythology. Here Belacqua meets Lord Gall, whose fantastic description inscribes in the folkloristic character of the story:

> Belacqua ... looked down on a bald colossus, the Saint Paul's skull gathered into ropy dundraoghaires and a seamless belcher, dangling to and fro that help to holy living a Schenectady putter, clad in amaranth caoutchouc cap-à-pie, a cloak of gutta percha streaming back from the barrel of his bust, in his hand a gum tarboosh (2014: 15)

On the phonetic level, the description attempts to imitate the Irish accent, suggesting references to the Irish folklore. The realm of Wormwood, as Lord Gall calls the place (2014: 15) is full of such fantastic creatures as the 'leprechaun' (2014: 11), 'John Jameson O'Lantern dancing before him' (2014: 11) 'mandrakes' (2014: 12), or 'Dáib i Seanacán' (2014: 29). The name of Lord Gall also epitomises the Irish connections, can either be juxtaposed with 'Gael,' a native Irish and 'Gall,' a foreigner (Nixon 2014: 75), even in the name of Lord Gall, one can notice the similarities to the symbol of the fence as the space of in-betweenness.

Nevertheless, the plot of the story is quite simple and imitates a fable.[9] Lord Gall is the ruler of Wormwood. He is infecund and does not have an heir. He knows that Baron Extravas will take control over the realm if Lord Gall does not have a son. Gall asks Belacqua to father a son with Lady Gall. Belacqua sets on a journey on an ostrich called Strauss to the castle where Lady Gall is waiting. Finally, Belacqua fathers a child but instead of a boy, a girl is born ("it is essentially a girl", 2014: 35). Lord Gall predicts the failure of his house when he talks about Byron's poem 'Mazeppa' that 'they can in no wise be translated into Gaelic.' (2014: 18). In this context Lord Gall symbolises the fall of a culture, in this case the Irish one, the failure that finds its origin in the dead language. The register and style applied to that story differs from other texts by Beckett of that time and appears to be a creative exercise of writing in a different style, the attempt that will be eventually abandoned.[10]

---

9 The Irish literature motifs in Beckett's text are examined, for example in Bixby, Patrick. 'Ireland 1906: 1945.' In: Uhlmann, Anthony (ed.). *Samuel Beckett in Context*. Cambridge University Press, Cambridge 2013: 65–75.

10 The analogue example of a 'non-Beckettian' register one can find in the short story 'A Case in a Thousand' published in 1934. Its structure inscribes in a psychological novel that can be found, for example in Virginia Woolf. Cohn notices that 'this short story is a new departure for Beckett in the simplicity of its diction, the lack of erudite reference, and the prevalence of dialogue' (2005: 67).

Coming back to Wiśniewski's observation on the importance of details that are scattered in different texts by Beckett, the example of Lord Gall will be a useful point in case. In fact, Lord Gall appears in *Murphy* as the lover of Miss Dew:

> The oui-ja board is how I live, I come all the way from Paddington to feed the poor dear sheep and now I dare not let her off, her is my card, Rosie Dew, single woman, by appointment to Lord Gall of Wormwood, perhaps you know him, a charming man, he sends me objects, he is in a painful position, spado of long standing in tail male special he seeks testamentary pentimenti from *au-delà*,... (2010a: 61)

Both in *Murphy* and 'Echo's Bones,' Lord Gall functions as the symbol of infertility; however, whereas in *Murphy* he is only mentioned and utters no single word, in 'Echo's Bones' he becomes one of the central characters. The episodic appearance of Lord Gall in *Murphy* just to later become one of the central characters of 'Echo's Bones' corresponds with Wiśniewski's recognition of atomistic compositional units that communicate with each other even though the units do not coexist in a near proximity of, for instance, one sentence or paragraph. In both examples it is visible that the construction of the character is built on the language, on the mix of French, German, English, and Irish, to be more precise. Nevertheless, Lord Gall's lack of reproduction power removes the character on the semantic level. Once his medical advisers inform Lord Gall that the girl was born, which means that he does not have a male heir, he remains silent. No other word by this character is uttered.

The objects that return and appear in other Beckett's texts are scattered through the whole 'Echo's Bones.' For example, in the opening scene of the story there is 'an urn,' an object that later returns in in *Play* (1963), where three characters sit in big urns and when Belacqua arrives to Wormwood he scents that 'the air filled with the camembert odours of goat' (2014: 14), the symbol of the goat is repeated during Lord Gall's conversation with Belacqua "We are quite alone" he said "except for a goat somewhere"' (2014: 18).

The goat can be also found in *Waiting for Godot* when the boy informs Vladimir that he minds the goats ('I mind the goats, Sir,' 2010c: 43). What is more, when one investigates the fragment of *Murphy* where Lord Gall appears, he or she can notice the symbol of the sheep (feed the poor dear sheep), the symbol that correlates with the boy from *Waiting for Godot*; the boy's brother, contrary to the goat, minds the sheep (2010c: 45). The above examples only illustrate that the compositional units in Beckett's texts are aimed at multiplying semantic relations and result in creating new meanings that build the structure of the text.

The final part of the story develops in the graveyard where Belacqua is described as '[a] free corpse, sat on his own headstone, drumming his heels against the R.I.P.' (2014: 36). The register of this part finds its roots in Gothic and Romantic literature (Campbell 2001: 456), the narrator even characterises the scene as '[a] classic-romantic' (2014: 36):

> What with the moon shining, the sea tossing in her sleep and sighing, and the mountains observing their Attic vigil in the background, he found it difficult to decide offhand whether the scene was of the kind that is called romantic or whether it should not with more justice be termed classical (2014: 36).

The Romantic associations are strengthened by the variation of the song *Je cherche après Titine* written by Léo Daniderff, and in 'Echo's Bones' translated and rewritten into German to imitate a love confession to a lover (Nixon 2014: 98). Belacqua meets in the graveyard a nameless groundsman, who echoes buried Belacqua in the story 'Draff' from *More Pricks Than Kicks*. However, this time we get to know that his name is Doyle: 'The next item on the programme turned out to be our old friend the groundsman, whom we did not bother to name in Draff, but now must: Doyle was his name.' (2014: 37). Once again a secondary object from one text is put into the core of the writer's interests. In that case, a certain degree of metatext is visible; the narrator is aware of the existence of the other self-referential realm that by being juxtaposed with the current artistic space, generates new meanings.

The other point worth noticing is the importance of naming objects to constitute their existence. We get to know that the narrator calls the groundsman Doyle, but a moment later Belacqua calls the man Mick ('My old friend Mick,' 2014: 37). Similarly Lord Gall starts calling Belacqua Adeodatus, using the name of Saint Augustin's son ('I was thinking, if you did not mind, of addressing you in future as Adeodatus,' 2014: 16). Such a measure suggests a fragile structure of symbols that appear in the text, the immediate change of the name moves the object to a new semantic structure that starts generating new notions, e.g., Belacqua (Dantean convention) – Adeodatus (Christian convention). The importance of naming objects to constitute their existence must happen though the voice, as the silence constitutes the non-existence, or nothing: '"Give it a name" said Doyle in a voice that he had some difficulty in recognising,' 2014: 50).

Belacqua, described by Doyle as '[a] spiritual body' (2014: 38), uses the groundsman to help him opening the grave in which the protagonist's natural body should be found. When he opens the coffin, he does not find any body but a pile of stones: 'In the coffin the handful of stones that Belacqua had found, the lantern lying on its side, the sweet smell of tubers killed in the snuff of candle' (2014: 51). The stones here work as a coda for the whole story, the symbol of death and the subject's neutralisation. Such a neutralisation is only reinforced by Doyle's behaviour who runs away from the cemetery ('Doyle stalking and rushing the tombstones, squatting behind them in ambush, behaving in a way quite foreign to his nature,' 2014: 51) as well as the Alba, Belacqua's lover from for example *Dream of Fair to Middling Women*, who has been watching the scene from a submarine and then departs with words: 'to hell with him so' (2014: 51).

Nevertheless, we cannot speak here about the full neutralisation of the object depicted by the heap of stones, due to the coexisting lantern with the snuff of candle. The still warm candle, juxtaposed with the neutralisation of the subject, can be deciphered as a symbol of possibility, the notion that accompanies to the concept of neutrum. Moreover, the example of the lantern inscribes in the already presented feature of atomistic compositional units in Beckett's works. The possibility that the sign of the lantern covers can be correlated, for example, with the figure of 'the boy' in *Endgame*. It is difficult to predict boy's nature, which is characterised in Hamm's words as follows: 'if he exists he'll die there or he'll come here. And if he does not' (2010c: 147). However, the symbols used in both texts are incomparable (the lantern, the boy), the idea that they convey, namely the notion of the possibility, make them compatible with each other.

Finally, the story ends with a sentence 'so it goes in the world' (2014: 51), the phrase that returns in the second part of 'Echo's Bones' as well as ends the story 'Draff' from *More Pricks Than Kicks*. The phrase, taken from the Brothers Grimm story 'How the Cat and the Mouse Set Up House' (Nixon 2014: 109), reoccurs as an echoic sentence and as such corresponds with Ovid's myth on Echo, who after death was transformed into a pile of stones. Overall, the sentence 'so it goes in the world' can be treated as a compositional unit that put in different contexts generates different meanings: Draff – an ironic viewpoint on the human condition, Lord Gall – a summary that reinforces the convention of a fable, the end of 'Echo's Bones'– reference to Ovid's Echo.

To sum up, the method of using signs for constructing the world of 'Echo's Bones' is similar to the one applied in *More Pricks Than Kicks* and *Murphy*, namely the writer incorporates symbols that belong to Judeo-Christian literary, philosophical and art traditions such as Dante, Ovid and Romantic paintings. All these symbols. Such as 'Echo's Bones' and the myth of Narcissus, the Gothic scenery of the graveyard, fantastic creatures from the Irish mythology, convey in themselves more general ideas associated with such terms as grief, love, loss or joy. Through the work on motifs that encapsulate the given themes, Beckett attempts to condense these essential notions to a single sign, a single word. The writer starts to use these symbols in the context of building his own universe only when the concept is reduced to singularity. For example, the relation between Belacqua and the Alba is a crooked romantic relation, a pastiche that on the one hand refers to *The Divine Comedy* Dante—Beatrice relation but on the other mocks the Romantic relation observed, for instance, in Goethe's *The Sorrows of Young Werther*. Owing to that the single sign in Beckett's text can accumulate a whole literary tradition that can start revealing itself once one symbol is juxtaposed in the text with the other (e.g., Lord Gall and Gaelic language, Zaborovna Privet and the fence, Wormwood and a purgatory). In the case of 'Echo's Bones' that work is even more visible as the accumulation of signs in the short story exceeds other discussed texts.

In addition, such an accumulation of signs originates in heterogeneous registers: the literary allusions ('Echo,' 'Dáib i Seanacán,' 'Mazeppa'), the Christian associations ('Adeodatus,' 'Saint Paul,' 'the Limbo') and self-referential indications. By the self-referential category I understand those signs that have already appeared in other Beckett's texts and function both as generators of new meanings and as connectors of at least two different texts of Beckett's universe, such as 'Lord Gall,' 'the Alba,' 'Belacqua,' and 'the goat.' What is more important, following Wiśniewski's concept of atomistic compositional units as well as Lotman' theory of constructing an artistic text, the signs play an indispensable aesthetic role in constructing the world of the story. Using the concepts encapsulated in separate symbols such as 'the stone,' 'the womb-tomb' or 'the lantern,' Beckett is exploring the motifs correlated with the human condition such as death, afterlife or possibility. A mind—body memory is also examined through the signs, as is the case in 'Echo's Bones,' the relation depicted in the character of Belacqua himself described both as a human in flesh yet in the lifeless condition. He is able to smoke cigarettes but simultaneously he cannot cast a shadow, nor hear other characters properly. Thus, his existence within the world of 'Echo's Bones' resembles an echo of past memories that is trying to constitute within the semi-opened, the half-light, zone of the Limbo.

Moreover, the symbols used in the story can allow us to answer the question why 'Echo's Bones' is a connector between Beckett's pre- and post-war texts. 'The urn,' 'the womb-tomb' and the 'the voice,' when read from the diachronic perspective, are the symbols that will be further examined by the writer. For instance, the appearance of urns in *Play* (a symbol of suspension between the worlds of life and death), the concept of the 'womb-tomb' (reduces the human existence) can be recognised in the construction of *Footfalls* and *Krapp's Last Tape*, finally, the concept of 'the voice' that appears to be one of major topics of Beckett's artistic exploration, e.g., in *Company*, depicts the attempt of capturing the subject's constitution through spoken words. All these aesthetic attempts that in due course were to become Beckett's signature can be observed in 'Echo's Bones.'

Conclusions

In the concluding section of my dissertation, I would like to summarise the main arguments of the preceding sections as well as indicate the general conclusions on Samuel Beckett's signature. The main aim of the argumentation presented in the thesis is to indicate that the elements that constitute Beckett's artistic signature, namely language, the neutrum and memory can be traced in the writer's pre-war works as central points of his interests. Thus, it would be indicated that in the case of Beckett's signature we can speak about a kind of a system, a system in which one can observe processes that through their continuous work, especially in the fibre of the words, are aimed at generating new meanings infiltrated through the artistic perspective of the author.

As far as the coined definition of the signature is concerned, I differentiate the term from apparently synonymous terms such as 'style,' 'manner' and 'poetics,' indicating that the act of signature should be treated every time as a singular event which offers a never-ending possibility of generating new meanings. Moreover, the signature understood as a singular event cannot be fully completed without two apparently contradictory notions, the surprise and the pre-assumption. The surprise is connected with the possibility that the signature offers, whereas the pre-assumption is a factor that requires from the receiver of the signature a certain amount of the artist's recognition. For illustrating that mechanism, one has referred to Lotman's theory of 'I' and 'other,' where these two spheres intermingle with each other. The 'I' of the artist becomes the part of the 'other,' the external world, where is further multiplied into many 'Is.' Similarly, the external world of the 'other' infiltrates new meanings to the internal world of the 'I,' which results in initiating the generation of new ideas.

The above mechanism of how the signature works is juxtaposed to Lotman's term 'semiosphere,' where the worlds of non-texts (external) and texts (internal) are filtrated through the boundary that separates these two worlds. In my definition of the signature both the receiver, such as a reader, and the artist himself function as a boundary. What is more, the receiver is the element without whom the signature cannot fully constitute – it is postulated that the signature deprived from the receiver remains in the realm of possibility where the processes of generating new meanings are in the suspended state.

Having defined the principles of the signature, the following aim of the thesis is to indicate how one can decipher Beckett's artistic signature. It has been indicated that the author recognises the pillars of the artist's signature in three aspects, the language, the neutrum and the memory. The importance of the natural language as a primary source that constructs Beckett's literary universe is depicted in the examples of words and expressions that are analysed in Chapters 1 to 4 of Part Two. Beckett's work in the matter of words is recognised as inexhaustible, where the words are continuously communicating with each other within the text resulting in the process of creating a structural relation that functions not only at the internal level of the text but also attempts to communicate with the words functioning in external texts (non-texts).

Moreover, the work in the structure of words has been recognised as a neverending process that is aimed at a maximum reduction of notions, ideas and associations that a particular word conveys to a single sign or symbol. Beckett's texts are fulfilled with such signs, such as the discussed example of the phrase 'womb-tomb,' which in its reduction is aimed at capturing the one's life span in a single symbol. The reduction of notions to a single sign has the other purpose, namely to approximate the subject, through the language, to the neutrum, the space in which only pure pre-contextual meanings function. Nevertheless, the attempt of approaching the neutrum is eventually not possible, primary due to the highly associative transmitter that the natural language is, and secondary due to the mutual communications that the symbols of a particular text are creating with the external non-texts.

One of the postulates of the neutrum is to create a closed space, i.e., the space that is not infected by any external signals. Only that condition should allow the subject to create a neutral environment in which the neutrum can function. The search of such a space is visible in Beckett's *Murphy*, where the subject eventually fails to enter the closed space being continuously disrupted by the external signs. In Beckett's signature one observes that symbols are in the state of the continuous in-betweenness, they are not able to constitute the hermetically closed system of a text as they continually communicate with the external symbols of the non-texts. That in-betweenness is located in Lotmanian boundary, the filter that works as a connector between the external and internal worlds of the text. Moreover, it is observed that Beckett is attempting to arrest the continuous, spiral work of memory using the symbols. Here, I find the parallel between the notion of the neutrum with Bergson's idea of the pure memory, in both examples, symbols serve a role of a device that Beckett uses to reach the non-contextual space. However, the idea of reaching the unreachable appears to be doomed to fail, it is recognised Beckett's endless attempts of establishing the neutrum as a central element of his artistic signature not only in the pre-war texts but in his whole *oeuvre*.

The above-presented principles of signature could be further developed and examined in the context of Beckett's post-war works. It appears to be intriguing to scrutinise to what extent the presented model is universal in the context of the author's whole work as well as which elements of the signature have become central in Beckett's late works. The other aim of my dissertation is to bring to Polish researchers' attention the still not fully scrutinised the pre-war period of the Nobel laureate's artistic activity. One can observe an extended interest in early Beckett's writing in Western research centres. For instance, The Samuel Beckett Research Centre at University of Reading in collaboration with Centre for Manuscript Genetics at University of Antwerp has been conducting since 2011 The Beckett Digital Manuscript Project which aims at digitalising all available Beckett's manuscripts, including the pre-war notebooks. Moreover, the publication and edition of source texts, i.e., *Samuel Beckett's German Diaries 1936–1937* (2011), *Samuel Beckett's Library* (2013), a short story *Echo's Bones* (2014), and *The Letters of Samuel Beckett Volumes I-IV* (2009–2016), implies that the tendency might be further continued. From the perspective of Polish scholarship, the main task in the following years appears to be connected with providing translations of the source texts which could help to increase interests in Beckett's early text. The latest translations of *Dante... Bruno. Vico.. Joyce* and *Proust* by Antoni Libera (PIW, 2017) and a complete translation of *Murphy* by Maciej Świerkocki (PIW, 2021) can be perceived as a good omen that can result in the increase of academic publications in the forthcoming years.

Bibliography

Ackerley, Christopher, J. *Demented Particulars: The Annotated Murphy*. Edinburgh University Press, Edinburgh, 2010.

Adorno, Theodor, W. 'The Stars Down to Earth'. *The Stars Down to Earth and other essays on the irrational in culture*. Routledge, London 2001.

Agamben, Giorgio. *The Signature of All Things. On Method*. Zone Books, New York 2009.

Alighieri, Dante. *Purgatory: Dante's Divine Trilogy Part Two*. Canongate Books, Edinburgh 2019)

Amiral, Eyal. *Wandering and Home: Beckett's Metaphysical Narrative*. Pennsylvania State University Press, 1993.

Anderson, Dustin. 'Zones of Indetermination: Beckett, Bergson, and the Monad of Murphy's Mind'. In: *Samuel Beckett Today / Aujourd'hui*. Brill, Amsterdam—New York, 25/2013, 75–89.

Ardoin, Paul, Gontarski, Stanley, Mattison, Laci (eds.). *Understanding Bergson, Understanding Modernism*. Bloomsbury, New York – London, 2013.

Aristotle. *Poetics*. Trans. by Joe Sachs. Focus Publishing, Newburyport 2006.

Atkins, Christopher D.M.. *The Signature Style of Frans Hals*. Amsterdam University Press, Amsterdam 2012.

Attridge, Derek. *The Singularity of Literature*. Routledge, London 2004.

Auckley, Chris. 'The Bible'. In: Uhlman, Anthony (ed.). Beckett in Context. Cambridge University Press, Cambridge 2013: 324–335.

Augustine, St. *Confessions*. Oxford University Press, Oxford 1991.

Badiou, Alain. *On Beckett*. Clinamen Press, 2003.

Bair, Deirdre. *Samuel Beckett*. Jonathan Cape, London 1978.

Bair, Deirdre. *Samuel Beckett*. Simon & Schuster, New York 1990.

Barthes, Roland. *Writing Degree Zero*. Beacon Press, 1970.

Beare, John, I. *Greek Theories of Elementary Cognition from Alcmaeon to Aristotle*. The Clarendon Press, Oxford 1906.

Beckett, Samuel, Auster, Paul (ed.). *The Selected Works of Samuel Beckett. Volume I*. Grove Press, New York 2010a.

— *Murphy*

Beckett, Samuel, Auster, Paul (ed.). *The Selected Works of Samuel Beckett. Volume II*. Grove Press, New York 2010b.

— *Molloy*
— *The Unnamable*
Beckett, Samuel, Auster, Paul (ed.). *The Selected Works of Samuel Beckett. Volume III*. Grove Press, New York 2010c.
— *Endgame*
— *Waiting for Godot*
Beckett, Samuel, Auster, Paul (ed.). *The Selected Works of Samuel Beckett. Volume IV*. Grove Press, New York 2010d.
— *'Echo's Bones'*
— *Company*
— *Dante...Bruno. Vico.. Joyce*
— *More Pricks Than Kicks*
— *Proust*
Beckett, Samuel, Nixon, Mark (ed.). *Echo's Bones*, Faber & Faber, London 2014.
Beckett, Samuel. *Dream of Fair to Middling Women*. Arcade Publishing, New York 2012.
Bénard, Julie. 'Dante... Bruno. Vico.. Joyce:' Samuel Beckett's 'Identified contraries.' In: *E-rea*, 15.2/2018.
Bennet, Michael. *Reassessing the Theatre of the Absurd*. Palgrave Macmillan, New York 2011.
Ben-Zvi, Linda. 'Samuel Beckett, Fritz Mauthner, and the Limits of Language.' In: *PMLA*, 95.2/1980: 183–200.
Bergson, Henry. *Creative Evolution*. Random House, New York, 1941.
Bergson, Henry. *Matter and Memory*. Zone Books, New York 1991.
Bergson, Henry. *The Creative Mind*. Philosophical Library, New York, 1946.
Bergson, Henry. *Time and Free Will*. Dover Publications, Inc., New York, 2001.
Bixby, Patrick. 'Ireland 1906: 1945.' In: Uhlmann, Anthony (ed.). *Samuel Beckett in Context*. Cambridge University Press, Cambridge2013: 65–75
Blanchot, Maurice, *The Space of Literature*. University of Nebraska Press, Lincoln, London 1989.
Blanchot, Maurice. *Faux Pas*. Stanford Univeristy Press, Standford 2001.
Blanchot, Maurice. *The Infinite Conversation*. University of Minnesota Press, Minneapolis – London, 1993.
Blanchot, Maurice. *The Space of Literature*. University of Nebraska Press, Lincoln, 1989.
Bogue, Ronald. *Deleuze and Guattari*. Routledge, London—New York 1989.

Boorstin, Daniel, J. *The Creators: A History of Heroes of the Imagination*. Vintage Books, New York 1993.

Borkowski, Rafał. 'Bergson—Beckett—Lotman: A Semiotic Analysis of Samuel Beckett's "A Wet Night" from *More Pricks Than Kicks*.' In: *Beyond Philology*, Gdańsk University Press, 14.2/2017: 9–30.

Borkowski, Rafał. 'Beckett przed Beckettem? Poszukiwania początków sygnatury Beckettowskiej na przykładzie opowiadania 'Echo's Bones" ['Beckett before Beckett? In Search of the Origin of Beckett's Signature based on 'Echo's Bones']. In: Wiśniewski, Tomasz (ed). *Beckett w XXI. Wieku. Rozpoznanie*. Gdańsk University Press, 2017, 87–104.

Bousquet, Mireille. 'Beckett and the Refusal of Judgment: The Question of Ethics and the Value of Art.' In: Feldman, Matthew, Mamdani, Karim (eds.). *Beckett / Philosophy*. ibidem-Verlag, Stuttgart 2015: 359–378.

Bowyer Bell, John. 'Waiting for Mario: The Espositos, Joyce, and Beckett.' In: *Éire-Ireland*, 30.2/1995: 7–26

Brough, John, Barnett. 'Art and Artworld: Some Ideas for a Husserlian Aesthetic.' In: Sokolowski. Robert (ed.). *Edmund Husserl and the Phenomenological Tradition*, Catholic University of America Press, 1988: 25–45.

Brzeska, Ewa. *Recepcja twórczości Samuela Becketta w Polsce*. Wydawnictwo Naukowe Uniwersytetu Mikołaja Kopernika, Toruń 2020.

Calder, John. *The Philosophy of Samuel Beckett*. Calder Publications, London 2001.

Campbell, Julie. "Echo's Bones' and Beckett's Disembodied Voices.' In: *Samuel Beckett Today/ Aujourd'hui*, 11/2000: 454–460.

Carrera, María José. "'Handicapped by my Ignorance of Spanish:" Samuel Beckett's Translations of Mexican Poetry.' In: Wiśniewski, Tomasz (ed.). *Back to the Beckett Text*. Wydawnictwo Uniwersytetu Gdańskiego. Gdańsk—Sopot 2012: 93–105.

Caselli, Daniela. *Beckett's Dantes. Intertextuality in the Fiction and Criticism*. Manchester University Press, Manchester—New York 2005.

Cerbone, David. *Understanding Phenomenology*. Acumen, Durham 2006

Cohn, Ruby (ed.). *Disjecta. Miscellaneous Writings and a Dramatic Fragment*. Grove Press, New York 1984.

Cohn, Ruby. *A Beckett Canon*. The University of Michigan Press, Michigan 2005.

Cohn, Ruby. *Just Play: Beckett's Theater*. Princeton University Press, Princeton 1980.

Connor, Steven. *Beckett, Modernism and the Material Imagination*. Cambridge University Press, 2014.

Cordingley, Anthony (ed.). *Self-Translation. Brokering Originality in Hybrid Culture*. Bloomsbury, London 2013.

Cornell, Drucilla. *The Philosophy of the Limit*. Routledge, New York – London, 1992.

Cornwell, Ethel, F. 'The Flight from Self.' In: *PMLA*, Modern Language Association, 88.1/1973: 41–51.

Cottingham, John (ed.). *The Cambridge Companion to Descartes*. Cambridge University Press, Cambridge 1992.

Cronin, Anthony. *Samuel Beckett. The Last Modernist*. Da Capo Press, New York 1999.

Czermińska, Małgorzata, *The Autobiographical Triangle. Witness. Confession. Challenge*. Peter Lang, Berlin 2019.

Dawson, Giles E. 'A Seventh Signature of Shakespeare.' In: *Shakespeare Quarterly*, George Washington University, 43.1/1992: 72–79.

Deleuze, Gilles. *Proust and Signs*. University of Minnesota Press, Minneapolis 2000.

Dennett, C. Daniel. *Consciousness Explained*. Back Bay Books, New York 1991.

Derrida, Jacques. 'A Certain Impossible Possibility of Saying the Event.' In: *Critical Inquiry*, Chicago Journals, 33.2: 441–461.

Derrida, Jacques. 'Signature, Event, Context.' In: *Margins of Philosophy*. The University of Chicago Press, Chicago 1982.

Derrida, Jacques. *Signéponge/Signsponge*. Columbia University Press, New York 1984.

Derrida, Jacues. *Memories for Paul de Man*. Columbia University Press, New York 1988.

Descartes, René. *Meditations on First Philosophy*. Oxford University Press, Oxford 2008.

Douglas, Paul. *Bergson, Eliot, & American Literature*. University Press of Kentucky, Lexington, 1986.

Dow Fehsenfeld, Martha, More Overbeck, Lois (ed.). *The Letters of Samuel Beckett. Volume I: 1929–1940*. Cambridge University Press, Cambridge 2014.

Eco, Umberto. *Lector in fabula*. PIW, Warsaw 1994a.

Eco, Umberto. *The Limits of Interpretation*. Indiana University Press, 1994b.

Eco, Umberto. *The Role of the Reader. Explorations in the Semiotics of Texts*. Indiana University Press, 1984

Engelberts, Matthijs, Everett Frost (eds.). *Notes Diverse Holo*. Rodopi, Amsterdam–New York, 2006. Anchor Books, New York 1961.

Esslin, Martin. *The Theatre of the Absurd*. New York 1961

Feldman, Matthew. 'René Descartes and Samuel Beckett.' In: *Beckett's Books: A Cultural History of Samuel Beckett's 'Interwar Notes.'* Continuum, London 2008.

Fernández, José Francisco "Echo's Bones: Samuel Beckett's Lost Story of Afterlife." In: *Journal of the Short Story in English* 52/2009, 115-24.

Fitch, Brian. *Beckett and Babel: An Investigation into the Status of the Bilingual Work.* University of Toronto Press, Toronto 1988.

Foucault, Michel. 'La pensée du dehors.' In: *Critique*, 229/1966: 523-546.

Foucault, Michel. *Maurice Blanchot: The Thought from Outside.* Zone Books, New York, 1987.

Foucault, Michel. *The Order of Things. An Archaeology of the Human Sciences.* Routledge, London – New York, 2005.

Freeman, Kathleen. *Ancilla to the Pre-Socratic Philosophers.* Harvard University Press, Cambridge 1948.

Frost C. Everett. 'Beckett and Geulincx's Ethics: 'my Geulincx could only be a literary fantasia'.' In: *Samuel Beckett Today/ Aujourd'hui* 24/2012: 171-186.

Genette, Gérard, *Narrative Discourse: an Essay in Method.* Cornell University Press, New York 1972.

Geulincx, Arnold. *Ethics with Samuel Beckett's Notes.* Brill, Leiden—Boston 2006.

Ghosh, Ranjan (ed.). *Edward Said and the Literary, Social, and Political World.* Routledge, London—New York 2000

Gillies, Mary Ann. *Henri Bergson and British Modernism.* McGill-Queen's University Press, London,1996.

Gontarski, Stanley. 'Trinity College Dublin.' In: Uhlman, Anthony (ed.). *Beckett in Context.* Cambridge University Press, Cambridge 2013.

Gontarski, Stanley. 'What it is to have been:' Bergson and Beckett on Movement, Multiplicity and Representation. In: *Journal of Modern Literature*, Indiana University Press, 34.2/2011: 65-75.

Gontarski, Stanley. *Creative Involution: Bergson, Beckett, Deleuze.* Edinburgh: Edinburgh University Press, 2015.

Gontarski, Stanley. *The Edinburgh Companion to Samuel Beckett and the Arts.* Edinburgh: Edinburgh University Press, 2014.

Gutorow, Jacek. 'Kartkując Becketta.' In: *Kwartalnik Artystyczny*, 4/2019: 108-112.

Harrison, Robert. *Samuel Beckett's Murphy: A Critical Excursion.* University of Georgia Press, Athens 1968.

Heidegger, Martin. *On Time and Being.* The University of Chicago Press, Chicago, 2002.

Heidegger, Martin. *The Basic Problems of Phenomenology*. Indiana University Press 1998.

Hejinian, Lyn. *The Language of Inquiry*. University of California Press, Berkley – Los Angeles 2000.

Herren, Graley. 'Working on Film and Television.' In: Uhlman, Anthony (ed.). *Beckett in Context*. Cambridge University Press, Cambridge 2013, 192–202.

Hesla, David. *The Shape of Chaos: An Interpretation of the Art of Samuel Beckett*. University of Minnesota Press, Minneapolis 1971.

Hill, Leslie *Beckett's Fiction in Different Words*. Cambridge University Press, Cambridge 1990.

Hill, Leslie. *Beckett's Fiction: In Different Words*. Cambridge University Press, Cambridge 1990.

Hill, Leslie. *Blanchot. Extreme Contemporary*. Routledge, London – New York, 2001.

Husserl, Edmund. *Cartesian Meditations. An Introduction to Phenomenology*. Springer Science+ Business Media Dordrecht 1960.

Husserl, Edmund. *Husserl: Shorter Works*. University of Notre Dame Press, 1981.

Husserl, Edmund. *Ideas Pertaining to a Pure Phenomenology and to a Phenomenological Philosophy. First Book: General Introduction to a Pure Phenomenology*. Martinus Nijhoff Publishers, The Hague–Boston–Lancaster 1983.

Husserl, Edmund. *Ideas: General Introduction to Pure Phenomenology*. Collier Books, London 1962.

Husserl, Edmund. *Logical Investigations*. Routledge, London – New York, 2001.

Husserl, Edmund. *On the Phenomenology of the Consciousness of Internal Time*. Kluwer Academic Publishers, Dordrecht—Boston—London, 1991.

Husserl, Edmund. *The Crisis of the European Sciences and Transcendental Phenomenology*. Northwestern University Press, 1970.

Hutcheon, Linda. *A Poetics of Postmodernism. History, Theory, Fiction*. Routledge, New York—London 2004.

Jakobson, Roman. *Selected Writings I: Phonological Studies*. Mouton & Co., The Hague, 1962.

Jakuszko, Honorata. 'Fritz Mauthner's Critique of Locke's Idea of God.' In: *Studies in Logic, Grammar and Rhetoric*, University of Białystok, 20/2010: 65–78.

Joyce, James. *Ulysses*. Oxford University Press, Oxford 1993.

Kaelin, F. Eugene. *The Unhappy Consciousness. The Poetic Plight of Samuel Beckett*. D. Reidel Publishing Company, Dordrecht—Boston—London 1981.

Kennedy, Sighle. *Murphy's Bed: A Study of Real and Sur-Real Association in Samuel Beckett's First Novel*. Bucknell University Press, Lewisburg 1971.

Kędzierski, Marek. 'Samuel Beckett i Polska (w latach 1981–2008).' In: *Tekstualia*, 4/2018: 63–76.

Kiely, Robert. 'Samuel Beckett's Murphy, Work and Astrology.' In: *Journal of Modern Literature*, Indiana University Press, 40.4/2017: 63–74.

Knowlson, James. *Beckett Remembering/Remembering Beckett*. Bloomsbury, London 2006.

Knowlson, James. *Damned to Fame*. Simon & Schuster, New York 1996.

Le Juez, Brigitte. *Beckett before Beckett*. Souvenir Press 2009.

Levinas, Emmanuel. *Otherwise Than Being or Beyond Essence*. Kluwer Academic Publishers, Dordrecht, 1991.

Libera, Antoni. *Błogosławieństwo Becketta i inne wyznania literackie*. SIC!, Warsaw 2004.

Libera, Antoni. 'Dante, Vico a Towarzystwo Becketta. In: *Kwartalnik Artystyczny*, 4/1996: 134–140.

Libera, Antoni. *Godot i jego cień*. Znak, Kraków 2009.

Libera, Antoni, Pyda, Janusz. *Jesteście na Ziemi, na to rady nie ma! Dialogi o teatrze Samuela Becketta*. PIW, Warsaw 2018.

Lotman, Yuri. 'On the Semiosphere.' In: *Sign System Studies*, 17/1984: 5–23.

Lotman, Yuri. *Culture and Explosion*. Mouton de Gruyter, Berlin – New York 2009.

Lotman, Yuri. *The Structure of the Artistic Text*. University of Michigan Press 1977.

Lotman, Yuri. *The Universe of the Mind*. I.B. Tauris & CO. LTD, London 1990.

Luce, Arthur Aston. *Bergson's Doctrine of Intuition. The Donnellan Lectures for 1921*. Society for Promoting Christian Knowledge, London 1922.

Lyotard, Jean-François. *The Inhuman: Conversations on Time*. Polity Press, Cambridge, 1990.

MacNeil, Heather. *Trusting Records Legal, Historical and Diplomatic Perspectives*. Kluwer, Dordrecht 2000.

Mali, Joseph. *The Rehabilitation of Myth. Vico's 'New Science.'* Cambridge University Press, Cambridge 1992.

Mander van, Karel. *The Lives of the Illustrious Netherlandish and German Painters*, Vol. 2. Davaco Publisher, Doornspijk 1994.

Massey, Heath. 'Bergson on Memory.' In: Ardoin, Paul, Gontarski, Stanley, Mattison, Laci (eds.). *Understanding Bergson, Understanding Modernism*. Bloomsbury, New York – London, 2013.

Maude, Ulrika, Feldman, Matthew (eds.). *Beckett and Phenomenology*. Continuum, New York, 2009.

Mauthner, Fritz. *Beiträge zu einer Kritik der Sprache*. J.G. Cotta'sche Buchhandlung Nachfolger, Berlin—Stuttgart, 1921.

Ponty, Maurice. *Phenomenology and Perception*, Routledge, 1981.

Momro, Jakub. *Literatura Świadomości. Samuel Beckett—Podmiot—Negatywność* [*Literature of Consciousness: Samuel Beckett—Subject—Negativity*]. Universitas, Kraków, 2010.

Mooney. Michael, E. 'Presocrtic Scepticism: Samuel Beckett's Murphy Reconsidered. In: *ELH*, The John Hopkins University Press, 49.1/1982: 214–234.

Moorjani & Carola Veit (eds.) Samuel Beckett Today/Aujourd'hui. Rodopi, Amsterdam, 11/2001: 454–60.

Moorjani, Angela, Veit, Carola (eds.). 'Introduction.' In: *Samuel Beckett Today / Aujourd'hui*, 11/2001: 13–15.

Moorjani, Angela. 'Beckett's Devious Deictics.' In: St John Butler, Lance, Davis, Robin, J. (ed). Rethinking Beckett. The Macmillan Press, New York 1990: 20–30.

Morot-Sir, Edouard. 'Samuel Beckett and Cartesian Emblems.' In: *Samuel Beckett and the Art of Rhetoric*. University of North Carolina 1976.

Nicholson, Graeme. 'The Ontological Difference.' In: *American Philosophical Quarterly*, University of Illinois Press, 33/4: 357–374.

Nixon, Mark. 'Belacqua Revididus. Beckett's short story 'Echo's Bones.' In: *Limit(e) Beckett 1*, 92–101.

Nixon, Mark. 'Between Art-world and Life-world: Beckett's *Dream of Fair to Middling Women*.' In: Maude, Ulrika, Feldman, Matthew (eds.). *Beckett and Phenomenology*. Continuum, New York, 2009.

Nixon, Mark. *Samuel Beckett's German Diaries 1936–1937*. Continuum, New York—London 2011.

Parker, Philip. *The Northmen's Fury: A History of the Viking World*. Vintage, 2014.

Perloff, Marjorie. *Differentials. Poetry, Poetics, Pedagogy*. The University of Alabama Press, Tuscaloosa 2004.

Pilling, John. *Beckett before Godot*. Cambridge University Press, Cambridge 1997.

Pilling. John. *A Samuel Beckett Chronology*. Palgrave Macmillan, New York 2006.

Pinsent, John. *Greek Mythology*. The Hamlyn Publishing Group Limited, London – New York 1969.

Pliny the Elder, *Natural History*. Harvard University Press, Cambridge 1979.

Pon, Lisa. 'Michelangelo's First Signature.' In: *Notes in the History of Art*, 15.4/ 1996: 16–21.

Porter Abbott, H., *Beckett Writing Beckett: The Author in the Autograph*. Cornell University Press, Ithaca 1996.

Pothast, Urlich. *Metaphysical Vision. Arthur Schopenhauer's Philosophy of Art and Life and Samuel Beckett's Own Way to Make Use of it*. Peter Lang, New York, 2008.

Preminger, A., Brogan, T.V.F. (ed.). *The New Princeton Encyclopedia of Poetry and Poetics*. Princeton University Press, Princeton 1993.

Proust, Marcel. *Swann's Way*. The Modern Library, New York 1992.

Rabaté, Jean-Michel. *Think, Pig! Beckett at the limits of the Human*. Fordham University Press, New York 2016.

Rabinovitz, Rubin. 'Repetition and Underlying Meanings in Samuel Beckett's Trilogy.' In: St John Butler, Lance, Davis, Robin, J. (ed). *Rethinking Beckett*. The Macmillan Press, New York 1990: 31–67.

Rabinovitz, Rubin. *The Development of Samuel Beckett's Fiction*. University of Illinois Press, Urbana 1984.

Ricoeur, Paul, *Time and Narrative I*, The University of Chicago Press, Chicago 1984.

Rowner, Ilai. *The Event. Literature and Theory*. The University of Nebraska, Nebraska 2015.

Rudnick Luft, Sandra. *Vico's Uncanny Humanism: Reading the New Science between Modern and Postmodern*. Cornell University Press, Ithaca – London, 2003.

Sailsbury. Laura. *Samuel Beckett: Laughing Matters, Comic Timing*. Edinburgh University Press, Edinburgh 2012.

Salisbury, Laura. '"What Is the Word:" Beckett's Aphasic Modernism.' In: *Journal of Beckett Studies*, 17.1–2/2008: 78–126.

Sartre, Jean-Paul. *Nausea*. New Directions Books, New York 1969.

Sartre, Jean-Paul. *The Transcendence of the Ego*. Routledge, London—New York 2004.

Schapiro, Meyer. 'Style.' In: *Theory and Philosophy of Art: Style, Artist, and Society*. George Braziller, New York, 1953.

Schmid, Wolf. *Narratology: An Introduction*. De Gruyter, Berlin—New York 2010.

Schmitt, Richard. 'Husserl's Transcendental-Phenomenological Reduction '. In: *Philosophy and Phenomenological Research*, 20.2/1959: 238–245.

Scott, David. 'Bergson on Intuition.' In: Ardoin, Paul, Gontarski, Stanley, Mattison, Laci (eds.). *Understanding Bergson, Understanding Modernism*. Bloomsbury, New York – London, 2013.

Scruton, Roger. 'Beckett and the Cartesian Soul.' In: *The Aesthetic Understanding: Essays in the philosophy of Art and Culture*. Carcanet Press, Manchester 1983.

Shakespeare, William. *The Tempest*. Yale University Press, New Heaven—London 2006.

Shelley, Percy Bysshe. 'A Defence of Poetry.' In: *The Selected Poetry and Prose of Shelley*. Wordsworth Editions Limited, Ware 2002.

Shestov, Leon. *Penultimate Words and Other Essays*. John W. Luce and CO, Boston, 1916.

Slote, Sam. 'Stuck in Translation: Beckett and Borges on Dante.' In: Journal of Beckett Studies, 19.1/2010: 15–28.

Spinoza, Benedict. *The Ethics and other Works*. Princeton University Press, Princeton 1994.

Steiner, George. *Real Presences*. University of Chicago Press, Chicago 1989.

Todorov, Tzvetan. *Introduction to Poetics*. University of Minnesota Press, Minneapolis 1981.

Tritt, William. 'Statistics on Proper Names in *Murphy*.' In: Morot-Sir, Edouard(ed.). *Samuel Beckett: The Art of Rhetoric*. University of North Carolina Press, Chapel Hill 1976.

Tubridy, Derval. *Samuel Beckett and the Language of Subjectivity*. Cambridge University Press, 2018.

Uhlman, Anthony (ed.). *Beckett in Context*. Cambridge University Press, Cambridge 2013.

Uhlmann, Anthony. *Beckett and Poststructuralism*. Cambridge University Press, Cambridge 1999.

Van Hulle, Dirk, Nixon, Mark. *Samuel Beckett's Library*. Cambridge University Press, Cambridge 2013.

Vico, Giambattista. *The First New Science*. Cambridge University Press, Cambridge 2002.

Wang, Aileen June. 'Michelangelo's Signature.' In: The Sixteenth Century Journal, 35.2/2004: 447–473.

Wegman, Rob C. 'Isaac's Signature.' In: *The Journal of Musicology*, University of California Press, 28.1/2011: 9–33.

Weingrad, Michael. 'New Encounters with Shestov.' In: *The Journal of Jewish Thought and Philosophy*, 11.1/2002: 49–62.

Weller, Shane. "'Gnawing to be Naught:" Beckett and Pre-Socratic Nihilism.' In: *Samuel Beckett Today / Aujourd'hui*, 20/2008: 321–333.

Whyte, Lancelot, L. *Essay on Atomism: from Democritus to 1960*. Wesleyan University Press, Middletown 1961.

Wiśniewski, Tomasz. 'Sposoby tworzenia znaczeń w twórczości Samuela Becketta' ['The Ways of Creating Meanings in Samuel Beckett's Work']. In: *Tekstualia*, 20.1/2010: 53–60.

Wiśniewski, Tomasz. *Kształt Literacki Dramatu Samuela Becketta* [*The Literary Shape of Samuel Beckett's Drama*]. Universitas, Kraków 2006.

Woodruff-Smith, David. *Husserl*. Routledge, New York 2013.

Żyłko, Bogusław. *Semiotyka Kultury. Szkoła tartusko-moskiewska* [*The Semiotics of Culture. The Tartu-Moscow School.*]. Słowo/ obraz terytoria, Gdańsk 2009

Index of Names

Ackerley, C. 11, 150, 152, 154, 157, 159
Adorno, T. 151
Alighieri, D. 9, 12, 14, 18, 29, 46, 53, 55, 75, 76, 105-118, 125, 127, 130-135, 137-144, 162, 165, 167-169, 172, 174, 175, 177, 180-182, 185
Aristotle 37-39, 157
Attridge, D. 10, 13, 17, 23-28, 31-36, 38, 41, 141
Auckley, C. 50
Augustine, St. 171

Badiou, A. 59, 77, 79
Bair, D. 45, 105, 107
Beckett, S. 9-14, 19, 22, 28-33, 39-62, 67-185
Ben-Zvi, L. 52, 53, 57
Bergson, H. 11, 86, 89-102, 120, 121, 124, 125, 159, 160
Blanchot, M. 13, 26, 60, 61-74, 79, 87, 101, 118, 124

Cohn, R. 11, 31, 49, 128, 135, 136, 140, 148, 153, 154, 156, 162, 167, 178
Coleridge, S. T. 37
Cronin, A. 46, 146

Derrida, J. 13, 17, 18-20, 23-25, 27, 28, 30-33, 41, 73

Eco, U. 13, 26, 27, 33-35, 41
Esslin, M. 29

Foucault, M. 64-70, 79, 101, 140
Genette, G. 27
Geulincx, A. 157, 161
Gontarski, S. 14, 53, 89, 90, 99, 102, 120

Heidegger, M. 76, 84, 85
Hejinian, L. 40
Husserl, E. 13, 77-86, 92, 101
Hutcheon, L. 40

Isaac, H. 10, 17, 18

Joyce, J. 9, 12, 14, 39, 43, 46, 53, 55, 90, 105-110, 115-118, 130, 154, 167, 185

Kaun, S. 55, 56
Kędzierski, M. 12
Knowlson, J. 45, 47, 84, 105-107, 110, 119, 127, 130, 145-147, 150-152

Le Juez, B. 11, 105-107
Lévinas, E. 28
Libera, A. 12, 185
Lotman, Y. 10-12, 20, 21, 23, 24, 28, 32-37, 41, 42, 93, 94, 109, 123, 127, 128, 135, 138, 143, 144, 176, 177, 182, 183
Lyotard, J-F. 73, 97, 98, 102, 120

Mauthner, F. 47, 52-56, 100, 112
Merleau-Ponty, M. 85
Momro, J. 63, 76, 82, 101
Moorjani, A. 82, 174

Nixon, M. 10, 13, 22, 47, 48, 52, 69, 77, 84, 119, 165-168, 170, 177, 178, 180, 181

Perloff, M. 38, 39
Pilling, J. 11, 46, 53, 69, 106, 107, 109, 147, 149
Porter Abbott, H. 131
Pothast, U. 125, 126
Proust, M. 9, 12, 14, 46, 69, 70, 89, 91, 105, 106, 119-127, 146, 185

Ricoeur, P. 26

Salisbury, L. 54
Sartre, J-P. 77, 78, 122
Schapiro, M. 22, 23

Shakespeare, W. 10, 14, 18, 21, 127, 139, 143, 144
Steiner, G. 19, 20, 41, 61, 64

Todorov, T. 39, 40

Uhlmann, A. 53, 74, 178

Van Hulle, D. 22, 48, 52, 69, 77, 119
Vico, G. 9, 12, 14, 53, 55, 56, 100, 105-117

Wegman, R. 17, 18
Wiśniewski, T. 11, 48, 80, 165, 168, 176, 179, 182

Żyłko, B. 109, 114, 115

Gdańsk Transatlantic Studies in British and North American Culture

Edited by Marek Wilczyński

The interdisciplinary series "GdańskTransatlantic Studies in British and North American Culture" brings together literary and cultural studies concerning literatures and cultures of the English-speaking world, particularly those of Great Britain, Ireland, the United States, and Canada. The range of topics to be addressed includes literature, theater, film, and art, considered in various twenty-first-century theoretical perspectives, such as, for example (but not exclusively), New Historicism and canon formation, cognitive narratology, gender and queer studies, performance studies, memory and trauma studies, and New Art History. The editors are leaving a broad margin for the innovative and the unpredictable, hoping to attract authors whose approaches will point to new directions of research as regards both thematic areas and methods. Comparative Polish-Anglo-American proposals will be considered, too.

Vol. 1 Mirosława Modrzewska: Byron and the Baroque. 2013.

Vol. 2 Andrzej Ceynowa / Marek Wilczyński (eds.): American Experience – The Experience of America. 2013.

Vol. 3 Marta Koval: "We search the Past…for Our Own Lost Selves." Representations of Historical Experience in Recent American Fiction. 2013.

Vol. 4 Tomasz Basiuk: Exposures. American Gay Men's Life Writing since Stonewall. 2013.

Vol. 5 Klara Naszkowska: The Living Mirror. The Representation of Doubling Identities in the British and Polish Women's Literature (1846–1938). 2014.

Vol. 6 Urszula Elias / Agnieszka Sienkiewicz-Charlish (eds.): Crime Scenes. Modern Crime Fiction in an International Context. 2014.

Vol. 7 Justyna Kociatkiewicz / Laura Suchostawska/Dominika Ferens (eds.): Eating America. Crisis, Sustenance, Sustainability. 2014.

Vol. 8 Agnieszka Pantuchowicz / Sławomir Masłoń (eds.): Affinities. Essays in Honour of Professor Tadeusz Rachwał. 2014.

Vol. 9 Janusz Semrau / Marek Wilczyński (eds.): Image in Modern(ist) Verse. 2015.

Transatlantic Studies in British and North American Culture
Edited by Marek Wilczyński

Vol. 10 Małgorzata Grzegorzewska / Jean Ward / Mark Burrows (eds.): Breaking the Silence. Poetry and the Kenotic Word. 2015.

Vol. 11 Dominika Oramus: Charles Darwin's Looking Glass. The Theory of Evolution and the Life of its Author in Contemporary British Fiction and Non-Fiction. 2015.

Vol. 12 Miłosz Wojtyna: The Ordinary and the Short Story. Short Fiction of T.F. Powys and V.S. Pritchett. 2015.

Vol. 13 Bartosz Wójcik: Afro-Caribbean Poetry in English. Cultural Traditions (1970s-2000s). 2015.

Vol. 14 Izabela Morska: Glorious Outlaws: Debt as a Tool in Contemporary Postcolonial Fiction. 2016.

Vol. 15 Edyta Frelik: Painter's Word. Thomas Hart Benton, Marsden Hartley and Ad Reinhardt as Writers. 2016.

Vol. 16 Małgorzata Grzegorzewska: George Herbert and Post-phenomenology. A Gift for Our Times. 2016.

Vol. 17 Anna Cholewa-Purgał: Therapy Through Faërie. Therapeutic Properties of Fantasy Literature by the Inklings and by U. K. Le Guin. 2016.

Vol. 18 Agata Handley: Constructing Identity. Continuity, Otherness and Revolt in the Poetry of Tony Harrison. 2016.

Vol. 19 Dominika Oramus: Ways of Pleasure. Angela Carter's 'Discourse of Delight' in her Fiction and Non-Fiction. 2016.

Vol. 20 Aneta Dybska: Regeneration, Citizenship, and Justice in the American City since the 1970s. 2016.

Vol. 21 Maciej Reda: The Apology for Catholicism in Selected Writings by G. K. Chesterton. 2016.

Vol. 22 Przemysław Uściński: Parody, Scriblerian Wit and the Rise of the Novel. Parodic Textuality from Pope to Sterne. 2016.

Vol. 23 Jadwiga Węgrodzka: Popular Genres and Their Uses in Fiction. 2018.

Vol. 24 Stephen Butler / Agnieszka Sienkiewicz-Charlish (eds.): Crime Fiction. 2018.

Vol. 25 Susana Nicolás Román / Marek Wilczyński / Łukasz Gałecki (eds.): Women in Edward Bond. 2018.

Vol. 26 Aleksander Bednarski / Robert Looby (eds): Redefining the Fringes in Celtic Studies. Essays in Literature and Culture. 2019.

Vol. 27 Krzysztof Filip Rudolf: Archaization in Literary Translation as Nostalgic Pastiche. 2019.

Vol. 28 Martin Potter / Małgorzata Grzegorzewska / Jean Ward (eds.): In Wonder, Love and Praise. Approaches to Poetry, Theology and Philosophy. 2019.

Vol. 29 Arkadiusz Misztal: Time and Vision Machines in Thomas Pynchon's Novels. 2019.

Vol. 30 Mirosława Modrzewska / Maria Fengler (eds.): Byron: Reality, Fiction and Madness. 2019

Vol. 31 Jelínková Ema / Sumner Rachael (eds.): The Literary Art of Ali Smith. 2019.

Vol. 32 Katarzyna Agnieszka Kociołek: Dress as Metaphor – British Female Fashion and Social Change in the 20th Century. 2020.

Vol. 33 Małgorzata Hołda: On Beauty and Being: Hans-Georg Gadamer's and Virginia Woolf's Hermeneutics of the Beautiful. 2021.

Vol. 34 Agata Handley: Constructing Identity in the Poetry of Tony Harrison. Revised and Expanded Edition. 2021.

Vol. 35 Grzegorz Koneczniak: Building (in) the Promised Land. Postcolonial Biblical Readings of Contemporary Irish Drama (2000-2015). 2022.

Vol. 36 Barbara Miceli: A 'Fourth Way' to Tell the Story. Fact and Fiction in Three Novels by Joyce Carol Oates. 2022.

Vol. 37 Rafał Borkowski: Samuel Beckett's Signature in Years 1929–1938. Reflecting on the Thought Process: Language, the Neutrum and Memory. 2022.

www.ingramcontent.com/pod-product-compliance
Lightning Source LLC
LaVergne TN
LVHW042246070526
838201LV00089B/47